Building a Healthy Business

FOR MASSAGE AND ALTERNATIVE HEALTHCARE PRACTICES

Jan L. Saeger

BA, LMT, NCTMB, CESMT, RYT

Lewis S. Rudolph

BS, AS, LMT

 **Higher Education**

Boston   Burr Ridge, IL   Dubuque, IA   New York   San Francisco   St. Louis
Bangkok   Bogotá   Caracas   Kuala Lumpur   Lisbon   London   Madrid   Mexico City
Milan   Montreal   New Delhi   Santiago   Seoul   Singapore   Sydney   Taipei   Toronto

BUILDING A HEALTHY BUSINESS

Published by McGraw-Hill, a business unit of The McGraw-Hill Companies, Inc., 1221 Avenue of the Americas, New York, NY, 10020. Copyright © 2010 by The McGraw-Hill Companies, Inc. All rights reserved. No part of this publication may be reproduced or distributed in any form or by any means, or stored in a database or retrieval system, without the prior written consent of The McGraw-Hill Companies, Inc., including, but not limited to, in any network or other electronic storage or transmission, or broadcast for distance learning.

Some ancillaries, including electronic and print components, may not be available to customers outside the United States.

This book is printed on acid-free paper.

1 2 3 4 5 6 7 8 9 0 QPD/QPD 0 9

ISBN 978-0-07-340191-1

MHID 0-07-340191-9

Vice president/Editor in chief: *Elizabeth Haefele*
Vice president/Director of marketing: *John E. Biernat*
Senior sponsoring editor: *Debbie Fitzgerald*
Director of Development: *Patricia Hesse*
Developmental editor: *Connie Kuhl*
Marketing manager: *Kelly Curran*
Lead media producer: *Damian Moshak*
Director, Editing/Design/Production: *Jess Ann Kosic*
Lead project manager: *Rick Hecker*
Senior production supervisor: *Janean A. Utley*
Senior designer: *Srdjan Savanovic*
Senior photo research coordinator: *Carrie K. Burger*
Media project manager: *Mark A. S. Dierker*
Cover design: *Jessica M. Lazar*
Interior design: *Maureen McCutcheon*
Typeface: *10/12 Palatino*
Compositor: *Laserwords Private Limited*
Printer: *Quebecor World Dubuque Inc.*
Cover credit: © *Rtimages/iStockphoto*
Credits: The credits section for this book begins on page 243 and is considered an extension of the copyright page.

Library of Congress Cataloging-in-Publication Data

Saeger, Jan L.
    Building a healthy business : for massage and alternative healthcare practices / Jan L. Saeger,
  Lewis S. Rudolph.
      p. ; cm.
    Includes index.
    ISBN-13: 978-0-07-340191-1 (alk. paper)
    ISBN-10: 0-07-340191-9 (alk. paper)
    1. Massage therapy—Practice. 2. Alternative medicine—Practice. I. Rudolph, Lewis S.
  II. Title.
    [DNLM: 1. Massage—organization & administration. 2. Complementary Therapies—
  organization & administration. 3. Practice Management. WB 537 S127b 2010]
  RM722.S24 2010
  615.8'22068—dc22

                                        2008044469

The Internet addresses listed in the text were accurate at the time of publication. The inclusion of a Web site does not indicate an endorsement by the authors or McGraw-Hill, and McGraw-Hill does not guarantee the accuracy of the information presented at these sites.

www.mhhe.com

Dedication

Jan Saeger: To Koda

Lewis Rudolph: To all those who need help in helping others

About the Authors

Jan L. Saeger

Jan L. Saeger is a co-author, with Donna Kyle-Brown, of McGraw-Hill's Massage Series flagship book *New Foundations in Therapeutic Massage and Bodywork.* She is an internationally trained and certified massage therapist who is licensed in the state of Florida and holds National Certification in Therapeutic Massage and Bodywork. Overseas credentials include training and certification in Thai massage from the Traditional Medicine Hospital and the International Training Massage Institute (ITM) in Chiang Mai, Thailand. Ms. Saeger received certification in Sen therapy from, and is certified to teach Thai massage by, ITM.

Ms. Saeger is currently a full-time instructor and the Massage Therapy Program Coordinator at Keiser University in West Palm Beach, Florida, which offers a 1,000-hour massage therapy and associate of science program. She has owned and operated a successful massage therapy practice for 14 years, working on amateur and professional athletes such as marathon runners, triathletes, and ballet dancers. Ms. Saeger specializes in the equestrian industry, working with professional trainers, riders, and show horses. Indeed, it was an idiopathic lameness in one of her horses that led Ms. Saeger to the healing arts field. She has since successfully combined therapeutic massage with Thai massage to rehabilitate countless show and pleasure horses and teaches other therapists these phenomenal techniques.

Additional business experience includes operating a robust practice in which she has been teaching yoga to people of all ages and walks of life over the past 33 years, and she is a former co-owner of an entrepreneurial company that imported unique and exotic gifts from Thailand for massage therapists. Prior to her work in the massage therapy field, Ms. Saeger was an editor and production manager in the magazine publishing industry in New York City. The majority of her time was spent with the American Kennel Club (AKC) as Managing Editor and Production Manager for its monthly publications. Ms. Saeger was one of the prime movers in overhauling the AKC magazine's design and purpose by splitting the magazine into three different publications, creating two statistical periodicals and one editorial or content-based magazine.

Ms. Saeger was Production Supervisor for Ziff-Davis, at the time New York City's largest magazine publisher, and was responsible for notable titles such as *Car and Driver, Modern Bride, Runner, Flying, Boating, PC, PC jr.,* and *Creative Computing.* Besides directly supervising the production managers for these magazines, she played a role in accounting for the four-color production costs on all 75 Ziff titles. With the sale of Ziff-Davis, Ms. Saeger moved to a Wall Street investment firm, Lord, Abbett & Co., where she functioned as Production Director for the Marketing Communications Department. At Lord, Abbett she was responsible for a $2 million marketing budget, and, as with her previous positions, she continued to provide the creative impetus behind everything from editorial concepts to printed pieces.

Work in the publishing field was a natural transition for Ms. Saeger after having graduated from Alfred University with a bachelor of arts in English literature and having grown up in her family's graphic arts and typesetting business.

Ms. Saeger currently lives in Loxahatchee, Florida, with her two Newfoundland dogs.

Lewis Rudolph

Lewis Rudolph received an associates degree in accounting from Mohawk Valley Community College and a bachelor of science degree in accounting from Rochester Institute of Technology in New York State. He is currently pursuing a master of arts degree in religion at Liberty University in Lynchburg, Virginia.

After graduating from college, Lewis joined a family-owned business in Utica, New York, where he advanced to the position of company treasurer. In 1991 Lewis moved to Florida and received his massage education, and he became a licensed massage therapist in 1992. Lewis became Director of Therapies for US Total Rehab in Palm Beach and Broward counties in Florida. Subsequently, he, along with his wife, Jill, established Southern Rehab and Therapy, Inc., which has operated in four locations in Palm Beach County, Florida.

Lewis has served as both Treasurer and President of the Palm Beach County Chapter of the Florida State Massage Therapy Association. Lewis also served the organization at the state level as Secretary and Treasurer.

Lewis has taught a variety of subjects in massage schools, trade organizations, and college programs. The courses include business, law, ethics, medical error prevention, and Intuitive Neuromuscular Massage, a massage technique that he has developed and trademarked.

Lewis currently resides in West Palm Beach, Florida, with his wife.

Brief Contents

Contents

CHAPTER THIRTEEN

CHAPTER FOURTEEN

CHAPTER FIFTEEN

CHAPTER SIXTEEN

CHAPTER SEVENTEEN

PART 3

Enjoying the Fruits of Your Labor

CHAPTER EIGHTEEN

APPENDIXES

Acknowledgments

Jan Saeger: I am grateful to the people in my life who have served as great business role models and those who have supported me in many ways, especially Rosann Richardson, Scott Stein, Miriam Morgan, and my esteemed co-author Lewis Rudolph.

Heartfelt thanks to all of my clients who have supported me over the years. Special thanks to Rosann Richardson and Elise Zudema, who have been pivotal to growing my business in many ways.

Lewis Rudolph: Many thanks to my co-author Jan Saeger for our seamless collaboration and great working relationship for my first book. To all of my customers and friends, for their endless support and encouragement. A special thanks to Dr. Tom Mullins and Charles Bronfman and Donal Ford, for their spirit of generosity and caring.

Also many thanks to my parents, Les and Bev Rudolph, and to my children, Louis Ray, Carre-Cross Duval, Bonny Belle, and Jeff Weido. An especially awesome thank-you to my grandchildren, Dylan Duval and Ava Weido.

To my wife Jill: Without your support, love, understanding, and confidence in me, I could not have accomplished this. I love you. Lastly, and most importantly, I thank you, God, for without your blessings, none of this would be possible. I raise this effort to praise you and your works done through me.

Reviewer Acknowledgments

Sandy Anderson, LMT
Truckee Meadows Community College

Carla Bashaw-Carriere, BA, LMT
McIntosh College

Patricia Berak, NCBTMB, BHSA, MBA
Baker College of Clinton Township

Bernice L. Bicknase
Ivy Tech Community College–Northeast

Susan L. Bova, BS, NCBTMB,
Massage Therapy Program Coordinator, Certified Master Medical Massage Therapist
Penn Commercial

Rebecca Buell, BS, LMT
McIntosh College

Michelle Burns, BSN, BS Alt. Med, LMT, MTI
Advanced Holistic Healing Arts

Jennifer M. DiBlasio, AST ACMT
Asst. Director of Education
Career Training Academy, Inc.

Lora Freeman, LMT
Chicago College of Healing Arts

Cindi Gill
Body Business School of Massage Therapy

Sam Gill
Body Business School of Massage Therapy

Robert B. Haase, LMP
Bodymechanics School of Myotherapy & Massage

Holly Huzar, LMT
Center for Natural Wellness School of Massage

Lynda Madnick, LMT
Palm Beach Community College Massage Therapy Program

Laura-Michelle Iacovone, BS, LMT
Center for Natural Wellness School of Massage Therapy

Lisa Jakober, NCTMB
Corporate Director of Education
National Massage Therapy Institute

Susan Kalchman, MT
American Institute of Massage Therapy

Julianne Lepp, CMNT
Independent

Maryagnes Luczak
Career Training Academy

Mary A. McCluskey, BS, MA, WRMT
Wisconsin School of Massage Therapy

Londyn Beck McGuigan
Lincoln Technical Institute

Tara G. McManaway, MDiv., LPC ALPS (WV), LMT (WV), CMT (MD)
College of Southern Maryland

Judy Moore, MPH, CMT
Consultant

Adam C. Nance, LMT
International Academy of Massage Therapy

Jay M. Nelson, LMT, CMP
Concorde Career Institute

Mercedes Nepute, LMP

Lesley M. Pearl
McKinnon Institute of Massage

Carissa Pohlen
Minnesota West Community & Technical College

Graham Rae, LMT
Manatee Technical Institute–East Campus

David J. Razo
American Career College

Dorothy Sala, LMT
Inner Journeys Holistic Care LLC

Rosemary Schliep, NCTMB
Minnesota State Southeast Technical College

David L. Sessoms, M.Ed., CMA
Miller-Motte Technical College

Cheryl L. Siniakin, PhD, LMTI, NCTMB
Community College of Allegheny County

Nancy Smeeth
Connecticut Center for Massage Therapy

Tina A. Sorrell, LMT, NCTMB, MTI
Independent Instructor

Steve Wiley
American Institute of Allied Health

Preface

Many students in health care and healing arts curriculums, including massage therapy, physical therapy, chiropractic, homeopathy, athletic or personal training, naturopathy, acupuncture, Reiki, and many more, possess a strong desire to help others but do not know how to create and maintain a thriving practice. Younger students often have not had financially astute role models, nor have they had personal experience in handling difficult monetary situations. Older students may have gone through changing life cycles involving family, career, and market fluctuations that may have wreaked havoc with their financial standing, leaving them leery and unsure of a nontraditional business structure.

A paradox begins to form as increasing educational requirements and increasing demands on students' time have resulted in fewer colleges or vocational schools including basic business courses in their curriculum. We can consider the biblical analogy of the man and the fish—"Give a man a fish and you feed him for one day; teach him to fish and you feed him for life"—and apply it here as "Give the students the skills necessary to practice their profession and you help them to be good therapists; teach them how to parlay those skills into a successful business and you help to give them a career." In other words, if we simply teach students the applicable courses for their discipline but do not teach them to profit from their course of study, we will not help them manifest their desires and create a viable means of support.

Along with not having good basic business skills, many new students, as well as those making a career change in later years, lack advertising and marketing training. This training is among the most essential factors in introducing yourself to the public and building a viable practice. Once your business is established, you will need to apply additional skills to constantly navigate often-treacherous waters. Each facet of business—keeping records, managing costs, buying supplies, maintaining ethical standards of practice, and understanding legal and tax considerations—can be the potential pitfall that sinks the business ship.

Personal computers and Palm Pilots are the latest hardware entries into the business field, leaving the old green accounting ledgers far behind. Almost any medical or health practice office you work in will have client records, insurance forms, and invoices on a computer program. This text will help you think about the many software options available for office management, billing, accounting, and overall organization.

Large corporations have dedicated enormous amounts of time and financial resources for their executives to acquire time management skills. Many students will leave school without having developed these essential skills, thereby increasing their chances of frustration or failure. This text will help you wade through these murky waters as well, by providing practical solutions to efficient time management in various forms of health practice.

About the Book

The quintessential bottom line is that this text, along with the pedagogy and ancillary material, is intended to help health care practitioners survive and thrive in the world of small-business management.

This book has incorporated into almost every chapter the following features to make it a practical and useful text:

- *Reality Check* boxes provide candid, anecdotal examples from the authors on what to do and what not to do in creating and running a business.

- *Tidbit* boxes offer valuable bits of information as short, concise tips. Many of these can be copied onto sticky notes and placed in various areas throughout an office, helping you remain on target and thereby meet your goals.

- *Checklists* at the end of all chapters aid you in evaluating whether or not you have met the chapter objectives.

- *So What Do You Think?* questions at the end of each chapter provide critical-thinking questions to reinforce what has been gleaned from the chapter.

- *Learning Outcomes* at the beginning of each chapter provide a glimpse ahead to important sections for quick understanding of the chapter's contents.

- *Key Terms* at the beginning of each chapter are in color when first introduced to familiarize you with important concepts.

Throughout the text, many chapters also include the following:

- *Tables and charts* that help you, as an entrepreneur, work through all elements from planning a budget to charting hours of operation.

- *Forms,* such as client intake/history and SOAP notes, that familiarize you with the various types of essential documentation. These forms are also online at www.mhhe.com/SaegerBusiness, so you can personalize each to include your own company information; the forms can then easily be printed out for use.

Appendixes with valuable information include:

- A *state-by-state resource list* gives each state's Web site information, allowing you to log on directly to the site for specifics on licensure/certification of various health care fields.

- *Budgeting and accounting forms* are provided for those individuals who would rather use the familiar pencil-and-paper worksheet.

- *Web sources and additional contact information* for companies and organizations mentioned in the text are included for further study.

Online Learning Center (OLC) www.mhhe.com/saegerbusiness

The OLC consists of the Instructor's Manual, PowerPoint presentations, numerous examples of forms, and EZ Test for the instructor. McGraw-Hill's EZ Test is a flexible and easy-to-use electronic testing program. The program allows instructors to create tests from book-specific items. It provides a wide range of question types, and instructors can add their own questions. Multiple versions of the test can be created, and any test can be exported for use with course management systems such as WebCT, BlackBoard, or PageOut. EZ Test Online is a new service that gives instructors a place online where they can easily administer EZ Test–created exams and quizzes. The program is available for both PC and Macintosh operating systems.

The OLC also has a student section that consists of PowerPoint presentations, quizzes, and numerous examples of forms needed to start and run your business. All the forms can be personalized and printed for use.

In Conclusion

Many health care and healing arts curriculums are inadequate in addressing business fundamentals; this text and its ancillaries and pedagogy, along with the Online Learning Center, are designed to help you understand, develop, and implement the skills necessary to enjoy a prosperous career whether you are a first-time student or someone who has had business experience in an unrelated field. Although this material was written by massage therapists, the information can be applied to various forms of health care practice, and it is our hope that this resource will become a trusted guide to many in the health care profession.

Introduction

From the Authors

One of the hardest things to do is to get your "head around" starting a small business, especially if you have not studied business in school or haven't had any experience in the business world. Starting and running your own business is a daunting and sometimes overwhelming task. If you take each task one step at a time it becomes easier for you to accomplish the overall task of running your business. When you get too bogged down in the "have to do's" of your business, you must remember that one step at a time works. A method that you want to remember is to take the easiest steps first. By starting small and simple, you will be able to build up momentum as you grow toward the bigger and more challenging steps that lay ahead of you.

Additionally, you need to keep moving forward. It is important that you keep your momentum and allow it to carry you forward when you don't have the strength to carry on by your own devices. Keep yourself ahead of the curve—in other words, try to stay ahead of what needs to be done—and you will be able to relax even when you are working very hard. There is nothing more stressful than trying to catch up. People who are always trying to catch up are always behind. When you are behind, you miss most of the opportunities that today presents, because you are still trying to make up for what you missed yesterday and the day before and the day before that and so on.

As the backlog of work increases, your effectiveness decreases. Take it one step at a time, and do plan for times when you stop walking. As much as you need momentum, you also need to be fresh and strong when you are taking those steps. If you are not rested and relaxed, you will lose many of the advantages that you have, such as a clear head, efficiency, effectiveness, and decisiveness. Do not just plan time to stop stepping; plan time to do things that you enjoy doing and that are not related to your business. It is important to be able to completely disengage from your work and engage in something that is good for you in another facet of your life. This is a function of a healthy, balanced life.

Being a business owner does not condemn you to a life that is single-minded, stressful, or too intense. Being a business owner gives you the responsibilities and rewards that the position has. It is up to you to make your position as successful as you choose it to be. Though success depends on many different variables, the most important ingredients for success are your abilities, both as a professional and as a business owner.

One of the things that you may notice in the text is our use of the words *customer*, *business*, and *establishment* more often than *client*, *patient*, *clinic*, *spa*, and the like. This is done for a specific reason, which is that for far too long, those in the health care service industry have forgotten that they are in the service industry at all. If you are not willing to provide the proper services at the proper time in the proper way, your business will fail. This is plain and simple. When reading this book, read it with that in mind. All of us are in the business of serving others. It is with that mind-set that we will be successful. We are to be servants to those who are our customers, our employees, and all those with whom we come into contact in our lives.

IT'S ABOUT THE SERVICE

I was working on a customer at his home and he told me that he thought that I was successful because I understood that good service was important in the service industry, while most other service people didn't understand that concept. I was upset that he called me a service person, and it seemed very demeaning to me, because I was a successful, accomplished massage therapist. He went on to state that if all the doctors would learn this lesson, then they would have greater success and an easier time of it in their professions. It then dawned on me that this customer of mine considered that the health care industry is a service industry like all other service industries. We are faced with the same problems, challenges, and issues that all other service professionals face. (LSR)

The best illustration of the true value of good service is the restaurant business. If you look at the restaurant business, you can see two concepts that translate very well to the service industry in general. The first is the type of restaurant that the owner is planning: Is it going to be inexpensive, fast, and basic, or is it going to be high-end gourmet? Where is the owner going to position the restaurant in regard to the competition? This is called *creating a niche*. The second comparative concept is the content of the service. The service that the owner is providing consists of the treatment, the atmosphere, and, lastly, the service itself. If people go to a restaurant and the service is not good, the food is not good, or the atmosphere is poor, they will most likely not go back. They have many other places that they can go to and will be happier with. The same goes for your business, no matter what it is. There are many other people and groups that are providing good service, treatment, and atmosphere. You have to be as good as they are, if not better. You don't have to worry about what the others are doing as much as about what you are doing and whether or not it is meeting your customers' expectations.

A Visual Guide to *Building a Healthy Business*

Every chapter opens with Learning Outcomes and Key Terms that prepare students for the learning experience.

Marketing Your Business

CHAPTER THIRTEEN

LEARNING OUTCOMES

After completing this chapter, you should be able to:

13.1 Learn who your customers are.

13.2 Find out what your customers value.

13.3 Successfully network and grow your business.

13.4 Understand what successful promotions and public relations entail.

KEY TERMS

customer referral

loyal customers

value

customer service

referral

networking

promotions

public relations

advertising

"The writing is very clear, very reader friendly and all chapters give excellent real life examples to consider."

Maryagnes Luczak, Career Training Academy

REALITY CHECK

MONEY WELL SPENT

Four years into private practice, I had the opportunity to make a second trip to Thailand to gain additional training and certification in Thai massage. Although I had just purchased a house and had all the expenses associated with being a new homeowner, I felt the additional training would be of benefit to the style of massage I was developing. (Besides, it was fun, and Chiang Mai had become a home away from home!) The money was well spent because the training further solidified the massage I performed and became an integral part of my practice. The monies gained have far exceeded the monies spent. However, if you are contemplating a considerable expense (at the time, my Thai training cost $2,500 versus $250 for a local seminar), make sure beforehand that you will be buying something that is going to be of great value and not just for fun. (JLS)

Reality Check boxes provide real-life examples from the authors' experiences so that students can envision typical business situations.

REALITY CHECK

IT'S MORE ABOUT THE EXPENSES

Both in our business and with therapists whom I have mentored, the time that it takes to break even financially varies quite a bit. The biggest factor in determining the amount of time that it takes to reach the break-even point is not the number of treatments but the actual break-even point. Very few therapists have had a difficult time increasing the number of treatments they perform, but they do have difficulty managing their expenses.

As our practice grew, we found that we were able to pay the expenses after about a year. This did not mean that after 12 months everything was easy, but there was a light at the end of the tunnel. There were months that it was easy to pay the bills, and there were months that the bills were not as easy to meet. Sixteen years later, the same thing pretty much occurs, yet, because of better planning, the good months and the bad months don't matter nearly as much. The difference is not in the income but in the expenses we incur and the planning we do for those expenses. Many of the people whom I have mentored have started single-person businesses or small group practices, and they have been able to become business-profitable within a year. On that basis, each has expanded into an overall profitable venture, including personal financial needs, within months after the business's break-even point. (LSR)

Tidbits provide students with valuable tips that they can implement in their businesses.

TIDBIT

It is important to listen to what your customers have to say, and it is much more important to listen to what they aren't saying. The complaint they don't share will be the reason they are leaving your business.

A working intake form

FIGURE 16.4

REHAB & THERAPY, INC.
437 West Main Street
West Palm Beach, FL 33415
(000) 000-0000 Fax (000) 000-0000

NAME ______ DATE ______
ADDRESS ______ PHONE ______
______ CELL PHONE ______
BIRTH DATE ___/___/___ SEX ___ MARITAL ___ E-MAIL ___
EMPLOYER ______ EMPLOYER'S PHONE ______
EMPLOYER'S ADDRESS ______
I WAS REFERRED TO REHAB & THERAPY BY ______
HAVE YOU HAD ANY OF THE FOLLOWING DURING THE PAST YEAR:

SEVERE HEADACHES	Y	N	TINGLING/WEAKNESS IN HANDS	Y	N	HAND SWELLING	Y	N
FAINTING	Y	N	TINGLING/WEAKNESS IN FEET	Y	N	FOOT SWELLING	Y	N
DIZZINESS	Y	N	BLOOD PRESSURE/ HEART	Y	N	CHEST PAINS	Y	N
PREGNANCY	Y	N						

NAME OF PRIMARY/FAMILY PHYSICIAN ______
ARE YOU BEING TREATED BY A PHYSICIAN? ______ FOR WHAT? ______
ARE YOU CURRENTLY TAKING ANY DRUGS? ______ PLEASE LIST ______
HAVE YOU BEEN TREATED FOR ANY OTHER MEDICAL CONDITIONS IN THE LAST YEAR? ______
HAVE YOU HAD MASSAGE THERAPY BEFORE? ______ HOW OFTEN DO YOU RECEIVE MASSAGE? ______
IS THIS VISIT A RESULT OF A WORK-RELATED ACCIDENT? ______ IF SO, DATE OF ACCIDENT ______
IS THIS VISIT A RESULT OF AN AUTOMOBILE ACCIDENT? ______ IF SO, DATE OF ACCIDENT ______
I AM SEEKING TREATMENT FOR: ______
PATIENT SIGNATURE ______ DATE ___/___/___
Logo and license number if required by state law

Form examples may be reproduced for student practice. All forms may be personalized for student use and are available in the text and on the Online Learning Center.

Checklists guide students in evaluating their completion of the chapter tasks.

CHECKLIST

Have you done these things yet?

☐ Have you selected team members for your team?

- A suit? Name _____
- An artist? Name _____
- A dreamer? Name _____
- A professor? Name _____

☐ Have you ensured that each team member understands and accepts his or her place on the team?

☐ Have you identified your strengths and weaknesses?

- My strengths are _____
- My weaknesses are _____

☐ Have you determined where you are going to fit into your team?

- Besides being the leader, I am also _____

SO WHAT DO YOU THINK?

1. You're entitled to terminate a professional relationship that you believe has become dysfunctional or unproductive, If you simply dislike a client, is that sufficient reason to terminate your relationship with him or her?

Critical-thinking questions at the end of each chapter reinforce the concepts that students have learned in that chapter.

"It is well written and thorough. The authors have a wide and deep knowledge base and communicate it to the reader in a friendly and easy to digest manner. The 'So What Do You Think?' questions give the student a chance to mull over the information and reflect on how it does or does not pertain to him or her."

Nancy Smeeth, Connecticut Center for Massage Therapy

Starting in the Business World

PART 1

Building a Strong Foundation

CHAPTER ONE

LEARNING OUTCOMES

After completing this chapter, you should be able to:

1.1 Visualize the importance of investing in yourself.

1.2 Describe the four aspects of self.

1.3 Understand how to create a vision.

1.4 Analyze a specific vision of your business.

1.5 Identify obstacles.

1.6 Define limiting beliefs versus empowering beliefs.

1.7 Explain the power of focus.

1.8 Recognize capabilities that assist in control of attention.

KEY TERMS

awareness

alignment

imagination

outcome

choice

beliefs

consciousness

internal dialogue

evidence

INTRODUCTION

Every creative project begins with a vision, a dream, a wish, or a desire. What we are creating from is an aspect of ourselves that feels larger and more expanded than our normal day-to-day selves. We are stretching ourselves outside our current "known" reality. The amazing process of creating is the ability to hold and sustain that vision and to keep our faith in our possibilities of success. When we begin a venture, the most difficult task is what we confront in ourselves. The key to sustaining our faith in our vision is our **awareness**. Awareness is what we are conscious of. Many of us, if not all, go into a healing profession to be in service to others and thus learn and grow ourselves. Our external world will reflect what is transpiring in our internal world. The goal of this chapter is twofold: first, to help you recognize that you are your greatest resource; second, to assist you in creating and grounding your vision by developing skills that will help you keep your focus as well as maintain your faith in what excites you about you (i.e., your passion toward any new venture you are contemplating beginning). The greatest foundation for your business is your investment in yourself.

When you are inspired by some great purpose, some extraordinary project, all your thoughts break their bounds. Your mind transcends limitations, your consciousness expands in every direction and you find yourself in a new, great and wonderful world. Dormant forces, faculties and talents become alive, and you discover yourself to be a greater person by far than you ever dreamed yourself to be. (Patanjali)

You as Your Foundation

You are the foundation of your life. The foundation is the ability to know and eventually manage all aspects of yourself and keep them in balance and **alignment**. You ultimately want to feel that you can stand on your own understanding of yourself—the authentic you. To create balance, you first must begin to understand what is taking place within you.

Four aspects exist within us: the spiritual, the mental, the emotional, and the physical. These aspects are intertwined together as our energy. They present as a whole picture. When one of these aspects is overdeveloped or underdeveloped, we have an imbalance that, in turn, affects our energy. We relate through our intuition of our energy and the energy of others. When we have greater balance, our aperture of our intuition opens and we begin to tap into a universal field that abounds and supports us in ways of which we may not be conscious.

At the beginning of any new endeavor, crisis, or transition, we are forced to connect with ourselves in a way that sometimes is very uncomfortable and unfamiliar. Sometimes we find we are forced to confront change and deal with ourselves on completely different terms after the loss of a loved one, a sudden job loss that leaves us without a familiar role to play, or a forced relocation due to a job change. In contrast, transitions can be rewarding experiences when we consciously choose to self-reflect and make personal changes. We begin to look at the world from the inside out. This begins the journey of utilizing your greatest asset—you.

> *Gnothi Seauton* (Greek for "Know thyself," inscribed above the entrance to the temple of Apollo at Delphi).

The tendency today is to get caught up in managing our external circumstances rather than accessing a greater realm, our internal world. Today, more than ever, we must hold our vision of what we want and what is important to us. The acceleration of the pace at which we are living provides a greater challenge, a greater contrast, in our ability to identify this vision within us. No one can access that vision, that realm, but you. Your greater self, your spiritual self, holds that vision within you.

In understanding the self, it is important to identify in greater detail the four aspects that exist within us.

- The *spiritual* is the unbounded. It encompasses all the unknown and all possibilities. It is often equated to the spark of divinity within each individual. Thus it is hard to define because it is so unique and personal. As William Blake wrote in "Jerusalem," "I rest not from the great task, to turn the immortal eyes inward, into the worlds of thought, the bosom of God, the human imagination." The spiritual, in essence, is your **imagination**.

  The imaginal ground, or imaginal field, is where we live, create, and have our being. It is the field where all other aspects can come and play in an uncensored manner—the best of all parts combined. The spiritual is the aspect of self that contains our intuition, which is our connection or conduit to the greater source of information. As the renowned scientist Buckminster Fuller once said, "I call intuition cosmic fishing. You feel the nibble and then you have to hook the fish." This statement describes intuition as sensing, something pulling you in a direction, a sense of a potentiality in a particular direction in which you have to use your other aspects to take action to pursue what it is you are sensing. Your spiritual self senses a tendency or a synergistic knowing, yet it still takes action to acknowledge, choose, or act decisively to confirm or manifest that intuition. Spirit is what sustains life. When we take our first breath, we are alive. Breath, our in-spire/in-spirit, gives us life until our last breath. Breath is the engine that powers change. We must breathe into (in-spirit) our imaginal hopes and dreams if they are ever to come to manifestation. Our connection with our spiritual selves fuels that energy source and allows us to tap into something much larger than ourselves. As written by Patanjali in How to Know God, "If the Reality exists at all, it must be everywhere: it must be present within every sentient being, every inanimate object."

  We hold a connection to a greater realm through our spiritual selves, however each individual chooses to define that aspect or whatever path is used to explore it (religion, yoga, personal development, etc.). It has been written in many books that the first step to creating is to become aware of your higher self. "Within you is a divine capacity to manifest and attract all that you need or desire" (Wayne Dyer).

- The *mental*, the mind, at first glance appears to be intelligent and planned, but it truly operates in response to the imagination. It is an instrument that is directed but seems as though it has a life of its own and is sometimes very difficult to control or direct. It is the program by which the subconscious attracts and creates what we manifest. It feeds information into your system. The mind has three components: the subconscious mind, the conscious mind, and the superconscious mind. The subconscious mind is power without direction and receives its direction from the conscious mind. It plays back what it receives like a computer and is very literal. It responds to repetition and feeling and interprets experiences that we attract according to our beliefs. The conscious mind has the power of choice and the free will to be directed or to direct. It can choose to suppress or express what is in our subconscious. And the superconscious mind gives us 100 percent of the information in the conscious and the subconscious—we tend to call it our "reality." The superconscious sees all things coming from itself.

- The *emotional* self comes from a response to the mental, physical, and spiritual selves. It is a commitment to a belief in something, 100 percent faith in it. An emotion is the physical manifestation of any idea that we believe in. It is instantaneous, whether it be positive or negative. It acts in response to our thoughts. This response is an indicator of where we are in our flow, our resonance. Paying attention to our emotional responses as directives is extremely helpful in aligning and balancing. They supply us with information as to whether we are in alignment with our vision or not.

- The *physical* self is the manifestation of the mental, emotional, and spiritual selves. It expresses in matter that which lives and plays out in those other aspects—hence, the saying "What the mind represses, the body expresses." The physical will always be a complete reflection of the internal aspect of ourselves. The physical also influences the mental and the emotional. Reflect on how you feel after a yoga class, or a massage, or a great walk. The physical activity may create the feeling of greater relaxation or expansion of your mental and emotional faculties. The body may be considered the mixing bowl into which we put our other ingredients.

The interrelationship of these four aspects is complex and intertwined. As you begin to have greater awareness of these aspects, you will begin to understand the forces within.

Your Vision

Everything in life begins with a seed. Our ideas, beliefs, and thoughts are the beginning of that seed, the vision. Our emotions and feelings enliven it. Our attention and conviction draw it forward to manifestation. The greater the degree of commitment and conviction to that vision, the more accelerated the process of manifestation. It is a continuous process to maintain attention on that vision to nurture its growth. The ability to control attention, the energy of your awareness, and the feeling of your wish fulfilled, your vision is what will determine your success or failure. "Always bear in mind that your own resolution to succeed is more important than any other thing" (Abraham Lincoln).

As we explore what it takes to create your business, we will expand on these areas in greater depth. For now, at the stage of inception, your greatest ingredient is your imagination.

Imagination is the ability to create an idea, a mental picture or a feeling sense of something. (Shakti Gawain)

Remember that as children we all played in and enjoyed the vividness of our imaginations. We could conjure up any picture, any image, without limitation. Imagination inspired us, energized us, and gave us great strength, buoyancy, and life. We were never figuring imagination out or planning the "how" or logistics of it. Watch children: They begin, they hardly take a breath, and off they go. Their energy and excitement are contagious and ignite their friends' imaginations as well. Imagination is magnetic and alive. But as we age, for most of us, that natural ability, that skill, becomes dull and faded. Some of us have even forgotten how to tap into it, but we all had and still have this ability. We may just need to remember or to be reinspired. "Your imagination is your preview of life's coming attractions" (Albert Einstein).

We will expand, later in this chapter, to removing some of the obstacles that may limit our imaginations. To explore creating your vision, begin by asking the question "What do I want?" Answering this question may be a difficult task for some and easier for others. We tend to fixate and focus on what we don't want. We push against all the unwanted that pervades our lives. All we need to do is, first, create the space to be able to reignite our imaginations.

We should also allocate time for this activity, giving it the importance it is due. If you are familiar with meditation, or even simple relaxation techniques, you may want to do whatever you do to naturally quiet your mind. "Before you can get what you want you have to know what you want" (Jeffrey Gitomer).

TIDBIT

Give yourself an optimum environment, one that relaxes you, feels good to you, and is free of distractions.

Ask yourself the following questions:

- What do I want?
- What is my vision?
- What does my vision look like when it is completed?

The goal is to work backward. Come *from* what you desire. Fill in the details such as:

- What does the environment feel like or look like?
- Who is there?
- What am I doing?

As you start to allow yourself to go into your imagined state, possibilities flow. Continue to allow yourself to explore the increases in energy of both expanded states and contracted states. Recognize that this is your creative process; have fun with it. This is your seed.

As you fill in your picture, you begin to plant your seed. As you feel what it's like to have your wish fulfilled, your feeling state of excitement, relief, passion begins to nurture that seed, to literally enliven it.

This picture becomes your *point of reference* in the future. This state of being, this feeling or imagined state, is the creation that you will continue to refer to when you get distracted from your vision.

Your Outcome

Write out your vision, your **outcome**, in detail. Elaborate specifically on the feeling of having accomplished your outcome, coming from that already successful state. "Be patient toward all that is unresolved in your heart and try to love the questions" (Rainer Maria Rilke).

Answer the following questions:

- How do you feel now?
- Where are you?
- Who is in your life?
- Who is in your business practice?
- Where are you living?
- Where is your office or center?
- What is new and different?

Pay attention to the sensory impressions, the sounds in the background. Feel them, and then write them down.

Write your vision as if it were happening now, in first-person ("I am") statements and present-time reality. Be committed to your highest choice. You are experiencing your vision as if it were occurring now, not in some future time.

Your Obstacles

We cannot impress on you enough the power of your imagination, your thoughts. At this stage, as you begin, fears may arise spontaneously. You may have questions such as "Am I capable?," "Will I have enough money to fund such a big dream?," "Where will I find the help I might need?," "What if I fail?," and on and on. As you start to focus on what you want, those fears and issues of the past may come up.

TIDBIT

Remember: You are in a state of coming from your outcome, not moving toward it. You are in a state of having your fulfilled vision, not attempting to achieve it.

EDUCATION SERVES ONE WELL

My father quit high school at 16 to join the Marines and fight in World War II. He never finished school after the war, nor did he acquire any further education before trying to run his own business. My childhood memories are of him always saying that his finances were no one's business, and he refused to get help from knowledgeable sources such as an adult-education business class or the Small Business Administration; he always handled money in secrecy. Therefore, I acquired the belief that money and anything related to it was of a dark nature and something to be feared. Only after I reached adulthood did I recognize that my fears were his fears of being thought of as not intelligent and not capable of being successful with money. (JLS)

What you may find is that the moment you begin to take charge of your attention, direct your thoughts, and focus on what you really truly want, what you don't want or haven't wanted in the past may become apparent. Look at this as an awareness process. To receive your heart's desire, you most likely have to clear out some congested areas. Someone once said that it is not failure we are afraid of—it is our success. If we do not allow ourselves to dream without any limitations, without any censoring, we limit ourselves to receive that which we are actually asking for. By expanding our dreams, we are opening a space within us, and consciousness will fill it with what we focus on.

Our indoctrination—what we grew up with, what we mimicked, what we thought we were rebelling against—influences us. In response to these influences, we developed a strategy as we grew to help us survive. This strategy becomes embedded as an automatic program that continues to run unconsciously. Our programs determine how we react and what we attract. There is nothing wrong with this or us; it is quite natural. It becomes a difficulty only when the program directs us rather than being directed by us. Feelings, judgments, and opinions that happen on automatic running are a result of the program. They are instantly there. When there is a *willingness to explore, it creates the space for awareness. Awareness affords us the opportunity to have choice.*

Herein lies the secret to tapping into our potential. Once we have a **choice**, we have options, and our window to possibilities becomes larger. We no longer act on automatic survival patterns. The world, our world, becomes a much brighter place. Where before we saw obstacles and problems, we now can see possible solutions, even exciting options.

Our strategies are made up of **beliefs**. Beliefs are our thoughts and ideas, which we may hold as true. Some are core concepts, often uninspected values within us. Other beliefs do not feel as solid and dense. Our beliefs translate into our thoughts and ideas, which occur very quickly, making up the chatter in our minds. In fact, for some of us, our minds produce these thoughts at an alarming speed, a chatter that may feel as though it never stops or we cannot even keep up with it. We do not need to know all our thoughts. The concept of the power of our thoughts and their influence on us is not new. Becoming aware of the influence they have on us is at times easier to understand intellectually than is our ability to stop them or redirect them. Truly, "thoughts are things," and powerful things at that when they are mixed with definiteness of purpose, persistence, and a burning desire for their translation into riches or other material objects. "Whatever the mind of man can conceive and believe, it can achieve" (Napoleon Hill).

The key to gaining some control and direction is that aspect of ourselves that brings everything to life—our *feelings*. We will feel either good or bad, expanded or contracted, empowered or limited; we will have the desire to move toward or away. Every belief has a feeling state associated with it. And the feelings act as an internal barometer that indicates which way we are going with our thoughts. We do not recognize that the elements of where we sit today, in this very moment—what surrounds us in our life, our home, our friends, our family; the shape and health of our bodies; our emotional and financial reality—are all manifestations of the thoughts we held or still hold as a result of the seeds we planted previously in our **consciousness**. Consciousness is the potential or reservoir of all possible states you could experience.

Letting Yourself Feel

It is worthwhile to explore the base you already operate from and then to deliberately redirect your attention to thoughts and beliefs you prefer for your foundation. Notice that you have conversations with yourself in your mind about your world and the people in it. We talk to ourselves. This is identified as our **internal dialogue**.

Identify any self-sabotaging internal dialogue you listen to:

- If you were to reduce the internal dialogue to a feeling, what is that feeling?
- Do you notice any pattern of that feeling repeating in your life?
- Do you notice something you swore you were never going to be like?

Once you have identified the feeling, take some space to feel the feeling, noticing where it lives in your body (do you have a sensation in your head, in your heart area, or in your stomach?). Notice how much space it occupies, and let yourself experience it, feel it, without resistance. If resistance appears, feel that as a sensation as well. As you do this, you may notice the feeling, the sensation, dissipate.

Usually it is our resistance to a feeling that doesn't allow us to feel it. Once we do allow ourselves the space to experience the feeling, it vanishes or begins to dissipate in that moment. When and if it reoccurs, do this process again.

Many are familiar with the expression "Don't think of the pink elephant." After hearing it, all that comes to mind is that pink elephant. Resist a feeling, a person, a memory, and all that comes to mind are those things. This sends a message to our subconscious, which then begins to attract those experiences. Unfortunately, most of us create much of our lives from resistance. The desire to have control over our experiences creates resistance to what is. To change this, we must be willing to feel, to experience, what we resist. When that happens, it becomes easier to see and possibly change our judgments, which may have caused the resistance to begin with.

> Everything in your life and the lives of those around you is affected by the Law of Attraction. It is the basis of everything you see manifesting. The more you come to understand this power of the Law of Attraction, the more interest you will have in deliberately directing your thoughts—for you get what you think about, whether you want it, or not. Without exception, that which you give thought to is that which you begin to invite into your experience. (Esther Hicks)

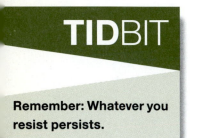

TIDBIT

Remember: Whatever you resist persists.

Limiting Beliefs versus Empowering Beliefs

Beliefs that serve us align with our vision. Limiting beliefs hinder our vision or whatever we may want for ourselves. Examples of limiting beliefs are "I can't," "I'll never be able to," "It's too hard," and "Nothing ever works for me."

"I can improve," "This is a process," and "I am learning about my strengths and weaknesses" are examples of empowering beliefs. Each of those beliefs has a very different feeling. Typically, an empowering belief feels expanded and gives a sense of relief and space (Figure 1.1), whereas a limiting belief feels contracted and negative. Only you can determine whether a belief is helping or hindering you. To find out, ask

FAMILY INDOCTRINATIONS

The only model I had seen for owning my own business was my father. He always had felt forced to have his brother-in-law as a partner due to the guilt and sense of responsibility inflicted on him by his sister. All of his family indoctrinations played on him, as he was an immigrant who was responsible for bringing his entire family to America after the war. He never felt that he chose his partner. He suffered greatly from feeling it was an unfair, financially inequitable arrangement. He created a victim identity in this relationship and felt like a martyr. He carried a lot of resentment about this arrangement. After my own business partnership ended, it was quite interesting to reflect how I had lived out exactly the same patterns and feelings I had observed in my father, no matter how much I disliked seeing them in him. (RB)

yourself "How does it feel?" Often we have conflicting beliefs. For example, when you begin a business venture, many beliefs can run rampant in your mind and some might seem to conflict with your venture. Consider the following conflicting belief: "To be in service to others, it is wrong to charge money." This belief will definitely affect your ability to generate a worthwhile income. Prosperity and good works can go hand in hand. If you feel guilty for charging for your services or if you do not value your own services, this will create a problem for your business. Identifying sabotaging beliefs is critical in establishing a healthy foundation based on beliefs that reflect what you really want to achieve.

Answering certain questions can help you focus on creating empowering beliefs about yourself that align with your vision of your ideal self. You want to connect feeling to the statements you come up with. How would it feel to be the person you are describing? Ask yourself the following question: "If I were to create myself today, anew, what kind of person would I choose to be?" Creating your ideal self is done from an originating perspective, rather than responding or reacting to something from the past. For example:

- Does my ideal person feel confident in the value of what he or she is offering?
- What are that person's qualities and characteristics?

Choose expansive beliefs that empower you to succeed

FIGURE 1.1

9

- What beliefs, thoughts, and ideas would that person have to have about himself or herself in order to have created the success he or she experiences?

You will notice from your answers to these questions beliefs you have about yourself that don't serve or align with your vision. These are limiting beliefs about yourself or your abilities.

How can you hold on to your vision despite those obstacles?

Focusing

Practice directing your thoughts to your outcome. Practice refocusing your attention as often as you remember to.

Whatever you put your attention on grows. Focus on weaknesses, and weaknesses grow. Focus on strengths, and strengths grow. Gaining control over your attention will take discipline and practice. It becomes easier when you have clearly defined goals or visions. They create a focal point for your attention.

Awareness of your thoughts is critical to helping you change. Ask yourself the following:

- Is my internal dialogue supportive of my vision or distracting and harmful to me? (Take a moment to reconnect to your vision. If you are hitting an obstacle, take a moment to upgrade your thoughts in a direction that offers relief.)
- What can I tell myself that could make me feel a little better?
- What evidence can support that better feeling?

Your Backdrop

Your vision becomes your backdrop. This backdrop is a story your subconscious will attract and collect the **evidence** to create. Evidence is any information that will support what you are focused on. Be aware of where and on what you are placing your attention. They will become part of your backdrop. Any event or situation may occur, yet our perspective of that event is what we potentially have power and control over. Whatever perspective or interpretation we choose, we will collect the evidence to support it.

When you are stuck or discouraged, don't invest in that version of the story. It may be challenging to feel you can change your perspective, yet you can begin by changing some aspect of the story you are telling yourself. If you feel something, tell a story about it—you are investing in creating it. Be deliberate in what you are choosing to tell yourself. Disciplining your mind, your attention, is like training an animal. It may be a wild animal at first, but it will learn. All you are doing is deliberately learning how to train your attention, direct it, and bring it back to your desired outcome. Do not invest in something you do not wish to have appear in your story.

Our innate being enjoys feeling good. The more joy and happiness you bring to your vision, the more your attention will align with that picture. Notice in the mornings, when you first wake up, what is automatically there. Is it something you choose to invest in? Don't ask yourself why it is there. Better questions to ask are "What would I prefer to focus on as my outcome for my day? and "What kind of feeling would I want to start my day with?" You could even begin by asking yourself "What was the best thing that happened yesterday?"

The point is we want to begin to retrain ourselves consciously to focus on what makes us feel good. The subconscious will then go about its job to collect the evidence to support that version of our reality.

Human beings have free will. When we consciously use our will, it then directs our attention. It is a "muscle" just like any other in our body. As we exercise it, it strengthens.

CHOOSING TO FEEL

I would often tell clients of mine a story to illustrate how we collect evidence. One morning when I woke up after a night of restlessness and bad dreams, I started my day grumpily. My husband was lying in bed, and as I looked at him, I began to tell myself a story about him. I didn't like how he spoke to the kids yesterday, I didn't like how he treated the dogs, and I particularly didn't like how he spoke to me. In other words, he was just awful yesterday. And there he was asleep in bed, and I was starting my day miserable. The next morning I woke up completely refreshed. I had a great night's sleep. I woke up feeling energized and happy. I looked at my husband lying in bed, and I saw the most wonderful man. I began to reflect on how he is my best friend, the greatest dad, and the love of my life. And there he was still sleeping in bed. I started my day with the greatest feeling and in the best mood.

I had to reflect. What changed? The body was the same body in the same bed on each day; yet I, dependent on my mood, looked to find the evidence, tell the story, that was going to support how I felt. It made me realize the power of my choice of feeling. How do I choose to feel? What is my preferred outlook? Whatever my choice is, I know I will collect the evidence to support it. So what evidence do I choose to collect? How would I prefer to feel? (RB)

Imagine you are sailing a boat in the middle of the ocean. How do you know if you are headed in the right direction? You have to continuously check your compass. Your life and the direction you choose to head in need the same kind of evaluation. Are you starting your day with the intention of holding to your course? You are strengthening your will to focus your attention on your course. Your vision is what you see on your horizon as your destination.

Remember you are only and always up against yourself and the restrictions and limitations you have created for yourself. *You are not a victim of circumstances; you are a creative creator.* "We are masters because we have the power to create and to rule our own lives. You create yourself, whatever you believe you are" (Don Miguel Ruiz).

We realize this is a small beginning in a lifelong adventure of discovering yourself. Your business, and any project, when viewed as a template for self-discovery can become a great adventure. If you enliven that picture with joy, enthusiasm, and happiness as your backdrop, all that you do will be a result of your curiosity. Keep curious, and do not get waylaid by taking yourself or any of what you do too seriously.

CHECKLIST

Have you done these things yet?

- [ ] Have you created the time and space to use your imagination to envision your business or project?

- [ ] Have you made time daily to reconnect with this image filled with feeling?

- [ ] Have you created and filled in the image with specificity?

- [ ] Have you identified your limiting beliefs regarding money, success, career, business, or any subject you wish to explore?

- [ ] Have you identified and written down empowering beliefs you choose to hold regarding the topics above or what you have added to your list?

☐ Have you felt the difference in yourself when you state a limiting belief rather than an empowering belief?

☐ Have you made a list of actions that would support your vision?

☐ Have you set a list of important versus not-important items in regard to prioritizing your time?

☐ Have you greater awareness daily of your thoughts (internal dialogue) that align and support your project? And of those that don't?

☐ Have you taken moments (time-outs) throughout the day to stop and feel where you are?

☐ Have you practiced being able to identify a contracted state, feel it, and pause to redirect your attention to a thought that will create relief or expansion?

☐ Have you written down your vision or some statements to use as a focal point for your attention?

SO WHAT DO YOU THINK?

1.   What are the benefits of noticing the four aspects of self that operate within you?

2.   Do you think you will set up a checks-and-balances system for referencing yourself?

3.   What are the benefits of writing down your limiting beliefs? What is the difference in writing down your empowering beliefs? Which feels better?

4.   Do you see yourself as the most valuable asset of your business? Why or why not?

5.   Do you see the value in practicing developing the use of your free will?

6.   Do you see an improvement in your ability to focus?

Creating a Mission Statement

CHAPTER TWO

LEARNING OUTCOMES

After completing this chapter, you should be able to:

2.1 Understand a mission statement.

2.2 Recognize the importance of a mission statement in business.

2.3 Develop a mission statement for your business.

2.4 Consider whether or not growth fits into your mission statement.

KEY TERMS

mission statement

simplicity

clarity

brevity

honesty

A **mission statement** tells you what you are in business for. A mission statement tells you what you want to accomplish in your business today, tomorrow, and far off in the future.

Mission statements for companies show what the company is all about. Ben and Jerry's Web site displays three mission statements. The following is their product mission statement:

Product Mission

To make, distribute & sell the finest quality all natural ice cream & euphoric concoctions with a continued commitment to incorporating wholesome, natural ingredients and promoting business practices that respect the Earth and the Environment.

Another cutting-edge company is Microsoft Corporation, which has this mission statement on it's Web site:

Our Mission

At Microsoft, our mission and values are to help people and businesses throughout the world realize their full potential.

These mission statements are very powerful (Figure 2.1), yet they are not meant to be specific about how the companies are going to accomplish their missions. Each statement is generic, and yet it provides a clear direction for the company. If a proposal is presented to the managers at Microsoft, one of the first questions that they will ask is, "Does this idea fit into our mission statement?" If it does not, then the idea will not be adopted by Microsoft.

For a massage therapist, a good mission statement would be:

To alleviate pain using the best massage therapy techniques, while providing a pleasant experience for people around the globe.

If, as a massage therapist, you ask yourself whether or not you should provide acupuncture treatments in addition to massage therapy, the answer would be no, because according to your mission statement you want to alleviate pain using the best massage therapy techniques. This mission statement can be adapted to fit other businesses as

Your mission statement should be one that you can envision rather than one that is esoteric

FIGURE 2.1

well, such as acupuncture, by removing the words *massage therapy techniques* and replacing them with *acupuncture*.

The previous example shows how important it is to create the correct mission statement. A mission statement is not set in stone, and it can be changed, but it is better to create the right statement and follow it throughout the life of the business. The mission statement is the vehicle by which your business decisions are going to be measured. By using the mission statement as your guide, you will create consistency and direction for your company. Even if you have already started a business and have been running it for years without a mission statement, you should create one now. It will help you keep on the right track as your business grows. You will be able to compare your decisions to your mission statement.

It does not matter whether you are a single-person operation or a multinational company, a mission statement will help you and those whom you deal with to understand what you are trying to accomplish in your business. This will create a clarity that will more easily enable you to accomplish things such as obtaining financing and developing partnerships.

Key Points in Writing a Mission Statement

Some of the most important things that you should think about when constructing your mission statement are:

- **Simplicity**. It is important to keep the message and wording of your mission statement straightforward. The statement should not contain anything that is difficult to understand.

- **Clarity**. It is important to keep the message and wording of your mission statement clear and concise. It is a statement that cannot be ambiguous at all. If any questions arise because the statement is not clear, it is important that you rework the mission statement.

- **Brevity**. If the mission statement is too long, it will lose its impact and focus. Too many words will cause the person who is reading it to lose the real meaning of what you are trying to accomplish.

- **Honesty**. If you are not completely honest in how you convey what your business means to you, your business will not succeed. Incongruities will show very quickly, and you and your business will suffer because of them.

It is a great idea to formulate this statement yourself after doing a little bit of research. The best way to research mission statements is to go online and look at the mission statements of some companies that you admire. Also look at the statements of some companies that do things that are similar to those you do. Remember that these statements define these companies and that you, too, will be defined by your mission statement.

Evaluation

Once you have formulated a mission statement, leave it alone for a day or so, and then go back to it to see whether it is still as good as you thought it was when you first wrote it. Do you think that it completely conveys what you want it to convey? If it does, take it to your team members (see Chapter 10) and see whether they like it as much as you do. If it conveys a clear, concise message of what you are about, you have created a masterpiece! Do not be surprised if each of your team members has a slightly different idea about what your mission statement should say, so take each of their suggestions and incorporate what you like and leave out what you don't want. Remember, you have the final say.

You may be asking, "I know what I am doing and where I am going, why should I go through all of this bothersome stuff?" The answer is that over time you may begin to lose clarity, because of a change in either the business climate or your circumstances, or you may even desire to do something different. A strong mission statement will be your fundamental guide and provide a strong foundation on which to build your business. At any given time, a review of your mission statement will tell you whether or not you are still on track. For example, you may realize that you are spending too much time on tasks that are not a part of your core business, such as selling products. Nowhere in your mission statement does it say that you are going to sell nutritional products to alleviate pain. It says that you are going to alleviate pain with *massage therapy techniques.*

This may not seem like a large problem to you, but let's take a closer look at what is involved in selling nutritional products, or in going beyond your original mission statement. In general, it involves additional work and therefore additional time. Specifically, selling nutritional products in your establishment requires that you:

TIDBIT

You can always go back and change your mind as conditions change, but your original decision is usually your best one, so carefully consider any changes that you want to make before you make them.

- Listen to salespeople explaining the advantages of their products over their competitors' products.
- Apply for all the legal paperwork needed for sales (credit applications, state resale certificates, etc.).
- Place orders, receive shipments, stock items, and sell items.
- Spend time with customers explaining the products, taking care of customer complaints, and answering questions about product usage.
- Place reorders, pay for inventory, and keep inventory current.
- Educate yourself and your staff about the nutritional products.

All of these tasks take time and effort away from your primary (and really only) purpose, according to your mission statement, which is to alleviate pain using massage therapy techniques.

This may seem like a small change that you can handle, but people have a tendency to continue to add things to their plate and fill up spaces with things just to do something. This new direction has nothing to do with the original mission statement for your business. Most importantly, it is something that is taking you away from something that you have a passion and talent for.

The loss that is incurred in this example is twofold. Not only do you lose time by doing these new tasks, but you also give your customers the perception that you are changing things that they are happy with. They will be the first ones to recognize that you are losing focus and possibly some of the benefits that brought them to you in the first place. You are sacrificing customers for something that you never intended to do in the first place. The problem manifests itself in a lack of focus for your business, which reduces the power that enables you to run your company successfully.

With the lack of focus, you are likely to lose the direction of the business also. A shift occurs in what the business accomplishes. Instead of spending the company's assets on alleviating pain through massage therapy, you increasingly spend them on other things. What begins to happen is that you start to compensate for the shortfalls that your customers are experiencing because of your loss of focus. The compensation is another item that is placed on your agenda, and it eventually becomes another thing that causes you to lose even more focus. Now that you have expanded from a few nutritional supplements in your store to many items, you are beginning to run out of room, so you start to look for a larger space. You are very happy because your business is growing both in gross receipts and in size. This growth, however, is not the type that necessarily makes you more money; quite frankly, it can reduce overall growth and profits.

Besides fitting in with your vision, which is described by your mission statement, an idea has to add value to the business. The way you know that value is added to your business is by creating profitable growth. If you decide growth would add value to your business, you must change the focus of your business by rewriting your mission statement. If you determine that adding products to sell fits with your mission statement, then by all means add them to your mix. There is no inherent problem with adding different revenue sources such as product sales. Doing so becomes a problem only if your mission statement does not include the sale of items in your business. Remember: A mission statement is something that all actions of the business are to be measured against.

Arguably, the most important function of the mission statement is to provide a framework for your business, but it also provides a framework for the growth of your business. A mission statement provides parameters for your business to grow and continue to be even more successful.

CHECKLIST

Have you done these things yet?

☐ Have you decided what the mission of your business is?

☐ Have you written out a clear mission statement?

☐ Have you determined whether or not your mission statement is realistic?

☐ Have you determined that growth is beneficial at some point?

☐ Have you rewritten your mission statement to include this growth?

SO WHAT DO YOU THINK?

1. What are the unexpected advantages that you have received from creating your mission statement?

2. Do you think that you should have a mission statement for your personal life? Does it have to match your business mission statement?

3. Do you have an idea of how you might revise your mission statement to accommodate growth? Or have you decided that growth would not be a good idea for you and your business?

Setting Goals

CHAPTER THREE

LEARNING OUTCOMES

After completing this chapter, you should be able to:

3.1 Define appropriate goals and explain their importance in business.

3.2 Recognize the importance of setting goals for yourself and your business.

3.3 Understand the difference between subjective and objective goals.

3.4 Develop subjective and objective goals for your business.

KEY TERMS

goal setting

goal

short-term goal

long-term goal

subjective goal

objective goal

gross sales

profit

number of customers

number of units sold

time amount per customer (gross)

time amount per customer (individual)

sale amount per customer (gross)

sale amount per customer (individual)

number of treatments

total hours worked

gross income

earnings per hour

earnings per treatment

total expenses

net profit

INTRODUCTION

For you to get to an endpoint, you first must know where you are going. You must specifically plan *how* to get to a certain endpoint. This is called **goal setting**. Planning, or setting goals, will minimize costly mistakes and help you fulfill the mission statement that you have just written. After creating a good mission statement, writing out goals will help you achieve your dreams for your business (Figure 3.1).

The key to success, above everything else, is planning for both the expected and the unexpected and having the people around you informed and in step with you on this journey. It does not matter how long it takes you to reach your goals as long as you plan for doing so. The less complicated and costly your business and personal life are, the quicker the break-even point will be and the easier it will be to achieve your goals. If you are in financial distress going into your new venture, you will put undue stress on the venture and undermine the future of your business. If you have personal financial issues, they should be controlled or eliminated before you head out on your own.

If you do not have good credit, take steps to repair it before going into a new business venture. You will have to take the appropriate measures even if this means taking on a second job. You must pay all of your bills on time to establish a record of good payment and good credit. It might be a bit disheartening to realize that you cannot immediately open your dream business, but it's better to get yourself in a more manageable position first and put the business off for a period of time. Remember, you can use that time wisely and creatively by doing all the necessary research or even designing your business, planning your marketing strategy, and shopping sales for office furniture and equipment.

The purpose behind defining goals is to help you achieve the following:

- **Focusing.** Goals help to give you focus today. They provide you with the reason for doing the things that you need to do *now* to get the job done.

- **Planning.** Goals help you to plan for your immediate and future needs. For example, if you have a goal that requires a certain amount of expansion in money and employees, you will definitely need to plan for that expansion well in advance.

Set goals that are high but not unattainable

FIGURE 3.1

- *Staying on target.* Goals keep you on target for where you want to be in the future.

- *Tracking your success rate.* Meeting measurable goals shows you whether you are successful or not at any given point.

Goals

A **goal** is something to strive for. Goals should be set high enough to be challenging yet not so high as to make them impossible to reach. They can be either long-term goals or short-term goals. A **short-term goal** is generally accomplished in less than one year, and a **long-term goal** spans more than one year. It is important to take into account the effects of your decisions with regard to both short-term and long-term goals. In addition to these goals, there are two other types of goals that you must identify: subjective and objective.

Subjective Goals

A **subjective goal** is a goal that cannot be measured in absolute terms. Examples of subjective goals are to be happy and to be successful. These are important goals, but how can you plan for happy? How many workdays are there in successful? Although it is difficult to *quantify* happy and successful, they are still very important goals and you should *qualify*, or ask yourself, what happiness and success really mean to you. Some other goals that are important but difficult to measure are:

- *Satisfaction.* Is your work challenging enough to keep you interested, or will you get bored easily? Are you satisfied with what you are accomplishing with your work, and are you satisfied with what the work is accomplishing in your life and the lives that are affected by you?

- *Life balance.* Does your work allow you to have the right balance in your life, with time off for family and other pursuits? This does not mean that you should be looking for an easy path that will allow you to do anything you want without regard to what your work demands of you. Balance does not mean that you will not need to sacrifice; it means that you are comfortable with the amount of sacrifice that you are planning to give. If you don't have balance in your life, you will fall over from lack of support both from your friends and loved ones and from yourself, due to mental or physical fatigue.

- *Comfort.* Will your work allow you to live comfortably right away? How long will it take before you will be able to support yourself, and do you have the funds to support yourself in the meantime? Is everyone else who may be affected by the lack of financial comfort in agreement with your decision?

- *Trade-off.* What will you be giving up, and are you going to be satisfied with what you are getting in return for it? Are you prepared to go all the way, through thick and thin?

So, if these goals are not able to be measured, what are you supposed to do with them? Think of all the subjective goals that you have in your life, and write them down on a chart, as shown in Table 3.1. Whatever you determine is important in your life should be written down in the left column as one of your subjective goals. The "Achieved" column calls for a simple answer of yes or no. There are no maybes here; subjective goals are either achieved or not achieved—no compromises. You cannot say they are almost accomplished. In the "Reason" column, explain why you answered yes or no in the previous column. Be honest with yourself. Summarize the

Tracking Subjective Goals			
Subjective Goal	**Achieved**	**Reason**	**Next Step**
Happiness	Yes	I am happy with my progress, even though I have had some setbacks. I am happy with where I am today and where I am going.	Keep up the good progress, and get past those setbacks.
Satisfaction	Yes	I am doing the work that I love to do, and I am impacting many people in a positive way.	Keep getting better at my work, and increase the impact that I have.
Life balance	No	I have lost contact with my family and regret that, even though they are OK with it.	Take time away from my work in a way that will minimize the effect on my business.
Comfort	Yes	I am really very happy because I haven't had to forsake too many material things.	Start thinking about the next step, saving for my future.
Trade-off	No	I used to be able to take the weekends off, but now I have to work all the time.	Take time off!

reasons that you feel you have or have not met each goal. In the final column, write down what you should do next. For each unmet goal, be sure to list a solution to what is keeping you from achieving it.

The subjective goals discussed above are by no means the only subjective goals that you may have in your life, whether in business or in your personal life. There are many possibilities that can be included in your subjective goals. Some of the additional goals that you could include are:

- *Ethics.* Are you being ethical in your dealings with the people whom you are doing business with?
- *Faith.* Is your faith growing stronger in your professional life as well as your personal life?
- *Stress.* Is your life as free from stress as you want it to be?
- *Future.* Are you comfortable with what the future seems to hold for you?
- *Movement.* Are you moving forward in your professional life, or are you stagnant and stale?

The list can go on and on. Your subjective goals need to be prioritized, starting with the most important ones at the top of your table and moving down to the least important at the bottom. You need to remember that you cannot have everything all the time but you can continue to strive toward the goal of having your list filled with a lot more yesses than nos.

Objective Goals

An **objective goal** is one that is quantifiable, that is, one that can be specifically measured. When determining your objective goals, you must keep in mind both your subjective goals and your mission statement. If your subjective goals lead you to a part-time profession, the same process of listing and determining the importance of the objective goals will apply. The only difference is the endpoint of the amount of growth that you will be planning for. The following are some examples of objective goals that can help to measure the success or failure of a business:

- **Gross sales**. This is the amount of money that you collect for the products and/or services that you provide to your customers over a period of time. It is a good indicator of how busy you are and how much money you can spend in the future, given how busy you are.

- **Profit**. This is the total amount of money earned less the amount of money spent to run your business over a period of time. Profit is the most important financial goal, for if you cannot make a profit, you will not last long in your business. Profit also shows how well you are using your assets to make money.

- **Number of customers**. This will allow you to see the overall growth of your company. It is called the *customer base*.

- **Number of units sold**. A unit could be a product or a service. The number of units sold is a good indicator of whether you are utilizing your assets (either products or employees) at the optimum level. For example, a hotel wants to have an occupancy rate of at least 80 percent as this shows that the hotel is using its asset of available space for its maximum benefit.

The goals listed above should be examined and compared on a monthly, quarterly, and yearly basis. The numbers will help you to see how you are performing and where you may be able to improve. By spending a few minutes each month, you will be able to avoid financial surprises.

Other goals that are not as obvious as those listed above should also be considered. These goals are important in the sense that they help to show whether you are maximizing your potential profit, and thus they should be reviewed periodically. These goals include:

- **Time amount per customer (gross)**. This is the amount of time that you spend *on average* with a customer during each customer visit. Some customers take up much more time than others. Though they may be great customers, you have to plan for time and organize yourself so that you can serve all of your customers properly.

- **Time amount per customer (individual)**. This is the amount of time that you spend with a *specific* individual each time he or she walks into your business. This measure allows you to plan for customers who take an extraordinary amount of your time. It will help you make proper business decisions as to whether or not such a person is profitable enough for you to keep on as a customer.

- **Sale amount per customer (gross)**. If you have a business that is product-based, this is the amount of money *on average* that a customer spends during each customer visit. This measure shows you what you are collecting from each customer who comes in your door. You could have all the customers in the world, but if you are not selling them any products or services, you won't be in business for very long.

- **Sale amount per customer (individual)**. This is the amount of money that a *specific* individual spends each time he or she walks into your business. It allows you to verify who is a profitable customer and who is not. This will help you make proper business decisions when dealing with scheduling and prioritizing your time.

Listed below is a sample schedule showing how often various objective goals should be reviewed.

WEEKLY GOALS

- Number of treatments per week.
- Total hours worked per week.
- Gross income per week.
- Earnings per hour.
- Number of customers per week.
- Number of new customers per week.

MONTHLY GOALS

- Number of treatments per month.
- Gross income per month.
- Total expenses per month.
- Net profit per month.
- Number of customers per month.
- Number of new customers per month.

YEARLY GOALS

- Number of treatments per year.
- Gross income per year.
- Total expenses per year.
- Net profit per year.
- Number of customers per year.
- Number of new customers per year.

All of the above numbers are very easy to acquire, but why should they be acquired? These are the most important financial and numerical indicators for the health of your business. In the category of weekly goals, the **number of treatments** is the best indicator of how busy you really are making money. You could be spending 20 hours a week playing video games, but that is not how you make your money as a therapist. It is important for you to see the trends of when you are busy and when you are not busy. Sometimes you may seem to be busier than you really are. With concrete numbers, there is no question as to whether or not you are busy and have met your goals. Remember, the key is to measure your performance against what you want to accomplish.

The **total hours worked** per week shows you the number of hours that you worked, both doing treatments and doing other things, for your business. If you find that you are working more hours outside the treatment room, you are shortchanging your ability to make money.

The next indicator is the **gross income** per week. This is simply the amount of money that you earned during the week that you have worked. It is a good idea to start the workweek on a Monday and keep it consistent throughout the year. *Income* is all money that you have received, even if it is for work yet to be done. Also, for the purposes of goal setting and tracking, money earned but not yet received is not included in this figure.

This brings you to the next indicators, probably the most important ones, which enable you to see at a quick glance what you have earned over a period of time. The first is **earnings per hour**, which is calculated by taking the gross income per week and dividing it by the total hours worked per week. This figure shows you how much money you earned per hour for the week that you worked. The second is **earnings per treatment**, calculated by dividing your gross income per week by the number of treatments per week. This measure shows you how much money you are making per treatment and whether you are discounting your treatments too much or giving too many free treatments. It is an important indicator of whether you are being compensated properly for the work that you are doing.

The last two indicators have to do with customers. The first is *number of customers per week*, which shows you how many different customers you are seeing each week. It enables you to see how spread out your customer base is and whether or not you are dependent on too few sources of income. As an example, if you are working for a doctor in his office four days per week and doing 90 percent of your treatments at his office, you may want to increase your production outside the doctor's office, for if you lose the doctor as a source of income, you will have very little income to depend on. This is not to suggest that you should decrease the amount of business that you do with this doctor, but you need to recognize that if you lose that particular part of your business, you may not be able to support yourself. You should be able to maintain and even increase your number of customers per week.

This brings us to the final indicator for this discussion, *number of new customers per week*, which shows whether or not your customer base is growing. If you are able to keep the same number of established customers while increasing your new customers, you will have a growing, thriving business. You have to keep your established customers happy, and, in addition, you have to attract new customers. Much of your customer base will cycle out over a period of time, so it is important to keep new customers flowing into your practice. Normal attrition can be due to any number of factors, such as the loss of a job, a child going off to college, divorce, or a move out of the area. In addition, you must keep in mind that there may be a seasonal factor in your business, as well as a limit on how many treatments you can provide per period.

When put together, the two customer indicators help to show you how potentially secure your business is. If you have many customers and you lose one, you have a better chance of getting past the loss than you would if you have only a few customers and you lose one. There are some advantages to having one large source for customer referrals and some individual customers, but they are completely dependent on the security that you have with the large customer.

As we move into the monthly goals, there are only two new goals that have to be addressed here in detail. All the other goals are just the weekly goals added together to get a monthly total. The first new goal in the monthly category is **total expenses** per month. It equals the amount of money that you have paid out during the period of time in question. This includes all the expenses that you incur and pay for. If you have not paid for an item, its cost should not be included for the purposes of monthly goals. For tax purposes, the amount may come into play, but that is not part of this discussion. Another thing that may confuse matters is noncash expenses, such as depreciation, which should not be included in calculating monthly goals.

Once the expenses are determined for the period, the **net profit** for that period can be calculated. This is done by subtracting the total expenses from the gross income for the period in question. Net profit indicates whether or not you have made any money during the time period in question. It is the number that you should be most concerned with, for without any profit you will not be able to stay in business for very long. Net profit enables you to see how you have done during a certain period of time.

The yearly indicators are a summation of the monthly numbers. All the goals should be considered when starting and running your business. Short-term and long-term effects should also be considered. If you don't reach your goals, find out

TIDBIT

One of the biggest pitfalls of small-business owners is spending money on the basis of anticipated profits that will be coming in, rather than income that has already come. It is dangerous, if not impossible, to play the catch-up game when it comes to finances. One only has to look at the credit card debacle to realize this fact.

why and change it! Don't wait and don't feel too bad; use the information that you have to make your business better. If you reach the goals that you have set for yourself, do two things that will help to ensure a more successful business. The first is celebrate! Enjoy your success! The second is create new goals that will challenge you even more than your previous goals.

CHECKLIST

Have you done these things yet?

☐ Have you developed and written long-term subjective goals for your business?

☐ Have you developed and written long-term objective goals for your business?

☐ Have you developed and written short-term subjective goals for your business?

☐ Have you developed and written short-term objective goals for your business?

☐ Have you prioritized your subjective goals for your business?

SO WHAT DO YOU THINK?

1. What have you learned from creating your goals and comparing the actual results to the goals that you set?

2. What are the most important goals that you have set for yourself? Why?

3. Do you think that long-term goals are as necessary as short-term goals? How long do you think you should have specific goals? Why?

4. Do you think that you should have goals for your personal life? Do they have to match your business goals?

Evaluation and Application of Goals

CHAPTER FOUR

LEARNING OUTCOMES

After completing this chapter, you should be able to:

4.1 Determine personal financial needs in order to develop goals.

4.2 Develop goals with regard to short-term, intermediate-term and long-term needs.

4.3 Evaluate the goals that you have set for yourself.

KEY TERMS

personal financial needs

business financial needs

other financial needs

total financial needs

INTRODUCTION

Goals should be looked at in at least two different time frames: short-term goals, which are usually accomplished in one year or less, and long-term goals, which span more than one year. Planning should be done from the beginning of the business and should cover at least five years, and longer if possible. The longer your plans for your business, the better off you will be. "Why is that so?" you are probably asking. The answer is very simple and can be illustrated best with an example, a vacation.

When you plan a vacation, you plan everything: You decide how you will get to your final destination, and you research and perhaps arrange accommodations. You then look for all the possible things that you can do during this vacation to maximize your enjoyment and produce the best outcome given your circumstances. The outcome is measured by the amount of fun, relaxation, and excitement that you experience. If you spend your time on your vacation looking for a place to stay and can't find any because all the rooms are booked, this will decrease the fun and relaxation of the experience. You might end the vacation on a dismal note if you neglected to arrange for the return trip back home and were stranded for several days. Though this may seem a rather basic example, hopefully it shows you that in planning for any future vacation, both the short- and long-term goal is very important. The goal is the end of your business cycle, not the end of the week or the end of the workday.

As shown in the above example, a perfectly good vacation or business can be ruined if not properly planned for from beginning to end. Planning is shown by the goals that you set throughout the whole business cycle.

The way that you map out your goals (Figure 4.1) can be as simple or as complicated as you want, but the ultimate objective is to give yourself a point to reach and a measuring stick to measure your performance (Figure 4.2). This chapter presents a step-by-step example of the objective-goal-setting process. Remember: If you follow a logical pattern, you can see your goals materialize right in front of you.

Mapping out your goals is a process

FIGURE 4.1

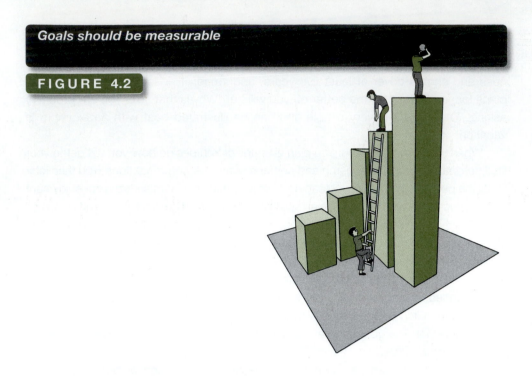

Goals should be measurable

FIGURE 4.2

It does not matter what type of business you are setting your goals for. Whether you are planning a part-time business or a multiple-location business, you use the same goal-setting and evaluation process. For any project, such as adding retail items or expanding to additional locations, the same process should be used in determining your goals and their evaluation.

Determining Objective Goals

The most important questions that need to be answered at this point are what are your goals, and when will you achieve them? The discusssion below explains how you can determine what your objective goals should be. The best way to determine goals is to work backward from the goals to what is necessary to reach those goals. If you approach your goals in this way, you will have a clear and specific plan of action for achieving them.

Step 1: Determine Your Personal Financial Needs
Personal financial needs include the monthly expenses you pay to run your household and support your family. The amount should be a number that you can live with, without causing any discomfort in the way that you live your life. There is a wide range of items and costs that can be part of your financial equation; they vary by individual and by location. Table 4.1 presents a representative example to give you an idea of how to determine your financial needs. This example does not include any other income that you may be receiving from a partner or from any other sources. As the table shows, your personal financial needs are $3,500 per month.

Step 2: Determine Your Business Financial Needs
Business financial needs are the expenses you incur to run your business, including paying yourself. Chapter 6 outlines what your business financial needs may be. For the purposes of this example, the financial needs for your business are $2,000 per month.

Monthly Financial Needs	
Item	**Cost**
Rent/mortgage	$850
Utilities	150
Child care	200
Telephone	50
Insurance (health, property)	500
Food	500
Repairs and maintenance	100
Medical expenses	150
Charitable contributions	200
Automobile (including insurance)	600
Other	200
Total	$3,500

TABLE 4.1

Step 3: Determine Any Other Financial Needs

Other financial needs include debt reduction or future growth or savings that you may want to distinguish from your personal and business financial needs. Examples of these needs are expenses for retirement, home improvements, and a college education, either past, present, or future. It is not necessary to include any of these items in this example.

Step 4: Determine Your Total Financial Needs

Total financial needs are calculated by adding your personal, business, and other financial needs together. We have personal financial needs that amount to $3,500 per month and business financial needs that amount to $2,000 per month. The total financial needs therefore are $5,500 per month.

Step 5: Determine the Number of Treatments Needed to Break Even

For this example, let us use $70 as the average price per treatment. To determine how many treatments you need to do to cover your expenses, divide total financial needs by price per treatment. Table 4.2 shows the calculation.

In this example, you need to do 79 treatments per month, or 943 per year, to break even financially. Thus, if we assume that you want to work for 50 weeks per year, you need to do approximately 19 treatments per week (943 treatments divided by 50 weeks). (If you wanted to work for only 45 weeks per year, you would have to perform 21 treatments per week—943 treatments divided by 45 weeks.) The break-even number of treatments should be the first goal that you want to achieve in your business. It is imperative that you are completely honest when you calculate this number, for if you are not, you will be facing financial shortfalls, which will lead to disastrous results.

Number of Treatments to Cover Expenses		
	Monthly	**Yearly**
Financial needs (break-even point)	$5,500	$66,000
Price per treatment	$70	$70
Number of treatments needed to break even	79	943

TABLE 4.2

IT'S MORE ABOUT THE EXPENSES

Both in our business and with therapists whom I have mentored, the time that it takes to break even financially varies quite a bit. The biggest factor in determining the amount of time that it takes to reach the break-even point is not the number of treatments but the actual break-even point. Very few therapists have had a difficult time increasing the number of treatments they perform, but they do have difficulty managing their expenses.

As our practice grew, we found that we were able to pay the expenses after about a year. This did not mean that after 12 months everything was easy, but there was a light at the end of the tunnel.

There were months that it was easy to pay the bills, and there were months that the bills were not as easy to meet. Sixteen years later, the same thing pretty much occurs, yet, because of better planning, the good months and the bad months don't matter nearly as much. The difference is not in the income but in the expenses we incur and the planning we do for those expenses. Many of the people whom I have mentored have started single-person businesses or small group practices, and they have been able to become business-profitable within a year. On that basis, each has expanded into an overall profitable venture, including personal financial needs, within months after the business's break-even point. (LSR)

Step 6: Determine the Number of Treatments Needed for the Profit You Want

Now that you have determined how many treatments are necessary to break even, you should also determine how much profit you want to build into your business. This is done in a manner similar to the break-even calculation. If you want to build in a $1,000 profit per month, you will have to perform an additional 15 treatments per month to accomplish this, bringing your monthly total of treatments to 94 and your weekly total to almost 23 treatments.

The next question that comes to mind is, "How long will it take to get to the break-even point?" This is a very difficult question to answer: The answer is completely dependent on what you are willing to do to get to that point. The most important factor is your willingness to work. If you are committed to building a successful business, you will need to put time and effort into your business. If you were working in another job and trying to get ahead, how many hours would you be willing to put in? You must be willing to work as many, if not more, hours in your own business to be successful. If you are planning to work a 40-hour week but you are only doing 5 hours of treatments, what are you doing with the other 35 hours?

The 35 hours that you have "free" should be spent increasing your business by promoting and marketing yourself (see Chapter 13). If you promote and market yourself, you will be amazed at how quickly your business will grow. You will find that the growth will be exponential as your focus on that growth becomes greater. If you develop and follow a marketing plan and stick to it, you will build your business.

This method works very well on paper, yet none of us practice on paper. There are always variations in the average price per treatment, the expenses incurred in the business, and personal expenditures. Steps 3 and 6 show how you can set goals and budget for your business. As you become more accustomed to setting goals and budgeting, as well as following a budget, the application of what you are budgeting for and your money outcomes will become more manageable.

Making goals a part of your everyday consciousness, seeing what your goals should and can be, will help you live a life that has less financial uncertainty and creates a greater ability to plan for whatever uncertainty comes to you. The more that you understand both what you need financially and what you can earn financially, the better you will be able to plan, live, and enjoy life. Financial problems are some of the most stressful problems that we encounter in our lives. Having an idea of where you are financially gives you power over your financial position by giving you the opportunity to change the things that make up your financial situation.

CHECKLIST

Have you done these things yet?

☐ Have you determined what your personal financial goals are?

☐ Have you determined what your business financial goals are?

☐ Have you determined what your other financial goals are?

☐ Have you determined what your total financial goals are?

☐ Have you determined how long it will take to reach the break-even goal?

☐ Have you determined how long it will take to reach your profit goal?

SO WHAT DO YOU THINK?

1. Do you think that it is possible to be able to determine what your financial needs are?

2. What other factors are involved in determining what your financial goals should be?

3. Do you think that your attitude about money will affect how you determine your goals?

4. Do you think that your attitude about what constitutes success will determine setting and achieving your goals?

Putting Together a Team

CHAPTER FIVE

LEARNING OUTCOMES

After completing this chapter, you should be able to:

5.1 Identify prospective team members for your organization.

5.2 Enlist team members and instruct them in what they are expected to do for the team.

5.3 Lead the team members effectively to better the business's position.

5.4 Recognize where members fit into the team, plug them in where they are needed, and be able to take advantage of their strengths.

5.5 Understand the importance of a team and the advantages that a team can provide, as well as the challenges a team can present to a leader and an organization.

KEY TERMS

suit

dreamer

artist

professor

communication

We are not islands unto ourselves. As much as we try to do things without the help of others, we are much more likely to succeed if we enlist the help of others in building and even running our business. We say "running" a business because operating a business requires some of the same characteristics as those needed to physically run a race. Many times we need help of some sort to finish the race; we know that we cannot do it alone. Sometimes support is needed to achieve the goal of winning the race.

Creating Your Team

Starting and running your own business can be a scary and lonely process. It is much easier if you bring along a team as you start your own business. The fact that you can't afford professionals, and you don't even know who should be on your team, should not be a barrier. Family members and friends will be glad to assist you if you approach them in the proper manner. You must also know whom to approach and when to approach them.

So how do you approach someone about being on your team? There are two very important aspects that you should include in your quest for team members. The first is to convey to your prospective team members that being a part of your team is something very special and an opportunity that they cannot possibly turn down. However, you must first convince yourself that *you* want to be a part of that team. You will not be able to convince anybody else to do something if you yourself are not convinced. Before you approach anybody about joining your team, write down all the benefits, or "selling points," that a person will receive by being a part of your team. These benefits can include the following:

- ***Broadening of the person's skills and knowledge by interacting with other intelligent people (you and other team members).*** If the person hangs around with people who have experience, and listens to them, he or she will learn something. The relationship will be equally beneficial not only to all of your team members but also to you.

- ***Connecting with others who can increase the person's professional endeavors.*** The person can capitalize on potential business through connections that he or she makes by being a part of your team. An example is a product supplier who has a great business mind. Your team members can use their new-found associates to increase their own business opportunities.

- ***Receiving any additional benefit that you are willing to give.*** This is not a benefit that is necessarily recommended, but there may be some things that you have that your potential team member values. Things such as free or discounted treatments, an old car that you have been holding onto for absolutely no reason whatsoever, or maybe some furniture that you don't need anymore. Please remember that one person's junk is another person's treasure. If there is something that your future teammate wants and you don't, then be generous. Often, the more generous you are, the more generous others will tend to be with you. Anything that is given or exchanged must be done so with complete agreement and knowledge of the terms of the transaction.

- ***Having a share in the business.*** If this person is integral to your success, you may want to consider giving him or her a piece of the action. For example, suppose a friend of yours happens to be a professional office or spa designer whose services you may not be able to afford in opening your establishment. You could offer your friend a share in the profits of your business in lieu of an up-front payment for the design services.

- *Participating in day-to-day perks.* Emphasize any other things that the person may see as a benefit, such as home-cooked meals, chocolate chip cookies, or whatever may be of interest to your prospective team member. It is important to think "outside the box" at times.

- *Receiving your gratitude.* Lastly, and most importantly, the benefit you should point out that the person will most appreciate and feel good about is your gratitude, appreciation, and thanks. You will always remember this person's help and relay to others that your success was due, in part, to his or her input.

The second thing that you must do when asking people to join your team is to be humble about it and honest about what you need from them. If you are neither humble nor honest about your needs, your relationship with your team will become more of a problem than an asset for you and your company. First, being humble just means that you are admitting that you need someone else's help, specifically the help of the person you have approached. If you are the type of person who finds it difficult to ask someone for help, now is the time to get over it. The future of your business depends on your ability to ask others for assistance. Second, you have to be completely honest and fully disclose what you expect from your potential team members. You must do your best to make them understand what is expected of them. Again, if they do not fully understand what is expected of them, the relationship will not last very long.

Having team members, both volunteers and employees, who "buy" into your business is very important. It is imperative that anyone who is working with you understands where you are going, how you want to get there, and why you are doing what you are doing. This is where a good mission statement and goal setting are important. If people do not understand and agree in principle with those things, they cannot go on the ride with you. By the way, do you agree with those things? If not, it is time to redirect and refocus what you are doing. Remember that it is never too late until it is too late. Explaining these things to prospective team members will help you solidify what you are trying to accomplish in your own mind. The more you explain what you are trying to accomplish, the more real it becomes and the more specific you will become in your direction.

Selecting Team Members

Though selection is not necessarily a formal process, you should think about many things before you choose the members of your team. The following is a short list of the things that you should examine when putting together your team.

Individuals' Strengths and How They Fit into Your Needs

You should look at your strengths and weaknesses and choose people with the traits that complement your needs. It is not necessary to look at specifics for the fit. What you need to look at is the type of person—whether he or she is a suit, a dreamer, an artist, or a professor.

- A **suit** will be able to tell you whether or not an idea makes business sense from a profit or loss angle. The suit is the person to whom you will be bringing all the numbers to examine and see if they make sense. The suit should also be able to help you with your overall business goals in regard to growth, planning, and strategies. Usually this person is able to review the details, whether big or small, to determine what should or should not be done.

OUR TEAM

In our company, we have three full-time members on our team and two friends who are also team members. The professor role is filled by me, while the artist role is filled by my wife, Jill. There's quite a bit of dreamer in each of us, so we share that position on the team. We have an accountant, who serves as a paid team member, and some very trusted friends who serve less formally as suits for our company. (LSR)

- A **dreamer** will help you to form your mission statement and keep your eye on that goal in your business dealings. The dreamer is going to be able to see the big picture yet usually does not have the gift to see the details needed to achieve the goals set forth in the big picture. Even if a dreamer gives you a picture that is far out of the realm of possibility for you in practical terms, this does not mean that the picture is worthless, for you might find that you can use part of what is presented to you. Remember that all of your teammates are there to give you help, not run your business for you. A dreamer is someone who looks for the big, optimal, and best possible option. Listen to a dreamer simply because he or she may know a better way to achieve something than you have ever thought of.

- An **artist** will show you how to be creative toward the goals that you have set in your mission statement. An artist gives you a more aesthetically pleasing way to do things, taking the functional and making it more enjoyable. A very good artist, for instance, is able to turn a waiting area into a place where your customers enjoy being, whether through decorations, interactive items, or just interesting features such as a tropical fish tank. Having an atmosphere that is comfortable and functional is imperative to the success of your business. Someone who is artistic can help you achieve that. Additionally, an artist person tends to look at things differently than do those who are suits or professors. When you enlist the artist in your business planning, you will be getting a different mind-set in the opinions that you receive.

- A **professor** will be your most trusted adviser as you run your business. Whatever the other members suggest to you should be presented to the professor, for she or he is the one who will give you an even, unemotional opinion about what makes the most sense. The professor is able to see the overall picture in a very different way than does the artist or the suit. The professor should be the most critical adviser that you have.

It is fine to have more than one person of the same type on your team, but it is best if your team does not exceed seven people, including yourself.

Good Team Member Interaction

Finding the right people is challenging and should be done with great care, for these people will be part of the foundation for your business's future. The best type of person is the one who is willing to be honest and also supportive (Figure 5.1). It is important to have someone who allows you to make the final decision and also lets you make mistakes as long as those mistakes are not of the crippling kind. As an example, it most likely will not matter if your logo is green instead of blue (though the artist may not like the idea for some reason), yet whether to buy a building without the proper financing really does matter. Also, team members should be used only when needed, not just for the sake of hearing applause for a decision. That would get tedious for the team members very quickly.

Your team members should be able to demonstrate the capacity to work well together toward the common good (your business)

FIGURE 5.1

TIDBIT

Instead of looking for others to serve you, be a servant to them. A successful leader is one who is willing to serve others.

It is important that you keep in contact with your team members and apprise them of what is going on. They may be able to see a different point of view or a potential issue that you have not considered. You have to be aware of the needs of your team members, because if you are concerned only about what they can do for you, the relationship will sour very quickly.

Individuals' Track Records in Business and General Life

It is important that people you are counting on for advice are successful in their own right. If they have failed in the area about which you are asking advice, it would be foolish to trust that they have all of a sudden become a lot smarter than they were in the past. The people you are seeking advice from don't have to be incredibly successful, but they should have shown that they know how to be successful. If a potential team member has had some difficulties in business, ask what happened and what he or she did to correct it or to try to correct it. A person who is inconsistent in the way that he or she lives his life should be looked upon as a less than optimal candidate, for such a person will also be inconsistent in his or her advice.

In addition, you will be working with the people you select for your team, so you must make sure that these people match your value system. It does not have to be a perfect match, but if there are extreme differences between your values and those of a team member, you will not be able to work together in a way that will be optimal for either you, the team member, or your business. For example, if one person regularly cuts corners on legal issues such as reporting income or following licensing laws and the other person feels that it is very important to report all income and follow all licensing laws, there will be a serious problem that will not be able to be bypassed at some point in the relationship.

You are not looking for perfection; you are looking for people who will complement your weaknesses with their strengths. If you understand what their weaknesses are and can work with them, despite those weaknesses, by all means get these people on your team now. Do not, under any circumstances, attempt to look past weaknesses that you cannot work with.

Team Members' Relationship to the Successful Outcome of Your Business

If a person is dependent on your successful outcome, this will most likely color the person's advice to you. You want your team members to want you to succeed for no other reason than success in and of itself. If they have a financial stake in your business, it should be a financial stake that they are not depending on for their livelihood. If they are, they should become investors or partners, not just advisers. The dual relationship of an investor and adviser is one that is fraught with potential problems, such as giving you advice for short-term financial gain while disregarding long-term benefits. A good example of this is the decision making in large corporations that often focuses on increasing the short-term value of the stock at the expense of long-term success.

Even more common is the problem of team members tending to become territorial with parts of your business. They may want certain things to happen for them, without regard for the overall health of the business. For instance, a risk-taking team member might push for a retail aspect in your operation, knowing the rewards from a retail component can be great, even though you clearly do not want one at this stage of your business. Though it may be something that you want to do in the next stage of your business, in 5 to 7 years, you deem it inappropriate now, and the risk involved is not something that you are at all comfortable taking at this point in time.

This is not to say that dissension is a bad thing. Having a diverse group of people will give a diverse set of opinions. That is an important positive aspect of having a team. Dissension does become a problem when a team member chooses not to want to see past a particular point in the business or the team. This will become a stumbling block that needs to be dealt with swiftly, by giving the team member a chance to change her or his thought process or by getting rid of the person.

Using Your Team

Now that you have created your team, you must decide how to use the team. There are many ways to use the team that you have created. Below are some suggestions that will help you to maximize team effectiveness in getting the best results for you and your business.

Make Sure That Team Members Understand Their Roles

It is important that your team members have a clear idea of what is expected of them and that they are not just willing to follow through in their responsibilities but are happy to do so. Each team member must know that she or he is important to you and, at the same time, should understand that all the other team members are also important. Each member should be informed of the other members' places on the team.

Team members must also understand the time commitment that is involved. The time commitment is the amount of time a team member has to accomplish what he or she is to do. Are you going to keep this team together only until your business gets started, or do you want to keep some or all of the members together forever?

Here are some of the questions that need to be answered about how you are going to use your team:

- How is your team going to accomplish what it needs to accomplish?

  —Are you going to have formal or informal meetings? Are these meetings going to be regularly held or held on an as-needed basis?

  —Are you going to use technology, such as e-mail?

- Is this going to be a formal team or a loosely related group of people?

  —The more formal the team is, the more preparation and work it takes to run the meetings and accomplish the goals set forth for the team.

  —It is more appropriate to have the team reflect the needs of the business. For the most part, a new or small existing business does not need a large, formal team.

- Will any team members grow into partners or employees? If so, then all group members should be made aware of that possibility prior to signing on.

  —If a team member is going to become an employee or a partner, it is imperative that there be a formal document outlining the parameters.

- Where does the role of team members fit in with your organization? Is it a primary role or a secondary one?

  —The role of team members should be secondary unless they are employees, partners, or future employees or partners.

Do Not Put Two Team Members in an Adversarial Position

The quickest way to hurt a team is to pit one member against another member. If there are any issues that come up, they should be taken care of through you and cleared up quickly to best satisfy any concerns for the sake of the overall team.

Clear **communication** between all team members is crucial. If two team members find it impossible to work together, you have some options: The first is to get rid of one of the members, the second is to get rid of both members, and the third is to keep both members. These are all viable alternatives, depending on the circumstances of the team.

It all boils down to whether or not the team members are valuable for your business even with the issues that they present to your business. One way to judge that is to see whether your team members save you time, money, work, or worry and increase your productivity and, ultimately, your bottom line. If your team members don't do that or they accomplish the opposite for your organization, they are not productive and should be gotten rid of.

Keep Communications Open at All Times with All Team Members

If a decision is made with input from the team or if any material decision is made about the business, all team members must be informed in a timely manner. With the Internet and conference calling, communication is easy, and there is no excuse for lack of communication. Group e-mails are perfect for this, simply because everyone gets all of the same information at the same time and no one feels as if things are being negotiated behind his or her back.

This does not mean that all decisions should wait for input from all of your team members. Some members may be involved in only part of your business activities and may have no expertise in other parts of your business. It is important that they have the information, even if they are not directly involved in that part of your business, because it may affect their thought process when presented with an issue about the organization. Also, you do not want to waste people's time by asking them about things that you have already received confirmation about.

There are some final thoughts about the group concept that you have to realize and accept if you are going to make the team concept work. First, your team members are not necessarily getting paid, and they most likely have busy, successful lives of their own that they are involved in. *You must use these people's talents keeping in mind their needs and limitations.* Second, you are going to depend on these people for information and opinions, sometimes more than other times, but you have to remember that *the final decision is yours and this is your business.* If any of your team members become integral in the running, planning, or overall shape of your business, they may be suited to become more formal parts of your business, such as partners, paid consultants, or employees.

Two or three can be much stronger and smarter than one alone. If you look at most successful businesses and business ideas, there is usually more than one primary person involved in the business. This doesn't mean that one person is not the "face" of the company or that one person is more important than anyone else; it means that one person cannot do everything and be everything. If a leader is a visionary, there needs to be a numbers person right behind the leader to keep that part of the business healthy. Sometimes it may be wise to start your business with a partner, as well as other team members who are not partners. The subject of partners will be discussed in more detail later in this volume; for now, just know that a business partnership is just like a marriage, for both the potential good and the potential bad that can come of it.

Why is it necessary to even have a team? The simple answer is that a team is more powerful and can accomplish much more than just one person. When you have someone walking next to you and you stumble, the other person is there to pick you up. A team gives you many advantages that cannot be ignored. Here are some of the advantages that are created when you create a team:

- Multiple perspectives arise when multiple people look at the same thing. Many eyes will see the same thing in different ways, so there is less chance that something will be missed. There is also less chance of making crucial mistakes if several people are looking at a situation independently of one another.

- Different people will give different answers for the same situation. If you give 10 people a business problem to be solved, chances are that you will come up with many more options for a solution than you will if you have only one person proposing different options.

- Having multiple people involved in a venture provides motivation for all involved to accomplish more, in a better way and in a more timely fashion. People are concerned with the way that they look to others around them; they do not want to look bad, so their performance will be enhanced by having other competent people around them.

- In addition to instilling motivation, a team can provide encouragement. What is the difference between motivation and encouragement? *Motivation* is being inspired to do something that you know others want and need you to do. In other words, you are accomplishing something because you are expected to do so by others. *Encouragement* arises when others are helping you for your own good, without primary regard for the team. They are helping you for you first. They are being positive for you and helping you to get to a place where you can then better help the team.

Potential Issues with Having Team Members

There are many other advantages to being a part of a team. There are as many different advantages as there are different teams. The advantages listed above are just some of the general ones. Sometimes, however, there can be issues with a team. The major issues that are listed below can be avoided, yet there is always a danger that they will occur at one point or another during the life of a team. Here are some examples of how teams can lose their advantages:

- Having a team can cause you to lose direction. A team can get sidetracked very easily if the members are not kept under control and on target. It can become a free-for-all, with each person attending to her or his own agenda. It is imperative that the leader keep the members of the team on track and on target. You do this by keeping the team's focus on the goals of the organization.

- Though we all like to think that we are good, even great, communicators, most of the time we are lacking in communication skills at some level. This is exacerbated even more by having other people, who are just as human as we are, with communication problems that come into play when working as a team. A great example of communication problems is shown with the children's game of "telephone." It starts with someone saying something to another person, who tells it to a third, and so on; by the time the message has been passed through a whole string of people, the message is completely different. Good communication is very difficult, to say the least. One way to help communication is to repeat the information given to you by others and have others do the same for you.

- Human beings are funny animals. No matter how good things are, no matter how much success there is, they generally become discontented with their situation. A leader needs insight into the others on the team to know what makes the members happy and to keep them happy. This does not mean that you have to keep them happy all the time, but you need to keep the people moving in a positive emotional direction. If a team member is an emotional liability, it is important that the leader let that person go. A positive motivating factor can be created by letting go of a negative factor.

- When two or more people come together, there is a surety of conflict. In fact, many of us don't need more than one other person to have conflict when making and realizing plans of any kind, let alone plans as complicated and important as providing a livelihood for ourselves and our families. Conflict does not have to be bad; it can have a positive effect in that it can create options through opinions. Conflict resolution needs to be quick and complete, and no one can turn his or her back toward it. As a leader, you must make sure that your team members know they need to cooperate for one reason and one reason alone: You are depending on them to do what they are supposed to do. You cannot accomplish anything if they are in conflict. If they cannot solve their conflict, you must decide who will continue to be a part of your team and who will not.

- If you have done your job really well in picking team members, you have picked people who are incredibly competent and capable—and more likely than not, they know it. You have picked them on the basis of their strengths and your weaknesses. To some degree, they will have an upper hand on you because they may have more knowledge or experience in a certain area than you do. There may even be some instances where your team members will use their expertise to gain a sort of control over you and your business. This does not mean that they are doing something that is cruel or sinister. It is, again, human nature. The good news is that this is your business, and the only way that you will lose control over your business is if you let that happen.

The bottom line is that having a team can and will enhance the chances for the success of your business. Creating a good team is not easy to accomplish, yet the upside of having people whom you can count on to help you when you need help is priceless. The extent to which you use team members can vary quite a bit. Depending on your strengths and weaknesses, you may need only to bounce your own ideas off team members most of the time. You may need to rely heavily on only one team member, who matches up with your weaknesses. Please remember, however, that even if you are relying on one member, all members of the team need to be kept abreast of what is happening.

CHECKLIST

Have you done these things yet?

☐ Have you selected team members for your team?

- A suit? Name _____
- An artist? Name _____
- A dreamer? Name _____
- A professor? Name _____

☐ Have you ensured that each team member understands and accepts his or her place on the team?

☐ Have you identified your strengths and weaknesses?

- My strengths are _____
- My weaknesses are _____

☐ Have you determined where you are going to fit into your team?

- Besides being the leader, I am also _____

SO WHAT DO YOU THINK?

1. Do you think that you would be better off working on your weaknesses to make them stronger, or do you think that it would be better to take advantage of your strengths and add someone else to help you with your weaknesses?

2. What do you think are the greatest advantages to having a team of people working with you?

3. What do you think are the biggest pitfalls to having a team of people working with you?

4. Do your perceptions of your strengths and weaknesses line up with others' perceptions? If they do not, why do you think they don't?

5. Is there something missing from your current team? What is it, and what can you do about it?

6. What are the most important traits to have as a business owner, and which traits don't matter as much? Why?

Living in the Business World

PART **2**

Budgeting

LEARNING OUTCOMES

After completing this chapter, you should be able to:

6.1 Determine what a reasonable budget is for your business.

6.2 Create a cost analysis formula for purchases.

6.3 Determine which cycle is optimal for your business to use in budgeting.

6.4 Recognize what items should be budgeted.

6.5 Differentiate between projected and actual income budgeting.

KEY TERMS

budget

one-time expense

recurring expense

cost-benefit analysis

recuperate

quality-of-life items

opportunity cost

INTRODUCTION

As you begin to plan for your business, one of the things that you are probably thinking is, "How much money do I have to spend for all of these things?" The way to determine what to spend is to set up a budget for starting your business. A **budget** serves as a guideline that will tell you how much money you have to spend on the items in your facility. So let's get started on setting up a budget for your establishment. This process can be used over and over as needed for special projects or expansions.

Creating a Budget

Creating a budget is a process that helps you allocate necessary monies for your business start-up and prevents you from spending too much money on things that you don't need. It also helps you to prioritize your needs and determine exactly what you are willing to pay for. As you create your budget, you should be organizing and writing down particulars, such as the equipment that you may be using in your practice. You should also prioritize the items in terms of need. For our purposes, let's assume that you will be opening a sole-proprietor massage therapy clinic. Here is a sample list of equipment that should be bought and expenses that you may incur:

- *Automobile.* This is the cost of purchasing or leasing a vehicle, as well as ongoing expenses that you will incur, such as gas and auto insurance.

- *Banking.* This is the cost of having a checking account, as well as any costs that you may have if your business accepts credit cards.

- *Decorating.* This includes any wall hangings, paint, carpets, and waiting room furniture.

- *Deposits.* Most utilities charge a deposit. You will have to pay a deposit for your rental premises, and if you are leasing any equipment, you may also be required to pay a deposit on it.

- *Electric.* This is a monthly expense, which will start as soon as the term of the lease agreement begins. Do not forget to call the electric company to turn on the electricity in your name.

- *Insurance.* Do not scrimp on your insurance. Make sure that your insurance will cover all problems. Many policies that are cheap do not adequately cover losses in many instances, and they may exclude the coverage that is the most important for you. Please speak with an insurance agent about the coverage you need. It is imperative that you know what is covered and what is not.

- *Licenses/fees.* Municipalities, such as towns and cities, require that businesses operating within their limits be licensed; so do counties and states. It is very important that you are properly licensed or registered in your jurisdictions, for if you are not, there will be fines and other potential repercussions that may affect you for a long time.

- *Massage equipment.* The most important piece of equipment that you will purchase is your massage table. Of all the purchases you will make, this is the one item that you have to extensively research, try out, and ask about. As an example, a concert violinist will not buy the least expensive violin to make beautiful music. The violinist will spend as much money as he or she possibly can to get the best violin available. The right massage table can make the difference between a treatment that is comfortable and one that will keep your customers from coming back. Other equipment that you might use includes hot packs, bolsters, support systems, and specialty items for doing specialty work (stones for stone massage, ayurvedic equipment, and so on).

- **Massage supplies.** The difference between massage *supplies* and massage *equipment* is that massage supplies do not last for more than a year. They are meant to be used and replaced over and over. It is very important that you use good supplies, particularly if the item is something that your customer can see, feel, or smell, such as a sheet for your massage table. The initial cost of a quality sheet may be high, but a good sheet will last hundreds of treatments. If you divide the cost of the sheet by the number of treatments you will use it for, the cost is negligible. If the life of a sheet is 100 treatments, a $10 sheet costs you 10 cents per treatment and a $20 sheet costs only 20 cents per treatment. Since a sheet can last far more than 100 treatments, the incremental cost of the sheet is even less. The overall point is that you should not be cheap with your supplies; your customers will notice if you are, and the cost per treatment is minimal.

- **Membership dues.** These are dues that you will pay for professional associations, local associations, and business associations. The point of joining these groups is to help you get business, network, and meet other professionals with whom you can exchange ideas and information. Professional associations can also help to provide you with other benefits, such as continuing education opportunities and insurance coverage.

- **Music.** Remember that the right music and musical equipment is very important for achieving the best environment for your treatments. If you are doing treatments outside an office setting, something very portable is important. Even in an office setting, portability is a good thing to have. A CD player is good, as is an iPod with a speaker system. Remember that the wrong music can ruin an otherwise good experience.

- **Office equipment.** Office equipment is all other equipment that is not related directly to massage. This could include desks, chairs, phones, computers, and the like. The most important characteristic that office equipment should possess is functionality. This functionality should not be exclusive of decor or taste. The office equipment should fit the type of facility that you are opening. Remember: When purchasing office equipment, you should determine your needs for each particular piece. As an example, it is not necessary to lease or purchase a large copy machine when a smaller machine that you can purchase for a few hundred dollars will do. Please remember that you must have a machine that can handle the amount of work that is needed will do. You can ask for advice from anyone at an office supply store and from other people who are currently in practice.

- **Office supplies.** The best thing you can remember about office supplies is "the less, the better." Businesses spend a lot of money on supplies such as paper, pens, and pencils, many times buying much more than they need, and the supplies just sit on a shelf and collect dust. It may not seem like a lot of waste, but it adds up. Office supplies should be bought four to six times a year; having much more than a two-month supply of any item is a poor use of your money.

- **Professional fees.** Professional fees are fees that are paid to professionals. The two best examples of professional fees are legal fees and accounting fees. The more time that you are able to spend doing the basic work, the less you will have to pay for professional fees. If you use an accounting program that has payroll capabilities, you will not need to have your accountant file quarterly returns for you. This can save a great amount of money for a relatively small amount of training and work.

- **Rent.** Rent is the cost you pay for using premises you do not own. It is usually based on the square footage of the space that you are renting. In addition to the rent that you will have to pay, you may also have to pay amounts for other things. These amounts can add up to a very large number, so you must pay very close attention to the lease and the amounts that you will be charged. Here are some other costs that may be included in your monthly cost according to your lease agreement:

— **Common-area maintenance (CAM).** This is the cost that your landlord passes on to you to maintain the common area of the property that you are renting.

— **Operating expenses.** These expenses can be carried through by the landlord to the tenant. Examples of these expenses are real estate taxes and insurance.

— **Utilities.** Most tenants have to pay for their own utilities. Make sure that you have a history of utility costs in the space that you are going to lease.

— **Taxes, insurance, and maintenance expenses.** Another lease term that you may encounter is the *triple net lease*. This is a lease under which you pay rent as well as all the taxes, insurance, and maintenance expenses that arise from the use of the property.

- **Telephone.** With new technology, the way we use the telephone and other associated things, such as fax machines and the Internet, poses a unique challenge as far as cost and usage are concerned. Many people use a cell phone for their office phone, and that's it. This is fine if you do not need any line for the Internet and a fax machine. As technology progresses, there will be a day in the not too distant future when you will be able to combine all of your needs any way that you want to. The important things that you will have to address are the cost and convenience factors.

This list is just a sample of items that you should budget. There are other things that may come up as one-time expenses or recurring expenses. A **one-time expense** is something such as a fire extinguisher (in some states fire extinguishers need to be recharged and tagged by an appropriate company or fire department on a yearly or biennial basis, so although it is considered a "one-time" expense, there are additional "maintenance" expenses associated with it). Another example is an installation charge for a simple plumbing or electric item. This would include the installation of a hot-water heater but not a complete electric overhaul of the space that you are leasing. A **recurring expense** is an expense that you have to pay over and over, such as the cost of Internet service.

Factors Determining the Purchase of Equipment

Cost-Benefit Analysis

A **cost-benefit analysis** is a means of determining whether something is worthwhile. It is not the only tool that you should use when deciding whether or not you should buy a piece of equipment, but it is a very important tool. Cost-benefit analysis is particularly useful for calculating whether or not a piece of equipment will pay for itself during its lifetime.

If a piece of equipment is supposed to add revenue to your business, the revenue it provides should be greater than the costs you incur to buy and run it. An example is a Hydrocollator: The cost of a simple Hydrocollator and packs is around $250. Will you be able to charge customers for the use of the hot packs? Are you going to be able to realize any additional income by having this piece of equipment in your establishment? Lastly, how long will it take you to pay for the Hydrocollator from the additional income that you are making? There may be less expensive alternatives

Calculation of Payback Time	
Cost of the equipment	$1,000
Additional income per treatment	÷$10
Number of treatments to break even	100
Number of treatments expected per week	÷5
Break-even point, in weeks	20

TABLE 6.1

that you can use instead of this piece of equipment, such as a Thermophore electric moisture-drawing heating pad. This heating pad is more than sufficient for the purposes of many practices.

You should have a specific period of payback time that you are willing to tolerate. Have a time in mind when you set up the payback equation. Follow the example in Table 6.1 for the purchase of equipment of this kind. Does it look similar to something that you have already seen in this book?

As Table 6.1 shows, it will take you 20 weeks to **recuperate**, or pay back, the cost of the equipment. If you want all of your equipment to be paid for in less than one year, you can go ahead and purchase this piece of equipment. It is very important that you include all the costs in determining the cost of the equipment. Some of the costs that you have to include, besides the purchase price, are the interest charges that you will incur if you are borrowing money to purchase the equipment, the service and upkeep cost for the equipment, and any incidental costs that you may incur when using the equipment, such as electricity or supplies that you have to purchase to use with the equipment.

The cost-benefit equation helps those of us who are impulse buyers. When the newest, greatest thing comes along, there are many who have to have that thing. When subjected to cost-benefit analysis, however, the newest, greatest thing may not pass the test.

Quality-of-Life Items

Quality-of-life items are items that you buy to make your life easier and to do your job better. Although they do not directly increase your income, they do a lot of work that saves you time and energy; thus, indirectly, they enable you to make more money doing the things that you do. The best examples are office equipment items such as computers, computer programs, and copiers.

In addition to adding quality to your business, some quality-of-life items are essential for your business. One of the most important things that you need to have is a functional and dependable car to use for your business. If you do work out of your car, your vehicle must be able to accommodate that work. You may need to spend more money than you want to on a vehicle in order to get one that meets your business requirements, but you should definitely take into account the quality-of-life and cost-benefit aspects of the vehicle when planning the purchase. There is nothing worse than spending money on an asset and then finding out that it does not suit your needs. It is especially painful if the asset costs as much as a vehicle.

Opportunity Costs

Opportunity cost is the last factor that needs to be looked at when considering the purchase of a piece of equipment. This is a difficult cost to directly determine, but it is a cost that has to be considered carefully. The opportunity cost is the cost of something that keeps you from doing something different either with the money or time invested. A simple example is the opportunity cost of investing money. If you can invest money in a savings account and earn 2 percent per year, you will make

SHOP WITH YOUR TABLE

A friend of mine purchased a new car close to graduation from massage school with the enthusiasm of preparing for home visits. She had not yet purchased a massage table, however. Needless to say, massage tables are a tight fit for most automobile trunks and just as difficult a fit for the back seat. The moral: Before accruing such a large expense, make sure it is an appropriate choice. It would have been a good idea for my friend to have brought along a massage table, as a prop, while shopping for her car. (JLS)

$20 a year for every $1,000 invested. If you invested the same money in a CD, you would have earned 5 percent per year, which amounts to $50. If you invested in the savings account at 2 percent per year you would earn $20, but you actually had an opportunity cost of $50 because you could have made $50 if you had invested in the CD, so in essence you lost $30 in the example.

So that piece of equipment—the Hydrocollator mentioned earlier—was paid off in 20 weeks, but what if you lost two hours a week because of the time spent cleaning and maintaining that equipment? You had an opportunity cost of $140 a week times 20 weeks, which equals a $2,800 opportunity cost! The cost is the amount of money that you could have made at $70 per hour instead of cleaning the equipment. That is a significant amount. Now, to be fair, you may increase your overall business simply by offering that new service, and this is why the opportunity cost is not as cut and dried as it seems on the surface.

Cost of the equipment	$1,000
Opportunity cost	$2,800
Additional income per treatment	÷$10
Number of treatments to break even	380
Number of treatments expected per week	÷5
Break-even point, in weeks	76

Whatever decisions about money you make, be sure they will multiply your dollars

FIGURE 6.1

COMFORT IS KING

When purchasing carpet for our current establishment, we decided to use a good-quality commercial carpet. In addition to that quality carpet, we also put good-quality padding under it, instead of just gluing it down. This was done for the comfort of our customers, but, more importantly, it was done for our own comfort. Since we spend quite a bit of time on our feet in our establishment, it was important to us that we did everything possible to keep ourselves as comfortable as we could. (LSR)

So the break-even point is now 76 weeks, when taking into account the opportunity cost of the lost income while you were maintaining the equipment, instead of the 20 weeks as shown previously. The opportunity costs can significantly affect the break-even point of a purchase, and therefore should always be considered.

Whatever you do in your business, you need to take into account the cost-benefit, quality-of-life, and opportunity-cost factors of your decisions (Figure 6.1). This applies not only to equipment but to everything that you do in your business. If you take just a bit of time following these guidelines, you will save yourself a lot of time and money.

Budgeting

We have all the components that we need for a budget, except the budget itself. Many accounting programs have budgeting capabilities, which are fairly easy to use, but it is a good idea to go through the process of budgeting manually at least once so that you can become better accustomed to setting up a budget (which is what we have just started). A budget is nothing more than a set of goals. It is a specific financial measurement of expenditures and income that you are trying to determine in advance.

A budget can be broken down in many ways. It can be broken down by the year, the quarter, the month, and even the week. It can be broken down as much as you want it to be. Any more than a monthly breakdown is not necessary. The reason that you may want a monthly breakdown is that most service businesses are cyclical, and it is helpful if your budget is able to reflect the cycles. If you do not budget, you will not be able to properly plan for the future of your business. You will not be able to save long-term for any assets that you want to add to your business or even short-term for seasonal changes in your business.

To make a budget from scratch, you need to research the items listed earlier in this chapter, determine the cost of each item, and enter that amount into your budget. Once all of the items are listed, you have created your very first budget! There are two budgets you should have when starting a business, the first being a start-up budget and the second being a working (ongoing) budget. Figure 6.2 is a sample of a budget for a start-up business.

This budget can be used for a start-up entity as well as a special project, such as a renovation project or a new-establishment project. The budget can be general, like the one shown, or it can have more detail. Some of the details that you may want to add just break down the expenses to a greater degree. As an example, the automobile expense can be broken down further into the detail shown in Table 6.2.

In addition to the start-up or special-project budget, there is also a budget that can be used in a periodic fashion. What this means is that you can do the budget

LEARN FROM YOUR MISTAKES

Hot-stone massage has become very popular, and it is a great treatment. My wife and I took a rather involved course, and we purchased equipment to be able to use this type of treatment in our business. The financial investment was significant, as was the time investment. After a short period of time, we both realized that for our business, hot-stone massage was not a good modality. There was a lot of time spent on cleaning the stones, with many of our customers not willing to pay extra for the service.

It did not take long for us to see that hot-stone massage was not the right kind of treatment for us to use in our business. It is a great treatment, but just not right for our circumstances. The important thing was that we did not try to get blood from a stone, so to speak. We did not keep trying when we realized that it was not going to work. We gave it a fair chance, and then we dropped it.

It was a great lesson learned, which I am sure that we will have to learn over and over. Do what you do best, and continue to get better at it. Whatever got you to where you are, keep with it! (LSR)

Example of a start-up budget

FIGURE 6.2

New Business (Project) Start-Up Budget:

Basic Expenses:	Budgeted	Actual	Difference
Automobile	$_____	$_____	$_____
Banking	$_____	$_____	$_____
Decorating (new office)	$_____	$_____	$_____
Deposits (phone, utilities, equipment)	$_____	$_____	$_____
Insurance	$_____	$_____	$_____
Licenses/fees	$_____	$_____	$_____
Treatment equipment	$_____	$_____	$_____
Treatment supplies	$_____	$_____	$_____
Membership dues	$_____	$_____	$_____
Music player, CDs, tapes, iPod	$_____	$_____	$_____
Office equipment	$_____	$_____	$_____
Office supplies	$_____	$_____	$_____
Professional fees	$_____	$_____	$_____
Rent (first, last, security)	$_____	$_____	$_____
Telephone	$_____	$_____	$_____
Other expenses	$_____	$_____	$_____

Other Expenses:

Equipment:

Refrigerator, fax,	$_____	$_____	$_____

Hydrocollator, electric heating pads, washer/dryer

Supplies:

Miscellaneous office supplies	$_____	$_____	$_____

Total Start-Up Expenses	$_____	$_____	$_____

51

MONEY WELL SPENT

Four years into private practice, I had the opportunity to make a second trip to Thailand to gain additional training and certification in Thai massage. Although I had just purchased a house and had all the expenses associated with being a new homeowner, I felt the additional training would be of benefit to the style of massage I was developing. (Besides, it was fun, and Chiang Mai had become a home away from home!) The money was well spent because the training further solidified the massage I performed and became an integral part of my practice. The monies gained have far exceeded the monies spent. However, if you are contemplating a considerable expense (at the time, my Thai training cost $2,500 versus $250 for a local seminar), make sure beforehand that you will be buying something that is going to be of great value and not just for fun. (JLS)

monthly, quarterly, semiannually, or annually. It is recommended that your budget be done at least quarterly, and even monthly if your business is seasonal or your expenses are seasonal. If the figures for your business change drastically from month to month, a monthly budget is necessary. If your business is relatively steady, a quarterly budget will suit your purposes.

Remember that a budget helps you to plan. It also helps you to measure your performance against what you wanted to accomplish. Once you start using budgets

Example of an expense budget

FIGURE 6.3

Expense Budget

Period: _____ to _____

	Budgeted	Actual	Difference
Automobile	$_____	$_____	$_____
Advertising	$_____	$_____	$_____
Associations	$_____	$_____	$_____
Banking	$_____	$_____	$_____
Education	$_____	$_____	$_____
Entertainment	$_____	$_____	$_____
Estimated taxes	$_____	$_____	$_____
Income distribution	$_____	$_____	$_____
Insurance	$_____	$_____	$_____
Interest	$_____	$_____	$_____
Licenses/fees/taxes	$_____	$_____	$_____
Treatment equipment	$_____	$_____	$_____
Treatment supplies	$_____	$_____	$_____
Office equipment	$_____	$_____	$_____
Office supplies	$_____	$_____	$_____
Payroll	$_____	$_____	$_____
Payroll taxes	$_____	$_____	$_____
Postage	$_____	$_____	$_____
Professional fees	$_____	$_____	$_____
Rent	$_____	$_____	$_____
Repairs/maintenance	$_____	$_____	$_____
Telephone	$_____	$_____	$_____
Utilities	$_____	$_____	$_____
Other expenses:			
_____	$_____	$_____	$_____
_____	$_____	$_____	$_____
_____	$_____	$_____	$_____
_____	$_____	$_____	$_____
_____	$_____	$_____	$_____
Total Expenses	$_____	$_____	$_____

KNOWLEDGE IS THE KEY

Two very important things that I use the monthly form for are anticipating the number of treatments that I will be doing during a certain period and seeing how much I am really charging per treatment on average. After a few years, I noticed a pattern in the number of massages that I was going to do in certain weeks of the year. Knowing that enabled me to plan vacation time better. I also tend to give a lot of my treatment time away to people. This form shows me when I start to do too much giving away. (LSR)

regularly, they will become very quick and easy to do. Figure 6.3 is an example of a periodic budget, one that you will use on a monthly, quarterly, or yearly basis.

For the first budget that you do, it is recommended that you break down the expenses in a way similar to that shown in Table 6.2. This will help you plan a little better, and you will be able to be more accurate in your estimates. Once you are sure of the components of the individual expense categories, it is not as imperative to be so specific. If you want to track individual components of the budget beyond the larger categories, then by all means do so.

Once you start budgeting, you need to actually do something with the budgets themselves. They are not there just so that you can keep yourself busy with another task. What you need to do is compare your actual and budgeted amounts and adjust your plans accordingly. If you notice that you are spending more money than you think you should be on a certain item, you can investigate and evaluate why. You may, and most likely will, find a way to save money through this method of goal keeping.

The last thing that you want to budget for is your income. Though this is not really a budget in the same sense as a budget for expenses, it is something that you need to keep track of, just like your expenses. If you do not plan for your projected income, you will not know how much money you will have to spend in your budget. Figure 6.4 is a sample form for keeping track of your projected income on a monthly basis.

This form allows you to estimate future daily income and number of treatments and then, for comparison, keep track of the actual money you received and number of treatments you provided each day. In a relatively short period of time, you will be able to see a pattern in the numbers, which will enable you to plan a lot better for things to come.

Detailed Budget for Automobile Expenses

TABLE 6.2

Automobile Expenses	Budgeted	Actual	Difference
Loan repayment	$	$	$
Insurance	$	$	$
Repairs and maintenance	$	$	$
Fuel	$	$	$
Total	$	$	$

Sample form for tracking projected income on a monthly basis

FIGURE 6.4

Monthly Income Projections vs. Actual

Month _____

	Number of Treatments per Day		Money Collected per Day	
	Estimated	Actual	Budgeted	Actual
Day 1	_____	_____	_____	_____
Day 2	_____	_____	_____	_____
Day 3	_____	_____	_____	_____
Day 4	_____	_____	_____	_____
Day 5	_____	_____	_____	_____
Day 6	_____	_____	_____	_____
Day 7	_____	_____	_____	_____
Day 8	_____	_____	_____	_____
Day 9	_____	_____	_____	_____
Day 10	_____	_____	_____	_____
Day 11	_____	_____	_____	_____
Day 12	_____	_____	_____	_____
Day 13	_____	_____	_____	_____
Day 14	_____	_____	_____	_____
Day 15	_____	_____	_____	_____
Day 16	_____	_____	_____	_____
Day 17	_____	_____	_____	_____
Day 18	_____	_____	_____	_____
Day 19	_____	_____	_____	_____
Day 20	_____	_____	_____	_____
Day 21	_____	_____	_____	_____
Day 22	_____	_____	_____	_____
Day 23	_____	_____	_____	_____
Day 24	_____	_____	_____	_____
Day 25	_____	_____	_____	_____
Day 26	_____	_____	_____	_____
Day 27	_____	_____	_____	_____
Day 28	_____	_____	_____	_____
Day 29	_____	_____	_____	_____
Day 30	_____	_____	_____	_____
Day 31	_____	_____	_____	_____
Total	_____	_____	_____	_____

CHECKLIST

Have you done these things yet?

- [ ] Have you listed the items you need to purchase?
- [ ] Have you used the three factors in determining what to purchase and what to wait on?
- [ ] Have you created a budget for your new business or project?
- [ ] Have you created a budget for your periodic expenses?
- [ ] Have you created an expense budget for your business?
- [ ] Are you comparing the projected expenses with the actual expenses?
- [ ] Have you started to fill in your treatment schedule, which will help you determine the amount of money that you will have to work with?

SO WHAT DO YOU THINK?

1. Does this sound familiar to you: "Opportunity costs are really important, but paying attention to them is bothersome, and it keeps me from doing the things I want to do." Why is this statement wrong?

2. What are the five most important reasons for writing and following a budget?

3. Have you heard the statement, "Budgets don't work"? Do you agree or disagree with this statement, and why or why not?

4. If you have had prior business experience, were you able to budget income, or did you take "what was left over"?

Customers, Services, and Location

CHAPTER SEVEN

LEARNING OUTCOMES

After completing this chapter, you should be able to:

7.1 Determine who your customers are.

7.2 Plan services you will be providing your customers.

7.3 Identify the various types of locations.

7.4 Design the location of your business.

KEY TERMS

customer

services

location

specialist

jack-of-all-trades

mobile business

INTRODUCTION

Who, what, and where are the first questions to be answered in regard to opening your business. Who your **customers** are, what **services** you are going to provide, and the **location** where you are going to provide these services are the basis for a successful business. These questions cannot be answered independently of each other. The process of answering these questions can be started with any one of them, but they are very dependent on one another. For purposes of this discussion, customers will be discussed first, with services and location coming second and third, respectively.

Who Are Your Customers?

How do you determine who your customers are before you even start your business? Many business owners may think they know who their customers are, but to accurately determine this, you must ask the following questions:

1. Whom do you want as your customers?
2. Are those customers available to you in ample numbers?
3. Are you qualified to work with those customers?
4. Do you have the facilities and equipment needed to work with those customers?

Whom Do You Want as Customers?

Whom are you trying to target as your customers? Are there particular characteristics that you are looking for in customers? Do you want customers who will be paying cash for your services, or are you willing to accept third-party reimbursement (insurance payments)? Do you want to work on sports injuries or automobile accident injuries, or do you want to perform stress reduction or spa services? It would be beneficial to outline the characteristics that you want in customers.

This does not mean that you should turn away customers who do not fit your initial customer profile, for that would be silly. You do, however, want to know where you should be focusing your attention when looking for potential customers. You may actually find that there is a group of people whom you haven't thought of as potential customers. The point is, as with everything else in life, there are things we know we want and there are also things we don't know we want. It is important to be open so that we can experience things that we may not necessarily be looking for.

Are Those Potential Customers Available for You?

Once you have decided what customer type you want to focus on, you must determine whether or not there is a large enough population of this type to support your business. If you are living in a community of people over 80 years old, prenatal massage would not be a good area to concentrate on. If there are not enough potential customers for the type of work that you want to do, you have three options:

1. **Move to a different location.** This is a possibility, yet it is an extremely complicated and disruptive choice.

2. **Change the customers whom you will be focusing on.** This is not a great alternative. The fact that you will not be able to do what you want to do will decrease the satisfaction you get from your work.

3. **Add another group to focus on that will increase your potential customer base to a more acceptable level.** This will allow you to work with people you want to serve and also allow you to grow your business in a good fashion.

Are You Qualified to Work with That Population?

Even if you have appropriate potential customers whom you can solicit business from, are you going to be able to legally and properly treat these customers? If you do not have the proper training and licensure, it does not matter how well placed you are to see customers. You must be aware of all of your limitations when promoting a specific therapy. Even if you can legally provide a specific type of therapy, if you are not proficient at it, then you will have unhappy customers who will not come back to you, who will not refer new customers to you, and who may actually dissuade others from seeking your services.

It may be frustrating to start without experience and not be able to promote yourself because of lack of experience. This lack of experience can easily be put behind you if you are willing to do some work to overcome it. Here are some great ways to gain experience that will make you more qualified and give you the ability to satisfy your customers:

1. **Take a class.** This is the best way to ensure that you have the basic knowledge in a particular treatment type. It may also be the only way to acquire the legal ability to perform the particular treatment. You can trade services with others from the class to gain experience.

2. **Read books and watch videos.** There is a plethora of books and videos dealing with all types of therapies. Choose a few different books and videos on the same topics. Always know your base subjects, such as anatomy, thoroughly. This does not necessarily give you the hands-on experience that you need, but it is a great way to gain knowledge.

3. **Use friends and family for practice.** This is easy, and you will be able to get more comfortable doing what you need to do. If you need better feedback or you need to hone your skills beyond just practicing, you can try option 4.

4. **Use a select few test people.** There may be friends or family members on whom you can try out new procedures. They can give you feedback and let you know how you are doing. A suggestion is to use these people consistently and let them know what you are doing prior to doing it.

Do You Have the Facilities and Equipment Needed to Service Those Customers?

If you do not have the proper facilities and equipment to do the services that you are promoting, you will create nothing but problems with your customers. If you cannot provide proper services with proper equipment in a proper environment, you would be better off not trying at all. If the facilities cannot handle a certain type of service, do not attempt to offer that service.

Services That You Are Going to Provide

Essentially, the questions that you had to answer about customers also need to be answered in terms of the services that you are going to provide:

STEP OUTSIDE THE BOX

When I was working almost exclusively with the equestrian community, international riders and their mounts, I had a few riders who allowed me to adapt what were normally considered modalities used on the human musculoskeletal system to their horses. These world-class horses were athletes in their own right and benefited greatly from my adaptation of Thai massage for them. (JLS)

1. What services do you want to provide your customers?
2. Are there customers who will take advantage of those services?
3. Are you qualified to provide the services to your customers?
4. Do you have the facilities and equipment to provide the services to your customers?

What Services Do You Want to Provide Your Customers?

The type of service that you want to provide your customers is what you should concentrate on first. If you enjoy doing rehabilitative work, it is imperative that you try to focus your attention on that type of service first. Figures 7.1 through 7.3 show different services you can choose. There are two options that you need to think about when deciding the services that you want to provide your customers. They are opposite approaches, and yet either of them can be used to your advantage. The first is the specialist, and the second is the jack-of-all-trades.

The **specialist** is someone who does one type of service and does it well. The service is one that fills a needed niche in the market, and the therapist is one who can be considered an expert or a leader in the performance of that type of service. The **jack-of-all-trades** is someone who does a lot of things well. A therapist of this type can perform different services that customers may need at different times. These approaches are extremes, and most people would do well to be flexible with the services that they provide.

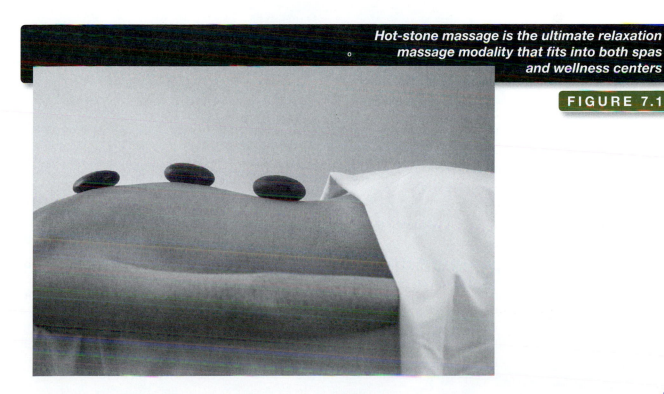

Hot-stone massage is the ultimate relaxation massage modality that fits into both spas and wellness centers

FIGURE 7.1

Wraps are offered in facilities that have access to showers, so be sure showers are available before offering "wet" treatments

FIGURE 7.2

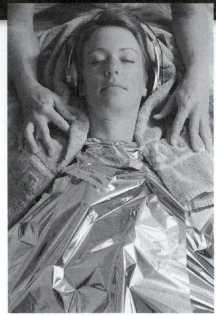

Acupuncture and herbal medicine are treatments found in wellness centers and clinics

FIGURE 7.3

One very important thing to consider is the type of service that the customers are expecting. If your customers are expecting a certain type of service and a different one is provided, they will be dissatisfied and will not return to your establishment in the future. The easiest way to determine what a customer wants is during the intake process, either by having the customer fill out a space on the form or just by asking the person. Also, knowing the referral source can be very helpful, because that will give you an idea of what the new customer is expecting. In general, customers will be expecting what their referral sources have told them they will be receiving.

Are There Customers Who Will Take Advantage of Those Services?

If there are no customers in your area who will take advantage of the services that you want to provide, you will have an uphill battle making a living by trying to provide those services. As in the customer discussion above, there are three options that you have when confronted with this dilemma:

1. **Move to a different location.** This is a possibility, yet it is an extremely complicated and disruptive choice.

2. **Change the services that you will be providing.** This is not a great alternative. The fact that you will not be able to do what you want to do will decrease the satisfaction you get from your work.

3. **Add other services that will increase your potential customer base to a more acceptable level.** This will allow you to do the services that you want to perform and will also allow you to promote additional services. This approach creates a greater demand for all of your services over a period of time, while still enabling you to support yourself.

Are You Qualified to Provide the Services to Your Customers?

The answer to this question has been discussed in the section above on customers. The bottom line is whether or not *you* would pay for the services that you are providing to your customers. If there is something lacking in your ability to perform these services, it must be corrected as quickly as possible.

Do You Have the Facilities and Equipment to Provide the Services to Your Customers?

This question has been answered in the section above on customers. Trying to do something that would endanger your customers or your business is foolish; therefore, it is imperative not only to have the proper equipment but also to have that equipment in good, clean working order.

Good Service

Providing good service means not only doing what you do well but also doing things right. Time is a very important element in all businesses. People do not want to waste time, and they do not want to have to wait. Make other people's time a priority for you. The following list constitutes good service to your customers:

1. Return phone calls promptly.
2. Show up for all appointments.
3. Keep rescheduling to a minimum.
4. Be friendly, fair, and honest in customer dealings.
5. Be on time.

Types of Location for Your Business

When speaking of the location of a business, we must first consider what we mean by *location*. The following are different types of locations:

1. **Mobile business.** You travel to your customers, providing services in their homes, places of business, or clubhouses.

2. **Sublet.** You rent part or all of an office from another professional who rents the entire space.

TIDBIT

All successful businesses are similar in that they have three important components: quality product, good service, and attractive delivery.

3. **Office sharing.** A group of professionals share space, and even treatment rooms, and share the costs.

4. **Renting/owning.** You are responsible for the payment of the expenses for the office space.

Mobile Practice

The same criteria that affect the opening of a fixed-location business also affect that of a **mobile business**. However, while the type of location has little effect on your customers, a mobile practice poses a number of extra challenges for you. The following are concerns that you will have when operating a mobile business:

1. **Travel cost can be considerable.** The cost includes fuel, tolls, and, most importantly wear and tear on your vehicle. For those who live in an area whose population is spread out, travel expenses become an even greater cost. Those who live in a metropolitan area may have to pay for cabs to get from one customer to another. These costs must be included in the cost of the services that are provided when at all possible.

2. **Time can be an even greater issue.** The time that it takes to get to a customer may be great. It is imperative that you schedule appointments so that the time that it takes to get to your customers is reduced. An example of this is organizing your schedule so that you go in only one direction each day of the week. Travel time should be accounted for when determining the cost of your services.

3. **Wear and tear occurs not only on your car but also on you, the therapist.** Carrying equipment to and from the vehicle to the customer can be difficult, to say the least.

There is such a diversity of situations with regard to mobile businesses and how they work, depending on the area that the business is in. The best way to confront all the individual issues is to speak with other therapists in your area and find out what they do about these issues. Each area has its norms and exceptions. Some of the most important issues that need to be researched are:

1. What is being charged for out-calls, and how are those charges determined?

2. How many out-calls is the average therapist doing? Are the therapists in the same type of situation that you are in?

3. What do customers supply, and what do you supply?

4. What is the length of a treatment?

This is by no means a complete list of questions that should be asked of other therapists in your area, but it is a good start.

Sublet an Office Space

Subletting is done quite often in the case of a therapist who rents space from a physician. A synergistic relationship between the two occupants of the office space can and should occur, with referrals back and forth being the greatest advantage to this scenario. It is a low-cost way to have an office space. Subletting must be done with great preparation, for there are pitfalls that can occur, such as incongruous hours of operation, level of noise in the office, space for other services that you wish to provide, reduced autonomy, and decreased rights as a leesee.

Subletting an office space is not a bad option for a first office space. Growth can occur if the primary office user grows and you grow with him or her, or you can grow out of the space completely and move into another space.

Office Sharing

Office sharing can be done a few ways. There are companies that bring together professionals in related fields and rent space to them. They share amenities such as waiting rooms, staffing, and bathrooms. You are responsible for your own space, and a part of your rent pays for the overhead of the rest of the office. Not all situations have the same amenities included, so the terms must be reviewed carefully before being agreed to. This is also done without the benefit, and expense, of a separate third party of people renting a space together without becoming a single business entity.

Other things that must be reviewed are the allowed hours of operation, limitations to the services that are being provided, and policies with regard to potential problems with other tenants (e.g., noise and odor issues) and how they are resolved. Shared office space is a great option to start with, especially if there is potential for growth.

Renting/Owning

This is the most costly and complicated way to acquire an office space, yet it is the one that will give you the most autonomy and freedom. You will have fewer problems in dealing with other people in your office, and you will be able to make decisions without having to consult a whole group of people, especially when it comes to decorating, services provided, and hours of operation.

Prior to signing a lease, it is important to determine whether or not it contains limitations with regard to any changes that you may be planning to make. It is also important to verify that you will be able to perform your services in the space and that you can practice at the time you want to practice. The same holds true if you are planning to purchase an office. Additionally, if you intend to purchase an office you need to investigate the future plans for the area that the office is located in, such as new building construction, road construction, or anything else that may affect accessibility, convenience, or the safety of your customers.

Where to Open Your Practice

Companies spend millions of dollars doing market studies and analyses of the potential customer base to determine where to open a business. Since you don't have that kind of money, here are some very easy steps for doing your own market study.

The best location is the one that has the highest number of potential customers for you to cultivate. If you have a specialty, other professionals can refer customers to you, but you also must be willing to refer back to them. A connection of professionals whom you can refer to is invaluable for your success. If other professionals are successful in a location, it has been proved for you that it can be a successful location.

About the Location

A location must be convenient to the customers you are trying to target. People in different areas of the country have different tolerances for traveling, so the same research that would be done with regard to travel by you as a mobile business should

SELECT AN APPROPRIATE SETTING

I had a friend who started a massage practice in a hair salon, with somewhat detrimental results. No matter how well the walls were insulated or how airtight the room was made, the noise and the strong fumes from hair dyes always seemed to seep into the massage space, rendering it less than desirable for therapeutic benefit. (JLS)

be done with regard to travel by your customers. In addition to being convenient, your location also must be easily accessible. In other words, access into your specific work area should not be a problem. Though your location could be on a busy street, which will give you a lot of exposure, do you want your customers to have to fight traffic to get a nice relaxing treatment? Would it be better for your business to be a little bit off a busy street, which would enable you to take advantage of a quieter setting, less expensive rent, and fewer intrusions during office hours, such as salespeople and curiosity seekers?

If you are trying to do a high-volume business, you want your location to be in a high-traffic area; but if you are a sole practitioner, you more than likely don't need to be paying a lot of extra money for a high-traffic location. The type of business that you are planning to run will help to determine whether or not you want a high-visibility location.

There are some very important factors that have to be considered when you are looking for a location for your business, no matter what type of facility you are planning:

1. ***Convenience for you to get to the business.*** If it is difficult or time-consuming for you to get to your job, you may not spend as much time there as you could.

2. ***Any noise factor that could impact the business.*** Noise is not good in a professional setting, and it could affect what you are trying to accomplish with regard to relaxation and professionalism.

3. ***Surrounding businesses and their customers.*** You want your customers to feel safe and comfortable getting to and from your business. Having your business next to a bar would be counterproductive, for example.

4. ***Convenient parking.*** This is a must. If a customer has to walk a distance or has a problem finding parking, the experience will diminish the probability of a return visit.

5. ***Safety and security.*** These feelings must be present. If a person does not feel safe coming to your business, or while at your business, because of its location, you will not keep that person as a customer.

6. ***The location should "fit" the type of customer you are trying to attract.*** If you are focusing on higher-end consumers, it is imperative that your location reflects that.

The who, what, and where of a business are very important. They are intertwined with each other and cannot be looked at in isolation to get the best answer for your business. As you start off, there may have to be some give-and-take when deciding the possibilities for your business, yet things can change as your business grows. You can incorporate changes when you are able to. Even if you cannot get everything that you want right away, you can plan to get some things in the future. It does not matter whether you are practicing full-time, part-time, or seasonally—the entire decision-making processes for customers, services, and location are the same.

TIDBIT

It is important to listen to what your customers have to say, and it is much more important to listen to what they aren't saying. The complaint they don't share will be the reason they are leaving your business.

CHECKLIST

Have you done these things yet?

☐ Determined the customer type that you want to target for your business?

- Type 1 _____ Type 2 _____
- Type 3 _____ Type 4 _____

☐ Determined what kind of location you are going to pursue?

- Type _____

☐ Scouted out the location of your business?

☐ Determined whether the location suits your customers' needs?

☐ Determined what services you are going to provide initially?

- Services _____, _____,
  _____, _____

☐ Determined what services you are going to provide at a later date?

- Services _____, _____,
  _____, _____

SO WHAT DO YOU THINK?

1. What are the most important characteristics of a successful location? List them in order of importance, and explain why they are in that order.

2. Do you think it is better to be a specialist or a jack-of-all-trades? Why?

3. What are the characteristics that you want in a customer?

4. What are some advantages and disadvantages of the different types of locations?

5. What is the difference between the number of treatments you can do working in an office and the number you can do with a mobile business? What does this mean in terms of income?

Layout, Look, Furnishings, and Equipment

CHAPTER EIGHT

LEARNING OUTCOMES

After completing this chapter, you should be able to:

8.1 Explain the importance of a functional layout and an appropriate ambience.

8.2 Recognize the importance of office size.

8.3 Understand the importance of properly furnishing and equipping the office space.

KEY TERMS

establishment

functional

ambience

micro view

macro view

massage equipment

office equipment

INTRODUCTION

How the business establishment is put together is a key element in the success of any business venture. The physical layout of the establishment must be designed well for the business to work optimally. The decor of the establishment has to fit the purpose of the business. The furnishings and equipment of the business must allow not only for the best use possible but also for the highest level of customer comfort possible. The goal is to have customers who come back, and part of their reason for doing so is that the establishment is a great place to be.

What Is an Establishment?

An **establishment** is a place in which you are doing business and you have some control over the environment. If you are providing services in customers' homes, on an out-call basis, those places are not considered establishments. This does not mean that the information regarding establishments can be ignored. The same principles apply to out-calls that apply to your own establishment. You will not have control over the situation to the degree that you have in your own place, but you can make changes that will enhance your performance and customer satisfaction.

The Keys of an Establishment

The physical layout of the establishment is very important. The most important aspect of the layout is functionality. The establishment is **functional** if the treatment rooms are big enough for the therapist to work in them comfortably and the waiting room is a comfortable size also. There needs to be enough room and a good room layout for the employees to work. All of the necessary facilities should be in their proper places.

In addition to functionality, you must take into consideration the **ambience** or "feel" of the establishment. The establishment should look good, clean, and pleasant. A facility should have all the things that you would consider important for making you feel comfortable. Everything from paint colors to the type of lighting is important for your facility. The furniture should be comfortable and functional.

Once the functionality and the ambience of the establishment are decided on, it is time to furnish your office. In furnishing, you can take micro and macro views of your establishment. A **micro view** is a view of one small aspect of the establishment, and a **macro view** is a view of the establishment as a whole.

The Macro View

The overall view of the space that you will be using has to reflect what you are trying to accomplish. If you are providing spa services or medically oriented services, the ambience should reflect that particular type of service. In other words, a spa/resort type of facility should be serene and relaxing; it should not have the look and feel of a medical or clinical office, which can be more austere. The functionality of the space is simply whether or not the space works easily for what you are trying to do.

The Micro View

The micro view of an establishment fits into the macro view of that establishment. Each micro component is a single aspect of the overall establishment and becomes part of the macro view. If the micro view does not work, the macro view will not work.

TIDBIT

No matter what the ambience is, the establishment has to be clean. Nothing can ruin an experience faster than an unclean environment.

WORKING IN A VASTU ENVIRONMENT

With my interest in and dedication to the principles and practices of yoga, I follow Vastu in my home and office. *Vastu,* Sanskrit for "dwelling" or "site," is the Indian science of design and architecture. Vastu is, in fact, the predecessor to *feng shui,* the Chinese science of organizing personal home and work space to maximize positive energy flow. When one applies the principles of Vastu, one does so with the entire property, home, or office building and each room in mind. Practitioners acquainted with modalities such as traditional Chinese medicine (TCM) and polarity recognize the "five basic elements." In Vastu the elements are space, air, fire, water, and earth. Space is the center of each property, building, or room and is where spiritual energies gather. Air governs the northwest area and inspires action or energy. Fire belongs to the southwest portion and is where anything related to fire or warmth is located, such as a fireplace or kitchen. Water governs the northeast and is calming; bathrooms and pools are located here. Earth is associated with the southwest area and is heavy and strong; any heavy pieces of furniture should be placed here.

My massage room is in the very center of the house, with the remainder of the rooms all located around the massage room. In Vastu, the center of the house, where spiritual energies gather, is considered the god-center and an area of healing (see Figure 8.1). My table is positioned southwest to northeast, with the head of the table being in the southwest. This is the position that Brahma, the Hindu god of creation, is believed to be lying in; it is the god-center. It also happens to be the "safe room" where my dogs and I rode out several hurricanes in Florida in 2004 and 2005! My writing desk is in the southwest corner of the house, the creative area; and the room where I teach yoga classes is in the northeast corner, the area for meditation. All of my clients comment on their experiences in the massage room, and I truly believe that they are experiencing the power of Vastu, not the massage alone. Following a prescribed arrangement for each room encourages peacefulness, harmony, well-being, and, most importantly for your office, prosperity.

Realize that clients sense the energy, the vibration, in your room. We live in a high-stress time when our senses are assaulted by many things: constantly ringing cell phones, a barrage of e-mails, ever-increasing commuter travel time. There are natural forces that govern the space around us and the space we place ourselves in. Aligning with and honoring this space creates an environment that not only is free of physical and mental clutter but also is one of respect. Whether your treatment room is more clinical in nature or more spiritual, clients will appreciate the positive forces they feel when in this space.

There are two excellent books on Vastu: *The Power of Vastu Living: Welcoming Your Soul into Your Home and Workplace,* by Kathleen Cox, and *The Vastu Home,* by Juliet Pegrum. (JLS)

The example that best shows this interdependence is the size of a treatment room with regard to the treatment provided: If the room is too small, the room will not work and thus the overall establishment will not work.

Putting the Views Together

It is time to put an establishment together using both the micro and macro views. If these views are combined properly, the establishment will be able to be used to its optimal level. The starting point is the macro view of what you are trying to accomplish. The plan calls for a small office for up to three therapists who perform different therapies. The office is not specifically medical, nor is it a spa; it does have components of each, however.

Attention to detail creates a warm and friendly environment and indicates professionalism

FIGURE 8.1

The overall size of the office space needs to be considered first. There are many considerations that need to be decided on to determine the optimal size. For example:

- **The number of treatment rooms.** There need to be a sufficient number of treatment rooms for the therapists to be able to work. Some therapists require only part of a room, for part-time work, while others perform work in more than one room at a time. It is important that the number of rooms that the establishment starts off with is more than adequate.

- **The size of the treatment rooms.** There is nothing worse than working in a room that is not the proper size. If the room is too small for your equipment, it will be impossible to work there effectively. A room always appears larger without any furniture in it. The best way to make sure that a room is large enough to be optimally functional is to lay out paper cutouts of your furniture and equipment so that you can actually see whether everything fits.

- **The area of the waiting room.** The area that is needed for the waiting room is wholly dependent on the number of people who will be waiting for your services or who will be with the people receiving your services.

- **Any space for back-office work.** If there is a need to have people doing any office work, such as billing or filing, which should not be done in front of the customers, then there needs to be a room designated for that. Additionally, if there is preparation for treatments that has to be done outside the treatment rooms, a space has to be made for this also. If there are to be laundry facilities or any other special needs, such as a refrigerator, these items should be located in a back room.

- **Restroom(s).** One or two restrooms, along with any other required facilities, such as showers, must be taken into account. If there are any shower facilities, there need to be multiple restrooms in your facility.

- **Storage.** Storage is a very important thing to have in any office. Files and supplies tend to build up, and it is important that you have the space to handle all the items that will be needed in the business.

The above factors constitute the micro view of the establishment. The macro view of the same establishment comprises factors such as whether the rooms are proportional to each other and the office as a whole. Another aspect of the macro view that needs to be taken into account is the cost of the area that is being used. It is very easy to say that you should have all the space you need, but space costs money, so the need for extra space must be balanced with the cost of that extra space.

Lastly, the space has to work well and be organized in such a way that all people who are in the space feel comfortable there. An example of poor organization is having the restrooms or the work space in the part of the establishment that customers first see when they enter. Common sense will dictate the overall organization of the space, but there is something even greater that will contribute to the shape of the space: The primary driving factor in the overall shape of the space is what is already available. For a small start-up venture, it is cost-prohibitive to build your own space; by finding a built space that meets your needs, you will save time, money, and aggravation.

When using someone else's space, you may have to compromise on one thing or another, but depending on the area in which you are planning to open your establishment, it may be the only real alternative that you have. Some creativity can come into play here, but please remember to walk away from anything that doesn't work for you, even if you like the overall space or the idea or something else about the space. If it is not going to work for a specific reason that cannot be changed, then walk away from it.

Furnishing Your Establishment

Depending on the type of establishment you are starting, the furnishings will vary tremendously. The furniture will become a large part of the ambience (discussed above) of the space. Some of the other things to take into consideration when purchasing items for your establishment are:

- **Ease of cleaning and maintenance.** You do not want to buy upholstery that is not washable. You do not want carpeting that cannot stand up to the wear-and-tear of heavy use.

- **Sturdiness.** You want to have items that are sturdy enough to be used over and over, without worry of breakage. Other people may or may not be as careful using the items as you would be, so please be aware of this when picking out items.

- **Replacement.** Some items that you purchase need to be available at a future time in case you need more of them. You may not need 10 chairs today, but you may need them next year. Will they be available, or will something complementary be available?

- **Compatibility with the scheme of your establishment.** Compatability goes beyond the decorating aspect of the purchase decision; it also includes whether or not an item is appropriate for your establishment. Are household couches appropriate for your waiting area? If they are, it would be fine to use them in that situation; if not, other options should be considered.

- **Compatibility with the needs of your customers.** Do your customers have any special needs that you have to consider in picking out your furniture?

When a business first opens, the amount of money available often necessitates a trade-off between having a fully finished establishment and having just the essentials. If funds are an issue, it is imperative that you prioritize the items that are needed in your establishment. Give top priority to customers' comfort and needs.

Proper seating in the waiting area is necessary, as are other appropriate furnishings, such as tables and lighting. The basic items that are needed with regard to furniture are as follows:

- *Chairs.* Between one and two chairs per person per session time are needed. So, if there are two customers each session time, there need to be at least two seats in the waiting area and there need not be more than four seats. If the waiting area is very large, additional seating may be needed to fill the space and make the size of the room look appropriate.

- *Tables.* Tables and/or wall racks are necessary for displaying magazines, brochures, and any other material that you want customers to see while they are waiting for you.

Other items for decorating purposes are pictures, wall hangings, and lamps. These items should be consistent with the macro view of the establishment. Your personal taste should be reflected, yet it is important to continue to recognize the purpose of the establishment.

Equipping Your Establishment

Prioritize which items your business requires immediately and which can wait for a future time. When it comes to your establishment, proper financial and business decisions should take precedence over "wants." Guard against falling into the "want, want, want" and "buy, buy, buy" mode; it is an easy trap to fall into. This will alleviate the financial and emotional stress that is inherent in purchasing too many things too early.

It is time to make a list and assign a relative importance value to each item.

Massage Equipment

Massage equipment is equipment that is specific to the performance of massage and has a useful life of greater than one year. Criteria to be used when you are selecting massage equipment are the quality, price, portability, and functionality of the items.

A *massage (treatment) table* is the most important piece of equipment that you will purchase. Figures 8.2 and 8.3 show different types of tables. The quality of the

Lightweight-frame
portable table

FIGURE 8.2

Hydraulic table with wooden frame

FIGURE 8.3

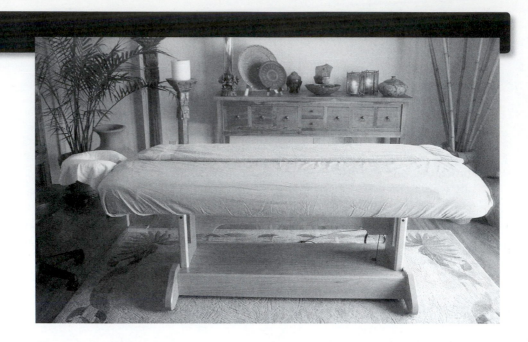

table is so important that you need to shop extensively, feeling and trying many different types of tables, before you buy one. If you are working in an office setting and plan on doing a volume business, you should use a hydraulic table. It not only will be the most durable but also will be a back saver for you, owing to the ease of adjusting the height and therefore the pressure during any given session. If you are going to be doing home visits, purchase a lightweight table that is portable. The weight, width, and ease of lifting your table are very important to the success of your practice. You should upgrade the covering on the table to the most comfortable materials. If possible, you should upgrade the foam used in your table. All of this is to do one thing, which is to make your customer more comfortable. If your customer is not comfortable during the treatment because of your table, you will lose the person as a customer, no matter how good your technique is. If possible, add either a table fleece or a table warmer to your table. Clients on the table get very cold very quickly because of a decrease in body temperature with increased circulation to the muscle. By keeping the customer warm with a table warmer, you will enable him or her to relax and enjoy the treatment even more. Remember to inform the customer that you have a table warmer, and be aware of any medical conditions your customer has that may preclude you from safely using a table warmer during the treatment.

Depending on the type of establishment that you will be running, you could need many other pieces of equipment. It is important that you use the same principle in shopping for and purchasing this equipment that you use in purchasing your table. Remember that you should list the items in order of importance of need, and purchase them in that order. Be ever cognizant of the balance you have to keep between the overall cost of the equipment and the items you "want to have" to open your establishment's doors. Other items include (but are not limited to):

- Hydrocollator/Thermophore or electric hot pads.
- Linens.
- Stereo/iPod and music.
- Exercise equipment.
- Electrical therapy (e.g., electric stimulator or ultrasound).

Figures 8.4, 8.5, and 8.6 show different types of equipment.

TIDBIT

If you happen to be in the market for a new car, take your table, and any other equipment that you use, along with you on demo drives. It is important that the table fit easily into the trunk or onto the back-seat. Many tables do not easily slide onto a back-seat or are too big for the trunk to close.

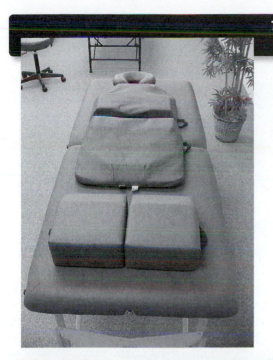

The bodyCushion for supportive and pregnancy massage

FIGURE 8.4

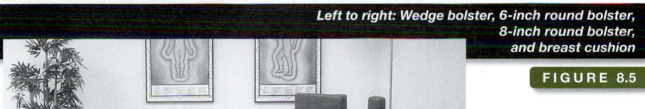

Left to right: Wedge bolster, 6-inch round bolster, 8-inch round bolster, and breast cushion

FIGURE 8.5

It is important that you balance the cost of the items with the monetary return that the items will provide your business. You do not want to spend a large amount of money on something that you will not make any money from. Doing so would be an indulgence that you may not be able to afford, and it could place the future of your business in jeopardy.

Office Equipment

Office equipment consists of items that last more than one year and do not directly involve any therapy. Office equipment is very important to plan for. The first and most important piece of office equipment is a computer. Even if you are antitechnology, you will find that a computer is essential for successfully running

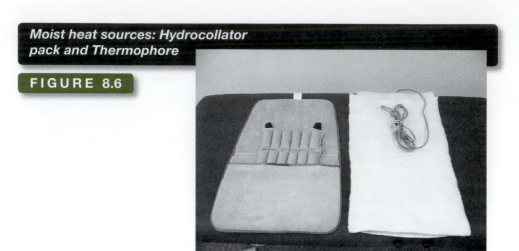

Moist heat sources: Hydrocollator pack and Thermophore

FIGURE 8.6

a business. Many computers come with software programs that can make life easier for you. If yours does not have the software you need to function properly, invest the money to purchase additional software. Technology will make you efficient by saving time and effort; you will be able to spend more time making money, instead of poring over books and sheets of numbers and information. You may also want to invest in a personal digital assistant (PDA), BlackBerry, or iPhone. These devices can be used for appointments and memos when you are out of the office, and they have the advantage of hotsyncing to your office computer; appointment lists and the like can easily be printed out to provide a hard copy for license renewal purposes.

If your business plan calls for you to do insurance work, purchase a program that will help you to do that. The programs range in cost from a few hundred to a few thousand dollars. The functions range from simply printing the HCFA (Health Care Financing Administration) forms to keeping track of past-due accounts, accounts receivable, billing cycles, and much more. Check with colleagues in your profession to determine the best programs to use. Be sure to ask what they like and don't like about the various programs. As with everything else you are planning to purchase, it is imperative that you do a cost-benefit analysis of the program that you want to purchase.

You should also consider purchasing an accounting program. You can ask your accountant which program she or he prefers that you use. Again, the cost can range greatly, and the programs' functions vary so much that you need to do a cost-benefit analysis based on your needs. Some of the tasks you may want the program to do are write checks, keep track of budgets, do payroll including payroll taxes, and do budget forecasting.

Most computers come preloaded with a writing program, which is more than sufficient for you to use. Please remember that flexibility is an important option. Have at least one person who has a background in computers, or at least a good amount of experience with computers, review the computer and programs you are planning to buy and your reasons for choosing those particular items.

After a computer, a copier is the next most important piece of office equipment. With today's technology, a multiuse printer, copier, fax, and scanner can be purchased for a relatively small amount of money, and for the purposes of a small office they are more than adequate. Leasing a large copier for speed or quality is an unnecessary expense, given the fact that you can go to a print shop for that kind of work when you need it. Generally speaking, buying a copier that will fit your everyday needs costs about the same as leasing a large copier for two months. This is a perfect example of options for which a cost-benefit analysis will show whether the benefit received justifies the cost of the purchase or lease.

Another item that you will be purchasing for your establishment is a phone system, which should be kept as simple as possible. For a small business, a portable phone system with an answering machine is sufficient, or even a cell phone alone can be a good option. If you are going to be making appointments from a certain system, it is important to have caller ID; people leaving messages often mumble their phone numbers or talk too fast for you to understand the numbers.

This takes us into the next group of items that you will need to consider purchasing for your establishment. If you are planning to purchase a desk and storage items, please make sure that they fit with the decor of the rest of the office. They need to be functional as well. You will need to have filing cabinets for paperwork, ideally cabinets with locks.

The most important thing to remember is that the micro needs to fit into the macro and the macro needs to fit into the function and look that you want for your establishment. If this is accomplished, your establishment will be a huge asset to your business.

CHECKLIST

Have you done these things yet?

☐ Have you determined what you want to do in your establishment?

- What areas and area sizes do you need in order to do what you want to do in this establishment?

  _____

  _____

☐ Have you determined the macro and micro views of your establishment?

- What furnishings do you want to include?

  _____

  _____

- What equipment do you want to have?

  _____

  _____

SO WHAT DO YOU THINK?

1. What are the most important items to have in your establishment? Why? List them in order of importance.

2. What type of atmosphere do you want to create in your office? If you are sharing an office, what if the other people have completely different tastes? How would you handle this?

3. If you are on a limited start-up budget, what items are crucial to your business? What creative combinations can you come up with to help curtail the amount of equipment you need to purchase?

The Legal Aspects

CHAPTER NINE

LEARNING OUTCOMES

After completing this chapter, you should be able to:

9.1 Identify the different business structures.

9.2 Decide what form your business will take.

9.3 Set up the appropriate business banking accounts.

9.4 Recognize additional legal obligations, such as licenses and insurance, in opening a business.

KEY TERMS

employee

independent contractor

entrepreneur

sole proprietorship

Schedule C

Schedule SE

general partnership

limited partnership

corporation

Employer Identification Number

C corporation

S corporation (or subchapter S corporation)

limited liability corporation (LLC)

doing business as (DBA)

INTRODUCTION

The legal structure of business and employment is very important and must be mapped out for all types of business, from a single-person operation to a multilocation operation with many employees. One thing can be done to make this job much easier: Find a good accountant and/or lawyer.

For purposes of this discussion, we will assume that an accountant is the professional you are going to hire, but the same process would be used for the hiring of an attorney. The first resource to be investigated is other people in your profession or in a similar profession. If they know of accountants whom they are happy with, those accountants should be considered. Word of mouth is a very powerful tool for you to use, both in acquiring help and in acquiring business. Here are some of the things you need to consider when looking for an accountant:

- ***Cost of the services to be provided.*** Some firms charge per form filled out; some charge a flat fee; others charge per hour, plus expenses. The overall cost of having an accountant do work has to be determined. If the cost is too high, some of the work should be done in-house, thus reducing the cost of the accountant's services. For example, you could use an accounting program, such as Quicken, to compile the figures in your office and then supply those figures to the accountant, instead of having the accountant spend the time on compiling those figures.

- ***Experience in your business type and ability to fulfill any special requirements that you may have.*** If the accountant has not worked with people in the health care profession before, it may be a good idea to find someone who has. If there are business or personal requirements that are specialized, such as a business in multiple states or countries, then the accountant should be set up to be able to do that work.

- ***Accessibility of the people who will be doing the work.*** It is imperative that all the people who will be working on the account are accessible and know what is expected of them. If these people are called, they should be available to answer any questions posed to them.

- ***Credentials of the people who will be doing the work.*** There needs to be a certified public accountant (CPA) working on the account. The CPA will be required to sign all forms that are submitted to the IRS and any other government agency, such as state, county, or city taxing agencies.

Other resources that you can use to find the right accountant are friends and family, the Yellow Pages, business schools, and the Small Business Administration (SBA). Questions on all the above factors are pertinent ones to ask potential hires. Another thing that needs to be done to help ensure a good hire is to check with the state regulatory agency in charge of the accounting profession. Also, check with the local Better Business Bureau and chamber of commerce to see whether the accountant's record is clear. Lastly, and most importantly, the accountant must have a clear understanding of the business and what his or her duties and responsibilities are. You are interviewing the accountant for a job, so if the person gets the job, then have him or her set up the business. If cost is a factor, do some of the work to reduce the accountant's charges. Ask the accountant what is the best form of business entity, and make sure that he or she explains why that form is the best. Some things to consider when forming a business entity include the cost, the time involvement, the future growth potential, the tax consequences, and the legal ramifications, such as liability.

Looking at each of the formal business and employment structures will provide a background that enables you to have an educated and productive discussion with your accountant.

Employment Structure

First, and foremost, the type of employment that will work best for you must be decided. This decision will lead to the structure of employment that you will be looking for. There are two basic ways that a person can be hired (Figure 9.1). The first is as an employee, and the second is as an independent contractor.

Employee

Depending on the employer, you will be brought onto a staff as an employee or independent contractor. As an **employee**, you will receive a W-2 tax form from the employer, who must report your earnings, withhold all relevant taxes including Social Security tax, and provide you with all the benefits that the other employees receive. Examples of these benefits are health insurance, retirement benefits, and paid vacations. There are specific criteria that you as an employee have to meet to receive these benefits, such as being a full-time employee. Individual states determine labor laws, so it is important that you research these laws. If you are an employee and you are being paid as such, there is a definite financial benefit for you. The Social Security tax (including the amount that is paid for Medicare) is more than 15 percent of your pay. When you are an employee, your employer pays half of that. That is an approximately 7½ percent benefit that you receive from your employer.

Independent Contractor

Some employers will bring you in not as an actual employee but, rather, as an independent contractor, in which case you will get a 1099 tax form and have to pay your own taxes and benefits, including the full Social Security tax, which is also called

Give careful consideration to whom you bring on board and under what conditions you hire them

FIGURE 9.1

self-employment tax. The rules that govern whether or not you are an employee are found on the IRS Web site, www.IRS.gov, under the category "employee/contractor." What needs to be noted here is that the employee/contractor distinction can be very complicated and is something that needs to be looked at very carefully.

In terms of your working for another company, you will not get into any trouble if you are working as an **independent contractor** and the IRS finds that you should have been paid as an employee, as long as you have been paying your self employment and withholding taxes. Your employer will have to reimburse you for the taxes that you paid, which the employer did not pay, if it is determined by the IRS that you should have been classified as an employee. It is important to note that your employer may also be responsible for making up for any other benefits that you did not receive as an independent contractor but would have received as an employee. You should know whether you are going to be paid as an employee or an independent contractor prior to your taking any job.

Other Considerations

If you are considering employing people in your business, you have to consult with your accountant to determine how to classify the people whom you have or are planning to hire. If you do not pay the people in your employ properly, the Social Security Administration and the IRS will not treat you kindly. In addition to the benefits that you will have to make up for your employees, you will most likely have to pay interest to your employees and fines to the IRS and the Social Security Administration. It can be very expensive when you have to pay for benefits to employees whom you no longer employ, as well as interest on the amount of money that you were supposed to spend for those benefits. The bottom line is that it is easier and far less expensive to get the proper information and do everything correctly from the start.

There are many advantages to working for someone else. As an employee, you have many things done for you—marketing, cleaning, booking, and so on. As an employee, you do not have to worry about setting up, acquiring customers, or handling business expenses. As an employee, you generally do not have the same risks and requirements that a business owner has. Perhaps after a few years' experience you will decide to take the plunge into opening your own business. This maturation process will give you time to put money aside and acquire the skills needed to open and run a business; perhaps you will even go back to school to obtain your first or an additional degree. Of benefit to you, you will have had the opportunity to watch other people make mistakes and decide how you can do things better.

Entrepreneur

Is entrepreneurial management for you? Not all of us possess the personality and skills required for entrepreneurial work. The term **entrepreneur** has many meanings, but it usually refers to one who is ideologically a capitalist or industrialist, has a high tolerance for risk, and enjoys being his or her own boss. Entrepreneurs come in many types. They can be one-person shows, or they can acquire venture capital to start something on a grander scale. They come in all different shapes and sizes, with different educational backgrounds and life backgrounds. One thing that an entrepreneur is *not* is someone who is not willing to put herself or himself in a position to fail. If you are reading this book now, you probably have a little bit of entrepreneur in you but you just don't know how to get things going. Congratulations! You

TIDBIT

Even if you don't identify yourself as an entrepreneur, if you are working as an independent contractor, or even doing part-time work, you are an entrepreneur.

CONFIRM CHOICES WITH A PROFESSIONAL

When we were running multiple offices, we would give our accountant all of our employee payment information and request a letter from the accountant stating whether or not the accountant, in his professional opinion, deemed that the people working for us should be classified as employees or independent contractors. We then paid them as such. We never had any issues, but if we had encountered any problems with the employees, we felt that the company was covered against an adverse decision by the Social Security Administration and the IRS. Additionally, if we had been found to be in noncompliance, we thought that we would not be treated as harshly since we had a certified public accountant sign off on the classification. (LSR)

have started the process. The entrepreneur can function within any of the business structures discussed below.

This book is not intended to replace any professional advice, such as that of an attorney or accountant, so please check with the proper professional to confirm the information stated in this volume. There are three basic types of business entities that you, as a new small-business owner, will have to consider. The first is a sole proprietorship, which is the most basic form of business entity. The second is a partnership, which, as the name implies, is started with two or more people. The third is a corporation, which is an entity separate from you as an individual. Each of these business types has advantages and disadvantages.

Sole Proprietorship

TIDBIT

When faced with the possibility of failure, do not freeze, but identify what the worst outcome would be and the worst result of that outcome. Generally, the worst outcome is not all that bad, and the result of the worst outcome is not as scary as one initially thinks.

In a **sole proprietorship**, one person has ownership of and liability for the business. It is the simplest form of business organization. As a sole proprietor, you can set your own schedule, work as much as you want or need to, take off when you want or need to, answer to no one but yourself, and have fewer government regulations to follow.

Many practitioners in the healing arts field are of an independent mind-set and therefore choose to work for themselves as sole proprietors. The simplicity of forming a sole proprietorship rather than a corporate entity has many advantages and disadvantages, depending on the financial backing you have and the level of risk you want to take with regard to personal liability. With a sole proprietorship, there are no legal papers to be filed through an attorney, as there are with a corporation. Creating this type of business is as easy as deciding you want to do it, selecting a name, opening a checking account, and, of course, following the other advice in this book. A sole proprietorship is a not a legal entity separate from you. You are the sole proprietorship. As a sole proprietor, you reap all the benefits of your business, but you also are the sole person responsible for the business and its legal liabilities. If your business closes and it owes money, you will be held personally responsible for repaying all debt that the sole proprietorship incurred. Once you are gone, the sole proprietorship is gone. This could create a problem if you have heirs who want to take over the business when you are gone or if you want to sell the business. Since all of the business assets belong to you personally, you have to sell them as an individual, not as a business, or they become part of your estate when you die, and without proper planning your heirs could lose the possibility of keeping the business going.

Another drawback to being a sole proprietor is the decreased ability to raise funds from external sources. It is very difficult to borrow for a sole proprietorship without attaching your personal property as collateral against the loan. This can create financial hardships and increased risk for not just you but your whole family. The best part of being a sole proprietor is that it is inexpensive and easy, which is something that you should take into account when starting your business. The best thing to do is to consult with your advisers about whether a sole proprietorship is the way to go for you and how long (if ever) it should be before you change your business entity. Additionally, in some states you can be a single-member (sole-proprietorship) limited liability corporation (LLC). An LLC may offer you corporate-type protection as far as liability is concerned. You must check with your individual state for details.

As a sole proprietor, you will file, along with your Form 1040, **Schedule C** to report business losses or profits and **Schedule SE** to report self-employment tax if there are net earnings. You will use a calendar year for filings: Form 1040 is due on April 15, with estimated taxes (Form 1040ES) being due April 15, June 15, September 15, and January 15.

Partnership

Partnerships are legal entities that can enter into contracts, borrow money, and obtain credit for the business. A **general partnership** has partners who share ownership and liability, whereas a **limited partnership** has partners who are financially invested in the business but do not play an active role in the operation of the business.

With both general and limited partnerships, a name under which to do business must be chosen and filed with the appropriate government agency, such as the county clerk's office. With a general partnership, the owners will operate the business with shared responsibility and authority specified in a written agreement. Debts and liabilities of the business are shared by all partners. With a limited partnership, the limited partners have a liability up to the amount of their investment and no more than that. General partners play an active role and have unlimited liability. In other words, a general partner in any partnership is liable for that partnership's debts, and any debtor can attach any general partner's personal assets to pay any of the partnership's debts.

There are some advantages to partnerships. The first is that it is still relatively cheap and easy to form a partnership. The next is that it is easier to raise capital for your business, simply by adding either general partners or limited partners to your business. Remember that a partnership, though not a haven against liability, is a separate entity that with proper planning can reduce the possibility of complete liquidation of a business if one of the principals dies or wants out of the business.

Along with the advantages of a partnership, there are also some disadvantages. The first is that a partnership has more than one person involved in it, and this can result in problems in the running of the business. If there are disagreements in the running of the business, the business may not survive long enough to become successful. Another disadvantage of a partnership is the liability factor. A general business partner can be held liable for all the debt of the business. Additionally, a general partner can be held liable for the debt of or legal action taken against any of the other general business partners; legal action could be in the form of malpractice or malfeasance lawsuits. All partners will be held liable for any contract that a general partner makes, as long as the contracting partner has the authority to do so in the partnership agreement.

Though the disadvantages of a partnership seem great, they can certainly be minimized by having a clear and concise partnership agreement. This agreement should outline the responsibilities, the liabilities, and the authority of the partners, as well as what happens at the conclusion of the partnership. This is a contract that needs to be worked out by all partners, accountants, and attorneys so that not only is there a clear understanding between the partners but also as many unforeseen events as possible are covered in the agreement. Additionally, some states allow for a limited liability partnership, which limits the liability of each partner.

Partnerships usually do not pay income taxes as a whole; each partner files Schedule K-1 (Form 1065) to report her or his share of the income as a partner. A partnership uses a calendar year for filings: Form 1065 is due the 15th day of the fourth month after the end of the tax year.

Corporation

A **corporation** is a legal organization whose assets and liabilities are separate from those of its owners. Each state has different laws and requirements for the corporation. These requirements include filing papers called *articles of incorporation*, electing officers, and obtaining an **Employer Identification Number** from the IRS [also commonly referred to as a *Federal Employer Identification Number (FEIN)* or a *Taxpayer Identification Number (TIN)*]. Check with the secretary of state in your state for specific requirements. A corporation must always file a federal income tax return and, where required, a state income tax return. A corporation may choose its fiscal year; Form 1120 is due the 15th day of the third month after the end of the tax year, and the estimated tax deposit form is due on the 15th day of the fourth, sixth, ninth, and twelfth months of the tax year.

The biggest advantage for owners of a corporation is protection of their personal assets from liability; only the corporation and its assets are held liable in legal proceedings. Corporations may also acquire equity through the sale of their assets. By being a completely separate entity, a corporation can do any legal activities, such as enter into contracts, sue, and own property. A corporation also allows its owners, who are called *shareholders*, to raise money either through a stock offering or a loan. It can be somewhat easier for a corporation to get a loan.

One disadvantage of a corporation is the complexity and expense of filing articles of incorporation through an attorney or an accountant. Corporations are also the most expensive type of business to run, but the advantages can be enormous. If your business has to deal with even one problem or financial setback, having a corporation could save you many times over the cost of running it. The biggest disadvantage of a corporation is double taxation. Since the corporation is a separate entity, it is taxed as such. If there is a profit and you want to receive that profit because you have earned it, you will receive that profit in the form of a dividend. That dividend is taxable income to you personally, so that profit has now been taxed twice. This occurs with a **C corporation**, which is a separate entity from its owners or stockholders formed in accordance with state regulation. The corporation pays income tax, and the owners pay tax on any dividends. You will file a C-corporation Form 1120.

An **S corporation (subchapter S corporation)** is a corporation that has to meet IRS size and stock ownership requirements. If the corporation qualifies, the shareholders may request S-corporation status. The corporation itself pays no taxes. The profit is passed on to the shareholders, who pay taxes directly on their individual tax returns but retain the advantages of a corporation. You will file S-corporation Form 1120. S-corporation status eliminates the double-taxation problem that C corporations have. This option must be requested at the time of incorporation. This is a very viable option that needs to be investigated.

Limited Liability Corporation

Often seen today is the **limited liability corporation (LLC)**, which is permitted in most states and generally must have at least two owners. Like the hybrid cars of today, this business structure seeks to employ the best of both operating systems, the partnership and the corporation. The owners are taxed as a partnership, while their liability is limited as in a corporation. There may be additional costs to form an LLC in the state that you live in.

The Mechanics

Business Checking Account

Once the initial work with the accountant is done, it is time to do some things that will help to start the business. It is time to open a checking account. The type of legal entity that is being started will determine the type of account that is opened. The most important thing to understand is that all business and personal expenses must be separated.

If a corporation is being started, a tax number from the government is necessary to open any accounts. Remember to keep track of any expenses that are incurred in this process, because these costs are deductible for tax purposes. The corporate account will have to be a business-type account at a bank. Business accounts usually have monthly fees and minimum deposits associated with them. Checks are signed by at least one of the appropriate officers of the corporation; signature cards have to be on file with the bank.

If a single-person business is being started, for example, a massage therapy business that handles out-calls, then it would be good to keep things simple and inexpensive. Open a separate, or second, individual account (a "personal" account, in banking nomenclature) in which to deposit all business income. Personal accounts are usually free of monthly service fees, so a few dollars can be saved if a personal account is opened. The important thing here is to keep all personal funds and all funds that are acquired from the business separate.

Business Name

In choosing a name for the business, select one that represents the profession but is not too "far out." If the name sounds too cute, it is most likely a great name to stay away from. The name should be a description of what is being done and be short and easy to remember. A name search can be done online through the Corporation Commission or secretary of state. If the name you want is not currently in use or has not been used within the past year, it is up for grabs. The name can also be trademarked for a hefty fee of $325 plus legal expenses, which could run into thousands of dollars. Most states require a doing-business-as designation if the business name is different from your own name; and some states require it even if you are doing business under your own name. A **doing business as (DBA)** is also known as a *fictitious name.* Contact the county clerk for specifics. The DBA is usually required on business accounts.

Licenses and Inspections

In addition to any tax numbers that may be needed from the federal government, any licenses that are needed for you to start in business should also be investigated. If you are opening a facility, you will also have to acquire local licenses and permits to operate a business. These may include state, county, parish, and city or township licenses.

States usually require a business license that is filed under the business name and ownership. Additionally, the professional requirements may include an establishment license, such as a massage establishment license. Depending on your state, these licenses may not be transferable to another name, person, or location without filing the proper papers and paying a fee. Check with your individual state's licensing board. States often require that the establishment license, any county or city licenses, and all practitioner licenses be prominently displayed. Practitioner licenses include but are not limited to those for massage, physical, occupational, and speech therapists; cosmetologists; acupuncturists; and naturopaths.

Most states or counties require a department of health inspection before opening the establishment's doors and yearly inspections thereafter. Inspectors will have a list to check off that includes items such as handicap-accessible bathrooms with hot and cold running water, cleaning supplies, document storage according to HIPAA regulations, safety precautions pertinent to the field (such as a "sharps" container for acupuncture needles), and fire extinguishers or sprinkler systems. Further, proof of insurance is dictated by the state. This may include liability, malpractice, and/or disability insurance.

Business Insurance

Having adequate business insurance is crucial. Review with an insurance agent the coverage necessary to protect you against things that may be detrimental to your business's continuing to operate. These risks may include fire, theft, product liability (if you sell products), and general liability. Check with your state's department of business regulation or the governing body of your field to determine what is needed. There is also the issue of malpractice or professional liability insurance. Check with the appropriate state board to determine whether this insurance is required. Whether you should carry malpractice or professional liability insurance is a business decision that you will have to make, and it is a decision that you should not take lightly.

BE A SMART CONSUMER

For many years we carried professional liability insurance, and as our practice grew, we thought that we should have even more coverage. I contacted an agent to ask about more coverage and was told to drop our coverage because if we had no coverage, we most likely would not get sued because we had no assets that could be taken from us in a settlement (in Florida, retirement and homesteaded properties are protected from judgments). If we had $2 million of professional liability insurance, we would be sued for at least that amount. I confirmed this with my attorney, so we dropped professional liability coverage. There is other coverage that is beneficial, such as sexual misconduct. It behooves you to be a good consumer and weigh the pros and cons of insurance coverage. We do carry an umbrella policy on our business that covers us for all general liability and loss. (LSR)

The Reality Check above presents a situation in which it was advantageous to drop professional liability coverage. In that case, not having professional liability insurance was a personal decision made under specific circumstances. Neither of this book's authors recommends that anyone drop this insurance without serious consideration and without conferring with professionals in your area. The important thing to take away from the Reality Check example is that you have to be aware of the options, the specifics, and the obligations that you have as a business owner. If you do not carry insurance that is customary in your profession, it is imperative that you inform your customers of this fact. If they are unaware of your lack of coverage, this could be considered unethical because you have not informed your customers fully so that they can make a decision to be treated by you that is based on all the facts.

It is important that all policies be reviewed for their coverage and exclusions (what is not covered). Many of the less expensive policies do not cover very much, so it is important that you know what is included and what is not. Like anything else in life, you get what you pay for. If you are satisfied with the coverage provided by less expensive insurance, that is fine. For many practitioners who do out-calls, work for others, or work part-time, such insurance coverage is most likely more than adequate. If there are a significant number of assets in the business, the coverage may not be adequate. Insurance policies and coverage need to be reviewed on a yearly basis. As the circumstances in your life change, your insurance needs should be reviewed.

Workers' compensation is required by law if you have employees, though many states do not require it in companies with very few employees. Florida, as an example, does not require workers' compensation in companies with fewer than three employees. Your building lease may also specify insurance coverage; be sure to check the lease if you have already signed an agreement or prior to signing. The insurance coverage is usually specified as a certain dollar amount per square foot being leased. In some instances, there is a minimum amount that the landlord requires regardless of the size of the leased premises. Insurance companies generally have a minimum that they will insure for. If you borrow money from a bank or other lenders, such as the Small Business Administration, the lender will require insurance coverage; many lenders stipulate that they be listed on the declarations page. Disability insurance may be something to consider if you are the sole owner and operator of your business. Disability insurance is a great thing to have, yet it can be very expensive, and your benefits are generally paid based on the amount of money that you pay yourself, not the amount of money that you bring into the business. Consider what you would do if you were hurt and couldn't work: Who or how would you pay your bills? Talk to your accountant and insurance agent about disability insurance; it may not be easy to file a claim and receive money, or it may be prohibitively expensive.

CHECKLIST

Have you done these things yet?

☐ Have you consulted the following, in order, to decide what business format you would work best in?

- Your "self" _____

- Your team members _____

- Your accountant _____

☐ Have you studied each business form or structure?

☐ Have you listed the steps involved in opening your chosen business form and started those tasks (e.g., need articles of incorporation filed through an attorney)?

☐ What is your business name going to be?

☐ Have you had partnership or corporate contracts written and reviewed?

☐ What other legal obligations do you need to meet before opening the doors (e.g., state and county licenses)?

☐ Have you spoken to one or more insurance agents?

SO WHAT DO YOU THINK?

1. Do you think you can manage a sole proprietorship or even a corporation, or would it be a better move, even if temporary, to be an employee?

2. Do you have an understanding of each task in the mechanics of putting together a business, and do you have the attention to detail needed to successfully complete the tasks?

3. Do you think that it is okay to learn the ins and outs of another person's business and then take what you have learned to start your own business?

4. Do you think it would be better to make your own mistakes than be a part of some-body else's mistake-making process?

5. Which business structure do you think is right for your business? Why?

6. What are the disadvantages of all the other business structures that are listed?

Getting Help

CHAPTER TEN

LEARNING OUTCOMES

After completing this chapter, you should be able to:

10.1 Differentiate between the various kinds of help.

10.2 Determine what type of help will be suitable for your purposes.

10.3 Decide what each person's role will be.

10.4 Recognize the vehicles through which additional help can be found.

KEY TERMS

limited partner

partner

compensation

employee handbook

Small Business Administration

Bringing someone new into your business is a very challenging thing to do, for this may be the first time that you have to share your business with someone else. Even though you have your team in place, they serve a very different purpose for you. You have a certain amount of responsibility for the people that you are bringing into the business. Their livelihood depends on your success or failure, so there is more pressure for you to be successful than there was with your team.

Finding Your First Help

If you are beginning to feel that you need some help in your business, you must first decide what type of help you are looking for. The following five examples are types of help that you may be looking for. Look over these types, and see if any of them meet needs that you want to fill.

1. Someone to bounce your ideas off of.
2. Someone to share the financial risk.
3. Someone to support the work that you are doing.
4. Someone to share the workload.
5. Someone who complements your weaknesses with his or her strengths.

If you are looking for someone who will consider your ideas and share the financial risk, you should most likely find someone who would be happy being a **limited partner**. This means someone who is not necessarily involved in the day-to-day operations. This person would most likely be a businessperson who does not necessarily have the desire or the ability to participate in the business on a daily basis. This person would have the ability to act as a mentor and would support you in your business. The person will benefit from this financially, because she or he will share in the profits from your business.

If you are looking for someone to support your work and share the workload, you will need to hire an employee. This person's skill is secondary to your skills. This does not mean that the person is not filling an important role; it means that he or she is dependent on your skills to be able to make money. The person will generally be compensated on an hourly basis. Whether you need this person on a part-time or full-time basis is based on the amount of work that needs to be done.

If you are looking for someone to share the workload and complement your weaknesses, you should be looking for a **partner**. This person will have more responsibility in the running of the day-to-day operations, along with a greater investment in the success of the operation. Her or his participation is not as limited as that of the first two types of people described above. This person will be compensated in like fashion to the way that you compensate yourself. You will depend on this person in more ways than just as an employee; you will depend on her or him as an equal in the running of the business and also in the risks and rewards of the business.

At this point you should be able to discern the differing needs that your business has. It is time to fit a person or persons to those needs. When looking for someone to work with in business, you should apply the same principles as you do when looking for a life partner. In fact, if you think about it, you may be spending far more time with a business partner than you do with your life partner. You have to make sure that the person you pick is someone with whom you can work with for a long period of time. It is imperative that you spend time and effort in communicating about many things with your potential partner and employees. You should discuss the following with each:

1. What you expect from the person. What are his or her specific duties?
2. What the person should expect from you.

3. Your business plan and where the person fits into it.

4. The things that are contractually important:

    a. **Time required for the job.** This can be on either a weekly or a one-time basis.

    b. **Compensation for the job that is to be done.** This is the amount of money that the person will be paid, either by the hour or the job.

    c. **Length of employment.** Are there any specific terms for the length of employment?

    d. **Type of employment:**

       (1) **Employee.** Will the person be paid a salary or an hourly wage?

       (2) **Shareholder (owner).** Will the person receive a portion of the profits or be responsible for a portion of a potential loss?

       (3) **Independent contractor.** Will the person be responsible for his or her own taxes and employment expenses?

5. The items that will be provided for the person to accomplish the job. What tools will the person be given to do the job?

You need to be open and honest right from the start, for if you are not, this will only cause trouble in the future. Also, it is of the utmost importance that you get everything in writing with regard to the people you are working with. An **employee handbook** or a document with clear job descriptions is a necessity (Figure 10.1). Whatever is in writing can be used as a guideline for how you work with the other people in your organization. Without such guidelines, there will be no rules specifying how the people in your organization are to do anything. Rules and policies are put in place for a reason: to protect everyone who is involved in the business. People know what to expect, they cannot be taken advantage of beyond the rules, and there is recourse for anyone who has been taken advantage of. Written rules and policies provide a safety net for all people in the business.

Once you have all of the important things outlined for the job or position of your new associate and you and your associate have agreed on everything, an intelligent

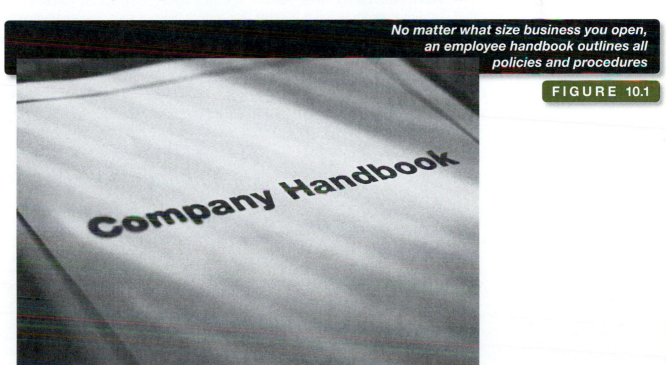

No matter what size business you open, an employee handbook outlines all policies and procedures

FIGURE 10.1

option is to have an attorney write the terms of the agreement as a simple contract. This will ensure that the document is legal and correct. If you cannot afford an attorney, you can use a boilerplate contract (available at office supply stores or online) or write your own (Web sites of various legal entities provide information on how to do so). You and your associate should sign the contract, and it should be notarized as well.

How You Find the Right Person

The way that you go about finding the person you want is dependent on the type of person you are looking for. As described above, there are five needs that you may be looking to fill. The person who will fulfill the first two types of needs will be found in a different way than people who will fulfill the other types.

There are companies that either will act as management or will provide financing for your business and act as a silent partner, or they will find you someone who will do the same. There are organizations, such as the **Small Business Administration**, that will act as a quasi partner for your business by giving you input on how to run your business and providing funds, in the form of a loan, for you to run your business. The Web site for the SBA is www.sba.gov. Friends and family members are also a good resource for this type of partner in your business. If there is a clear understanding of what is expected by all parties concerned, the people who are the closest to you are the best resource for you. This option does present some issues, but if clear communication and understanding are present, then many problems can be avoided.

If you are looking for someone to support you in your business or share in the workload, the following ways to contact candidates are suggested:

- *Newspaper ad.* When advertising for a position, be clear, concise, and specific about what you are looking for. No matter what position you are offering, ask potential employees to fax a résumé to you. Do not put any phone number in the ad, unless you have a person who will be able to answer the phone specifically for applicants' calls.

- *Friends and family.* Your friends and family are a great resource. Just be careful not to promise anything that you cannot deliver, such as a guarantee of employment.

- *Associations.* These are great places to get to know other people in your industry, and they are a great source of potential employees.

- *Word of mouth.* Asking other professionals, customers, and service providers for recommendations can be helpful. People who frequent your establishment and know what you are about can be very helpful to you in the search process.

- *Local schools.* Schools have lists of people who are looking for work. They can also provide you with other services, such as continued notification of potential employees for your business.

- *Online.* There are many online services that provide names of people looking for work, as well as providing a place for you to advertise openings.

The last type of person, someone who will complement you, will be a partner and thus should not be found directly through any of the ways described above. While this person may be found initially through the methods mentioned above, he or she needs to grow into the position of a partner. As the relationship grows, you will be able to see whether the person is what you want in a partner.

Sometimes you may be "forced" into making someone a partner because your business depends on them heavily. You end up with two choices: either a weaker

BE CAREFUL HOW YOU ASK

The first time that I wanted to hire a therapist, I put an ad in the paper. I was inundated with over 100 calls in the first two days. There was no way that I was going to be able to call those people back in a reasonable amount of time, so many people never received a call back from me. From that point on, when I had to advertise for any position, I asked for a résumé to be faxed. The response was much more manageable, and I was able to reduce the number of call-backs based on the information on the résumés. (LSR)

business, because of the loss of that person as an employee, or a stronger business, at a cost, because you have made that person a partner. There are times when you could lose a strong employee and continue to have a strong business, so it is not always bad to lose a good employee. Do not let the fear of losing somebody good force you to make a bad business decision by giving away your business.

The Bottom Line

The bottom line is that as your business grows, the need for additional help will grow. It is imperative that you identify the place of need, the type of person that can fill that need, and the type of legal arrangement that you would prefer for that position and then fill it. You should use the outlines described above to fill the needs of your business and enable the continued growth of your business.

CHECKLIST

Have you done these things yet?

☐ Have you made a list of the specific functions you need help with?

☐ Have you identified who may be able to fill those needs?

☐ Have you written an employee handbook or clear descriptions of what each party will be responsible for?

☐ Have you determined which sources to use to find help, if needed?

SO WHAT DO YOU THINK?

1. What would happen within your organization if people did not have a clear idea of responsibilities? Make up some scenarios.

2. What are the best types of arrangements for your business? Why?

3. How do you know when to hire additional people for your business?

4. Are there any instances where a partnership is not a good idea? Why?

Success through Ethics

CHAPTER ELEVEN

LEARNING OUTCOMES

After completing this chapter, you should be able to:

11.1 Explain why ethical practices are critical in your business.

11.2 Define basic concepts in professional ethics.

11.3 Distinguish between a *boundary crossing* and a *boundary violation.*

11.4 Ask appropriate questions in ethically difficult circumstances to navigate potential conflict.

11.5 Judge when to seek the professional guidance of a supervisor or mentor or turn to other appropriate resources for professional assistance.

KEY TERMS

professionalism

ethics

Hippocratic Oath

fiduciary relationship

therapeutic relationship

power differential

paternalistic

boundaries

transference

countertransference

dual-role (multiple) relationship

conflict of interest

Professional ethics in health care is the application of guiding principles of right conduct to the study, practice, and business of health care (Figure 11.1).

Why Success through Ethics?

Ethical considerations should be part and parcel of any business decisions you make—not only because this is the right thing to do, safeguarding the integrity of your business, but also because it is likely to contribute to your success. A number of recent studies agree; companies displaying a "clear commitment to ethical conduct" financially outperformed companies that did not have ethical codes. A meta-analysis (research that looks at combined studies of common factors) noted that businesses with ethical codes were significantly more likely to show strength in four key areas of financial performance: economic value added, market value added, price-earning ratio, and return on capital.

Why do businesses with ethical codes do better? Their success is likely due to a complicated interplay of factors, but it is understandable that clients would value ethics in their caregivers. Wouldn't *you* rather work with ethical people? A study released in 2001 supports the assertion that the vast majority of clients care about ethics. Over two-thirds (71 percent) of prospective clients surveyed (defined as Americans who report receiving massage and bodywork treatments each year) considered ethics "extremely or very important" criteria in their choice of practitioner.

Concepts in Professional Ethics

This chapter will discuss the role of professional ethics in your practice. **Professionalism** is a combination of individual responsibility—personal responsibility on the part of each member of the professional community—and the collective responsibility of a formal group or association of practitioners. The term **ethics** refers to principles of right or good conduct. Professional ethics in health care is the application of

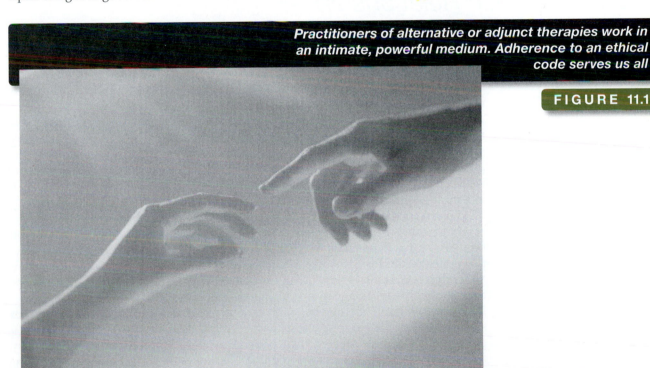

Practitioners of alternative or adjunct therapies work in an intimate, powerful medium. Adherence to an ethical code serves us all

FIGURE 11.1

guiding principles of right conduct to the study, practice, and business of health care. Unlike personal ethical codes, which are flexible and open to debate, professional ethical codes are formally defined, mandatory standards of conduct established by and for members of professional associations to ensure quality and integrity in their profession.

This chapter will equip you with the basic concepts and rationale for ethical decision making in your practice. It will help you navigate unknown ethical territory, identify questionable behavior, and develop a sense for "red flags" of potential conflict, as well as take steps to resolve these issues. Even more important, it will help you know when to seek the professional guidance of a supervisor or mentor or turn to other appropriate resources for professional assistance.

Since all state licensing authorities, certifying or accrediting agencies, and professional associations establish their own standards of conduct and ethical guidelines for their members, you will need to refer directly to the organizations and academic or training institutions with which you are affiliated, as well as state, local, and national associations, to review the ethical guidelines that apply specifically to you and your practice. You may also want to refer to the literature (e.g., journals and newsletters) or Web sites of prominent professional organizations, which typically post their ethical codes and standards of conduct.

Formal ethical codes and standards of conduct have a long history in the business of health care. Many of the values, obligations, and rights we have come to identify with contemporary wellness are rooted in the **Hippocratic Oath**, a 2,400-year-old ethical code that directed physicians, above all else, to "do no harm." Today, health care ethics (also called *bioethics* or *medical ethics*) is a vast field of study, with categories and subcategories relating to every conceivable topic and issue. Most medical and health-related disciplines establish their own ethical codes and standards of conduct, which encapsulate the compiled wisdom of countless individuals and years of professional experience. Studying these codes and standards offers practitioners the opportunity to learn from their predecessors' mistakes instead of their own.

The Therapeutic Relationship

Health care professionals have weighty responsibilities to their clients, colleagues, and the profession. The focal point of these interrelated responsibilities is a relationship of trust, or **fiduciary relationship**, in which the client puts his or her trust in a professional practitioner with the expectation that both client and practitioner are working in the client's best interests.

This expectation is the foundation of a **therapeutic relationship**, one that cures or restores health. While the practitioner and client share the same primary concern and objective—the client's welfare—it is the practitioner, by virtue of his or her professional status, who is ultimately responsible for the client's safety, security, and well-being. The practitioner bears the burden of accountability because he or she is in a position of authority or power in relation to the client.

Interpersonal dynamics exist in all relationships, and they are a normal and necessary part of a therapeutic relationship between client and practitioner. An important part of this dynamic is the **power differential**—the imbalance in authority or power that results from the practitioner's greater expertise in a health care discipline. Your education, skills, experience in the field, and professional certification give you an authoritative advantage over your clients.

In the past 40 years, the role of health care professionals and the relationships they share with their patients and clients have changed dramatically. Some decades ago, physicians commonly treated their patients in a **paternalistic**, or parental, way, sometimes keeping details of the condition or illness from the patient and making medical decisions with little or no patient input. Today, physicians are encouraged to speak openly with their patients regarding health and treatment options, and patients are encouraged to ask questions and discuss their concerns with health care professionals. Both are emblematic of a health care system fraught with potential liability and of the realization that patients who take an active interest in health concerns tend to make better, more informed health and medical decisions.

Ideally, your relationship and interactions with a client are a partnership that ensures the client's voice is heard, thereby promoting healthy behaviors and sound, informed health care decisions. Encourage reluctant or shy clients to become well-informed, active participants, rather than passive observers, in their own health care decisions. You can play a significant role in ensuring that your clients understand their medical conditions and treatment options, their questions and concerns are heard and addressed, and their voices and votes are part of the decision-making process.

Some clients will welcome the opportunity to take a more decisive role in their health care decisions; others may be intimidated or overwhelmed by the responsibility. Remember that your client's best interests should always be your primary goal and the guide for all your actions and decisions. If you suspect any other interest is taking priority over your client's welfare, review your rationale. For example, are you recommending frequent treatments because they benefit your client and are appropriate to his or her condition or because you're strapped for cash? When in doubt, ask yourself, *What is optimal for my client's health and welfare?*

Professional Responsibilities and Boundaries

The concept of "profession," with its fiduciary obligation, gives rise to the notion of **boundaries** in the client-professional relationship. While this concept is understood in several different ways in the health care literature, there is consensus regarding one of the defining characteristics of professions and professionals: commitment to serve the profession's clients and to place clients' interests ahead of those of any individual professional or, indeed, the profession. The *professional boundary* defines the extent and limitations of the relationship with your client. It preserves your client's confidentiality and creates a "safe space" for your client to receive professional services.

Concerns about professional boundaries in the relationship between clients and health care providers—and the damage that results when boundaries are transgressed—usually capture public and professional attention following reports of inappropriate sexual relationships between health care professionals and clients. However, relatively little attention has been paid to the "boundary question" outside this context, and many other interactions raise concerns about boundaries as well. Practitioners need guidance if they are to avoid engaging in interactions with their clients that may prove ethically problematic.

A variety of standards establish the limits of appropriate professional behavior, whether those limits are explicitly enumerated in standards of conduct, codes of ethics, or law or tacitly conveyed through professional training and widespread acceptance. Individuals who seek help must rely on the professional they consult to be trustworthy. When practitioners behave in ways that call their professional judgment and objectivity into question, the trust on which the relationship depends is compromised. And when trust is compromised, the efficacy of the therapeutic relationship is undermined.

Standards regarding professional boundaries are found in a variety of sources. Directly or indirectly, professional codes of ethics, consensus statements, position papers, policies, and laws define the boundaries of appropriate behavior. These various codes, consensus statements, and position papers can assist practitioners to maintain boundaries in their professional relationships with clients. Some standards are concrete, setting specific thresholds for professional behavior, often by proscribing particular activities or relationships, such as sexual relationships. Often, the standards set by professional organizations carry sanctions for professionals who violate acceptable behavior.

Other standards, however, set out only general values and principles that should guide the professional's conduct and decision making, and they rely on health care professionals to use good judgment in applying those values and principles. While practitioners in many fields are prohibited from engaging in dual or multiple relationships with clients or former clients in which there is a risk of exploitation or potential harm to the client, these regulations only broadly define "dual or multiple relationships" and rarely suggest criteria by which professionals should assess the nature or level of risk a particular dual relationship would pose for a client.

State and national guidelines offer specific guidance to help practitioners avoid inappropriate conduct, such as recommending that professionals restrict contact with clients to appropriate times and places. Violations of these guidelines could result in probation, limitation of practice, and suspension or revocation of licensure. Practitioners should be aware, moreover, that inappropriate sexual or physical contact can also result in clients' suing practitioners.

The nature of professions is such that they demand expectations of a higher morality and a greater commitment to the good of others than do most other human activities. The health care relationship is one of both great intimacy and great disparity in power and knowledge, giving rise to special obligations for health care professionals. The practitioner-client relationship entails special obligations for the practitioner to serve the patient's interest because of the specialized knowledge that the practitioner holds and the imbalance of power between practitioner and client.

Relationships and interactions that may be ethically unproblematic among nonprofessionals may be unacceptable when one of the parties is a professional. An individual may have a personal interest that is perfectly acceptable in itself but that conflicts with an obligation the same individual has *as a professional.* For example, under circumstances in which it would normally be acceptable for one person to ask another individual for a date, it is not acceptable for a health care professional to ask a *client* for a date, because doing so might compromise the professional's fiduciary commitment to the client's welfare.

Transference and Countertransference

The intimate nature of therapy involves practitioners in clients' important and sometimes highly stressful life events, and the mutual dependence of practitioners and clients working in close concert presents the potential for blurring of limits to professional relationships. Remaining within the bounds established by the purpose of the relationship can be especially difficult in prolonged or long-term relationships. Even so, in all encounters, *practitioners are responsible for retaining their professional boundaries.*

As we have discussed, with any position of power comes potential for abuse. When health care professionals forge close relationships with people in their care, the combination of physical and social interaction between practitioner and client can trigger strong emotional responses in one or both parties, leading to small improprieties as well as egregious misconduct.

It is not unusual for clients to unintentionally test professional boundaries or for practitioners to unknowingly relax them. When practitioners and clients are motivated by countertransference and transference, respectively, they are more susceptible to inappropriate impulses that can lead to misconduct. The term **transference** refers to all the feelings experienced by the client, related to his or her past experiences and relationships, stirred up by or in the session; transference also refers to a situation in which the client tries to personalize the therapeutic relationship based on his or her projection of emotions from the past. Transference is neither negative nor positive, but it is "always a distortion; a projection of emotions from the past to current objects." The term **countertransference** refers to all the feelings experienced by the practitioner, related to his or her previous relationships and experiences, that are stirred up during the session, including the practitioner's conscious and unconscious response to the client's transference of emotions. Countertransference also refers to a situation in which the professional tries to personalize the therapeutic relationship based on conscious or unconscious responses to the client's transfer of emotions.

Be aware that transference and countertransference can activate strong emotional reactions and/or feelings of sexual attraction, raising unrealistic expectations on the part of clients and practitioners. Learn to identify emotional red flags of blurred professional or personal boundaries in your behavior. If you overreact, are preaching or lecturing, or are uncomfortable, unsure of yourself, or dissatisfied in your interactions with a specific client, you may be experiencing countertransference, bringing emotions and reactions from your personal life into your professional environment.

Boundary Crossings and Violations

Boundaries are breached in two ways. Some breaches are inadvertent or not intentionally exploitative. These are known as *boundary crossings*. Commonly cited examples are a good-bye hug initiated by your client at the completion of treatment, nonsexual physical reassurance at times of extreme stress, running a session overtime, or selective self-disclosure. Repetitive boundary crossings are potentially harmful because they blur the boundary, thereby increasing the chances of boundary violation.

A *boundary violation* is a significant and potentially harmful breach in which the practitioner's behavior goes beyond appropriate professional limits, overriding the client's rights or actually doing harm to the client. Boundary violations generally arise when a personal interest displaces the professional's primary commitment to the client's welfare in ways that harm the client or the client-practitioner relationship. Some examples are affectionate or flirtatious communication, self-disclosure about the practitioner's personal problems, or breaking confidentiality.

Interactions between health care professionals and clients are ethically problematic when they can reasonably be expected to affect the care the individual or other clients receive or the health care professional's relationships with colleagues—or when they give the appearance of doing so.

Asking your client, who is a lawyer, for free legal advice; requesting a church donation; mentioning personal details about a client or repeating what was said during a session to a friend or spouse—all are subtle ways practitioners take unfair advantage of their relationships with clients. Even when clients appear to welcome, rather than resent, them, such requests or behaviors are never appropriate and do not belong in a professional environment. It is equally inappropriate for practitioners to accept favors, free merchandise and services, or confidential information (such as stock tips) from a client. Such interactions can distort the therapeutic relationship and obscure its primary objective.

Boundary violations not only harm individual clients but carry consequences for others when they erode trust and confidence in the profession more broadly. Practitioners' obligations to society parallel their obligations to individual clients. Practitioners' conduct as professionals should merit the respect of the community. Clear—and scrupulously adhered to—boundaries thus protect health care professionals as well as clients, helping to sustain the public trust on which the free-dom to practice rests.

You will sometimes need to respond to situations in which the boundary becomes less defined. These situations may seem ordinary and potentially harm-less. For instance, would you accept a gift from your client? Your answer might depend on the context. An inexpensive token of thanks at the last session may be different from a gift on your birthday or one offered by your client at some other point in treatment.

You are responsible for maintaining the protective boundaries that ensure your client a physically and emotionally safe environment. Part of your responsibility in that role is to protect the client from you, should you act or speak inappropriately or be motivated by anything but your client's best interests. Although practitioners and clients may be similarly affected by these psychological processes and equally capable of showing poor judgment or acting irrationally, licensed health care practi-tioners are bound by their professional affiliation to act responsibly, even when the client does not.

Beware of corrupting influences and motivations that jeopardize your profes-sional relationship with the client. If you suspect you are acting out of an unhealthy need or motive, or feel your interactions or relationship with the client is impeding rather than facilitating the therapeutic process, seek assistance and/or supervision. Consult a mentor, supervisor, or professional organization with which you are affili-ated for assistance, supervision, referrals, and other professional resources.

Personal Boundaries and Self-Disclosure

Self-disclosure is the process in which the practitioner reveals personal (rather than general or professional) information about himself or herself to the client. Inappro-priate self-disclosure is done for the benefit of the practitioner rather than the client and may burden the client unnecessarily. Sometimes self-disclosure leads to role reversal, a case in which, for example, the client feels he or she must take care of the practitioner. This unnecessary disclosure is a boundary violation.

There are many different motivations for and types of self-disclosure. Self-disclosure may be deliberate or accidental, may be initiated by either the cli-ent or the therapist, and can be spoken or unspoken. An example of unspoken intentional self-disclosure is how you choose to decorate your workplace. Infusing your work space with items that express your personality is fine, but make sure this doesn't cross the line. A sticker with your political affiliation or a photo of a politi-cal candidate is inappropriate. Some self-disclosure is unavoidable, as your presence communicates facts about you such as your approximate age.

Some disclosure is accidental because it is not meant to be shared but is com-municated through body language or tone of voice. Accidental self-disclosure also occurs in cases where a practitioner runs into a client unexpectedly, when both are sitting in their doctor's waiting room, for example. The practitioner may or may not want to disclose information about why she or he is there, and it may be difficult to find a safe middle ground, revealing enough to be professional and friendly but not enough to compromise personal space and privacy. Consider personal and pro-fessional boundaries when you develop a Web site or promotional materials. The Internet is a great way to get information "out there," but it is difficult to take the information back, so consider that content carefully.

There is some debate regarding the extent to which practitioners should dis-close personal things to their clients. We all know someone who self-discloses too easily or inappropriately and the awkwardness that can result. Also, there is the risk of taking time and attention away from your client's treatment and burdening him or her with knowledge of your own problems. Self-disclosure signals that the relationship is becoming more personal, and it can be interpreted as an invitation for your client to ask further personal questions or seek friendship with you. Exactly where should you draw the line?

It is helpful to ask yourself two questions before self-disclosing: (1) How will self-disclosure benefit the client?; and (2) how will it affect your professional boundaries? You should also consider your own privacy. For example, what if you and your client attend the same Alcoholics Anonymous meeting? Would this make it hard for you to get the full benefits of attending the meeting during times of stress or relapse?

Whenever there is an interaction between you and the client, personal information is shared, some intentionally, some accidentally. Boundary crossings may be more likely to occur in situations of transference (the client's personalizing of the relationship) and countertransference (the practitioner's personalizing of the relationship). You may have a momentary incident in which you share something, which later you wish you had not. Self-disclosure is not always conscious and deliberate. Of course, it is impossible to take words back once they are spoken. When in doubt, do not self-disclose.

It is usually best to allow the client to direct the conversation and avoid obviously controversial topics. If the client shares information, it is easy to give noncommittal responses that show you are listening and interested, but do not expand on the conversation. Train yourself to avoid reflexive emotional responses or judgments (both negative and positive). A good rule of thumb is to monitor your own feelings without imposing them on your client. If you are distracted by a strong feeling (e.g., a spark of attraction) mentally put it to one side. Wait until after the session; then talk with a peer or supervisor or deal with it personally. As with other boundary crossings, self-disclosure should be client-focused, based on the welfare of the client. Different clients and practitioners have different personal boundaries, so appropriate boundaries must function within each client's comfort zone.

Remember that personal and professional boundaries exist for the benefit of both the practitioner and the client. Changing or moving boundaries, which are the limits within which the therapeutic relationship occurs, results in an unclear or ambiguous relationship that is a risk to the safety of the client, although it may not appear to have negative repercussions at the time. Transgressions often have delayed consequences that may not initially appear harmful.

Boundaries are signified and reinforced by the temporal and spatial routines of the treatment process: regular appointment times, consistent length of sessions, and a dedicated treatment room.

They are also reinforced by appropriate behavior. Try to maintain the same structure and rules of conduct in each session, with each client. Examine the rationale and potential repercussions of any changes or exceptions you make for specific clients, even at their request, before you implement them. Bending a rule may not always endanger the therapeutic process, but impropriety can be a "slippery slope." If you uncharacteristically deviate from normal session structure or protocol, suspect your impulses may be motivated by self-interest, or are having strong emotional responses to a client, seek peer support or supervision. Detecting boundary violations is complicated by the fact that transgressions are more often a process than an individual event or occurrence. Boundary violations may be subtle or be masked by the professional-client relationship.

Inappropriate behavior tends to make people uncomfortable. If you notice that a client is not responding positively to treatment, make sure your behavior or comments are not contributing factors. Relieving stress, physical stiffness, or pain should be a relaxing and comfortable experience. If your behavior is appropriate but your client appears anxious or uncomfortable in the session, discuss your concern with the client.

Dual-Role (Multiple) Relationships

A **dual-role (multiple) relationship** occurs when an individual, either at the same time or at different points in time, engages in two role categories; for example, in addition to the professional therapeutic relationship, there is also another relationship, such as relative, friend, student, business partner, or instructor. While it is perhaps best to avoid dual relationships, it is not always a possible, or practical, ideal. In a small town, for example, avoiding dual relationships may be more difficult than doing so in a large city.

There is a great range of opinion regarding the propriety of dual relationships. Some professional associations consider that although not all dual relationships are negative, all have that potential. Other organizations suggest that dual relationships are acceptable if they are not at exploitative. Similarly, some professionals consider it unethical to treat friends, while others consider it acceptable to proceed as long as appropriate measures are taken to ensure there are no detrimental effects to the therapeutic or preexisting relationship. To ensure that the relationships do not cross the line into exploitation, it is important to follow recommended procedures including informed consent, open discussion, consultation, supervision, and examination of personal motivation—*all of which should be documented.*

It is always best to avoid multiple relationships if it appears likely that the dual relationship might interfere with the therapeutic relationship. Existence of a dual relationship, however, is not necessarily a violation of boundaries. A dual relationship that violates boundaries is usually referred to as a *prohibited dual relationship.* This is a dual relationship that might impair objectivity or effectiveness, permit exploitation, or create an actual, apparent, or potential conflict of interest.

It is your responsibility, not your client's, to maintain appropriate boundaries in your professional relationship. If a complaint is filed, it will be your responsibility to demonstrate that a client has not been exploited or coerced, intentionally or unintentionally. Be especially vigilant regarding any conduct that could impair your objectivity and professional judgment in serving your client and any conduct that carries the risk and/or the appearance of exploitation or potential harm to your client.

Recognize and avoid the dangers of dual relationships when relating to clients in more than one context, whether professional, social, educational, or commercial. Dual relationships can occur simultaneously or consecutively. Prohibited dual relationships can include, but are not limited to, the following:

- Forming a sexual relationship with a current client or someone who has been your client if the client-therapist relationship has not thoroughly ended.
- Treating clients to whom you are related by blood or legal ties.
- Entering into financial or business transactions with clients (other than the provision of therapeutic services).

Other situations that complicate the therapeutic relationship are lending and borrowing money, meeting at inappropriate places or times, giving or receiving gifts, soliciting donations, inappropriate self-disclosure, socializing with clients, and inappropriate use of language.

It is not unusual for massage therapists to work with family and friends when they are building a client base for their practice. As a student, you may have provided services free to those you knew well. When you begin your practice, you will want to use a sliding scale, eventually increasing the rate to your full price when you feel your experience justifies it. While these are, by definition, dual relationships, they are not necessarily unethical.

Before engaging in a dual relationship, ask yourself the following questions to determine whether the dual relationship is in the best interests of the client and practitioner:

- Is the dual relationship necessary?

Unnecessary dual relationships are associated with unnecessary risk. It is usually in the best interests of the professional to avoid a dual relationship, if possible. If the dual relationship is deemed necessary, ask:

- Who benefits from the dual relationship?
- Will the dual relationship cause risk to the client?
- Will the dual relationship disrupt the therapeutic relationship?

These questions should be revisited throughout the treatment process to ensure that the relationship remains in the best interests of the client.

- Am I conflicted or objective in my reasoning?

Because objectivity is an ideal that we can only approach, it is useful to discuss this subject with a supervisor or peer counselor. Review this list of questions and the answers in consultation with a trusted adviser, and document the discussion.

Documentation should record each portion of this decision-making process, reflecting the choices that led to the dual relationship. Good documentation acts like a witness to the event, and it should, in retrospect, support the practitioner's choice. Evaluations of boundary violations in professional practice usually occur long after the fact—they are often arrived at retrospectively by an ethics committee, so the rationale should be clear.

Finally, if you proceed with treatment, ask:

- Does the client understand the significance of the dual relationship, and did he or she give informed consent regarding the risks associated with the relationship?

The following examples describe potential ethical dilemmas relating to dual relationships. In each case, the dual relationship causes boundary confusion because the two relationships have different boundary rules. Consider how you would handle this scenario:

You need some painting done in your office. Your client is unemployed, short of money, and underconfident. You are thinking about hiring your client to do the paint job since it could have therapeutic benefits. What if your client does a bad paint job? How would this impact the therapeutic relationship? What if your client discloses that she has been drinking heavily? What impact might this have on your trust in her as a painter? What about these negative disclosures?

Consider how you might react to some of the following scenarios:

- Your child becomes friendly with your client's child.
- You bump into your client while you are both drinking alcohol at a party.
- A mutual friend introduces your client as his new girlfriend.

Many kinds of interactions potentially interfere with the primary therapeutic relationship between practitioner and client and pose concerns about acceptable conduct for practitioners. Becoming socially involved or entering into a business relationship with a client, for example, can impair, or appear to impair, the professional's objectivity. Accepting a gift is sometimes an appropriate way to allow a client to express his or her gratitude but at other times is problematic.

Showing favoritism—by giving a particular client extra attention, time, or priority in scheduling appointments, for example—can cross the boundary between action that is appropriate advocacy on behalf of a particular client and action that is unfair to others. Such interactions or activities are ethically problematic when they can reasonably be expected to affect the care received by the individual or by other clients or the practitioner's relationships with his or her colleagues or when they *give the appearance* of doing so. Yet not all behavior that might be considered

Mr. D, an independent contractor, has been the practitioner's (Mr. H's) client for three years. During a visit, Mr. D overhears Mr. H talking to a colleague about some remodeling for Mr. H's home. Later in the visit, he hands Mr. H his business card and tells him that he will do the remodeling for a great price because he appreciates the care he has received from Mr. H. The client's offer of discounted service may contain an implicit agreement—Mr. D may now expect Mr. H to provide special services or reduce his fees, for example. How does this change the client's expectations of the client-practitioner relationship and put the practitioner's objectivity in question? The client may perceive that the practitioner's personal interests can be appealed to for care that is outside accepted professional norms.

inappropriate necessarily violates professional obligations. Although it is frequently difficult to draw clear lines, the examples below highlight some of the considerations at stake.

Health care professionals should be alert to situations in which they may be likely to be motivated to behave in ways that violate accepted ethical standards. Ambiguous interactions and relationships, for example, have the potential both to impair the professional's objectivity and compromise his or her judgment and to give rise to conflicting expectations on the client's part, which can contaminate the therapeutic relationship and potentially undermine the client's trust. Multiple or ambiguous relationships raise other concerns as well. Consider the case of Mr. D and Mr. H in Ethical Quandary 1.

It is not always feasible for a practitioner to bracket his or her interactions with a client from other interactions he or she may have with the same individual outside the health care setting. While any practitioner may face the challenge of navigating multiple, overlapping, or ambiguous relationships, the problem may be particularly acute for practitioners in small communities, many of whose clients are also the tradespeople, shopkeepers, bankers, or others with whom they must do business regularly. But that does not obviate the professional's responsibility to be sensitive to the ethical concerns at stake and take appropriate action to withdraw from or manage social or other relationships in ways that minimize the possibility of harming clients, interfering with the care of others, or disrupting relationships with colleagues.

Defining what counts as a violation of professional boundaries simply by referring to "dual relationships" or to the *kinds* of relationships between clients and health care professionals (e.g., business or social) may cast the net too widely. Determining whether any given interaction is or is not appropriate behavior for a health care professional calls for careful, critical reflection on the particular circumstances. Consider the scenario presented in Ethical Quandary 2, for example.

Gifts from clients may be problematic if they carry with them an expectation of return favors, or they might influence a practitioner's judgment even when there is no expectation of return. But like Mrs. O, many clients wish to express gratitude to their practitioners, and allowing them to do so accords them a measure of empowerment and mutuality in the client-practitioner relationship and can foster greater trust and a stronger clinical bond. In other situations, however, gifts *are* ethically problematic, as in Ethical Quandary 3.

Not all gifts are the same (and a gift is not always valued in the same way by giver and recipient), and some can actually benefit the client-practitioner relationship. Thus, whether a gift or gift relationship violates ethical professional boundaries should be evaluated on a case-by-case basis. Small gifts of food may be acceptable because they are unlikely to affect a practitioner's objectivity or judgment, while larger gifts may do so. It is always the practitioner's responsibility to safeguard professional objectivity by being cautious when accepting or giving gifts.

Mrs. O's daughter has been Ms. K's client for many years. The O's have a cottage several hours from the city where they spend the summers and where Mrs. O is an avid gardener. At the end of every season, Mrs. O makes sure to bring flowers and home-grown tomatoes for both Ms. K and the office staff.

Ms. M sits on the board of a nonprofit community group that serves inner-city adolescents through after-school and summer activity programs. Mr. G, a local businessman, has been her client for some time. When Mr. G comes for a routine visit during the group's annual fund-raising drive, Ms. M asks him for a contribution. Soliciting a gift in this way takes advantage of Mr. G, who may feel uncomfortable declining a request from his practitioner or may worry that he won't receive the same attention from Ms. M if he doesn't contribute to the community group. Conversely, a practitioner's gift to a client may create confusion about roles or engender a sense of obligation on the part of the client that adversely affects his or her openness in the therapeutic encounter.

Finally, seeming to "play favorites" by accommodating individual clients in special ways can also raise concerns about ethical professional boundaries. Health care professionals commit themselves to treating all clients fairly. Clients often need more than just clinical care, and it is not necessarily inappropriate for professionals to provide help in other ways. But their actions on behalf of a particular client must not adversely affect the therapeutic relationship with that client or compromise the care available to other clients or appear to others to do so. Just what activities might constitute a violation of professional boundaries depends very much on the specific context in which such actions take place and their foreseeable likely consequences for others.

In Ethical Quandary 4, giving Mr. J a ride home would probably be acceptable if it did not place additional burdens on other staff or mean that Ms. K is not available to other clients. Obviously, if Ms. K were regularly to extend the kindness of a ride home to certain of her clients, she would be compromising her professional commitment to be fair to *all* of her clients and would potentially impede the efficient functioning of the clinic.

The basic general principle underlying all these guidelines is that the practitioner must give priority to the client in any conflicts of interest. A **conflict of interest** is a situation in which an individual has a private or personal interest that is substantial enough to influence or appear to influence the individual's professional practice. This definition has three components: (1) The professional has a private or personal interest (by itself, not a problem); (2) the personal or private interest conflicts with the obligation of professional objectives; and (3) the conflict interferes with or intrudes on the individual's professional responsibilities.

Avoiding conflicts of interest requires maintaining professional and clinical independence from commercial interests and ensuring that relationships do not lead

Mr. J is ready to be picked up after a treatment session. His daughter calls the office complaining of car trouble and saying she won't be able to pick Mr. J up. Ms. K (the practitioner) is thinking about driving the client home herself.

to any action that is not in the best interests of the client. In particular, practitioners should not rely on company representatives or industry-sponsored promotional events for their knowledge of products and should not endorse or attempt to sell these products to clients.

Health care professionals should beware of interacting with any client in ways that could reasonably be expected to create awkward situations for either party, compromise the professional's primary commitment to client welfare, or call the professional's objectivity into question. While not every business or social interaction or relationship between a health care professional and a client *necessarily* violates ethical professional boundaries, professionals should critically examine their own actions by considering the following:

- Is this activity a normal, expected part of practice for members of my profession?
- Might engaging in this activity compromise my relationship with this client? With other clients? With my colleagues? With my institution? With the public?
- Could this activity cause others to question my professional objectivity?
- Would I want my other clients, other professionals, or the public to know that I engage in such activities?

If the answers to these questions indicate that an activity *may* violate professional ethical boundaries, the practitioner should:

- Determine whether there are applicable standards.
- Consult a trusted and objective peer for a second opinion about the activity.
- Seek assistance from a supervisor or ethics committee.
- Communicate his or her concern to the individual involved.
- Transfer the client to another practitioner's care if the professional relationship has been compromised or if avoiding the violation will damage the relationship.

As well, it is imperative that health care professionals be familiar with:

- Relevant professional codes of ethics, standards of practice, guidelines, and position statements.
- Applicable policies in their facilities.
- Laws pertaining to relationships between clients and health and personal care professionals.

Drawing distinct lines is possible only with regard to the most egregious transgressions of professional ethical boundaries, and health care professionals must always exercise judgment in their relationships with clients. Consultation with a more experienced colleague is an excellent way of getting support and guidance to help you make competent, ethical decisions. Peer supervision and case conferences also offer opportunities to discuss and clarify ethical matters.

You may find it useful to develop your own list of decision-making criteria, questions to help you determine when an ethical boundary is being tested in your own practice. Here are some of the types of questions you might want to ask to clarify situations when the ethical option is not obvious:

- Is this situation in the best interests of the client; does it preserve and maintain his or her safety and well-being?
- Am I taking advantage of the power imbalance or feelings of transference?
- Does the situation complicate or impinge on the therapeutic relationship by creating a dual relationship?
- Is it outside my scope of practice?
- Could it pave the way for future transgressions (a "slippery slope")?
- Does it violate informed consent?

We have focused on obligations that flow from the notion of "profession," but the analysis offered here is equally relevant to all caregivers, whether they are licensed practitioners or other staff. Understanding and respecting professional boundaries is part of professional competence. Maintaining those boundaries is an essential part of compassionate, effective, and ethical treatment.

CHECKLIST

Have you done these things yet?

☐ Have you become familiar with the ethical standards associated with your state and national licensing requirements and/or professional affiliations?

☐ Have you minimized your ethical risk-taking behavior (maintaining appropriate boundaries, limiting self-disclosure, etc.)?

☐ Have you developed a list of questions to ask yourself when confronted with a dual relationship?

☐ Have you developed a list of questions to ask yourself when confronted with other kinds of ethical dilemmas?

☐ Have you considered how you will respond to gifts from your clients?

SO WHAT DO YOU THINK?

1. You may have grown up with and/or been trained in the paternalistic tradition prevailing until recently. However, this chapter has focused on boundary issues in a health care environment that, in general, values more patient awareness and dialogue between practitioner and patient. How do the different paradigms (paternalistic versus communicative) relate to potential boundary abuses of different kinds?

2. Do your ethical boundaries toward your clients apply equally toward clients' family members or friends? (Your answer will no doubt depend on the boundary and each specific client's relationship with the other people.) Consider the painting scenario mentioned in the chapter: Would you hire your client's equally despondent cousin to paint your office? Would you accept a gift costing over $50 from a grateful spouse of a client, given without the client's knowledge?

3. If you realize you have inadvertently transgressed an ethical boundary with a client, such as revealing some personal information, which factors should influence your decision about whether to acknowledge the breach with the client?

4. Transference and countertransference reactions inevitably alter over time as you work with a particular client. As a practitioner, how do you self-monitor these inevitable shifts in your relationships with clients?

5. After your therapeutic relationship with a client has formally ended, does the scope of your ethical boundary obligations change as well? For example, may you ethically make or accept a dinner party invitation from your former therapy client?

6. In most court cases, the defendant is presumed innocent until proven guilty (the "burden of proof" is on the party bringing suit, the plaintiff). However, if a patient alleges in court that a practitioner maltreated or coerced her, the burden of proof shifts to the practitioner, who must prove himself or herself innocent. Is this fair? Why or why not?

7. Suppose you are not certified in a subject but have extensive experience regarding it. For example, a massage client mentions she's been diagnosed with sarcoidosis, a rare chronic condition, and asks if you know anything about the disease. You do; you have sarcoidosis yourself. Is it ethical to share your expertise? To reveal your own condition?

8. Is it ever acceptable to continue a therapeutic relationship with a client to whom you are attracted?

Ethical Business Practices

CHAPTER TWELVE

LEARNING OUTCOMES

After completing this chapter, you should be able to:

12.1 Define more basic concepts in professional ethics.

12.2 Implement basic ethical practices in all business operations.

12.3 Explain how professional accountability is maintained in your discipline.

12.4 Explain the significance of one's scope of practice.

12.5 Develop a business code of ethics, consulting relevant professional affiliations, personal beliefs, and state and national regulations as a guide.

KEY TERMS

professional accountability

scope of practice

misconduct

harassment

desexualizing

autonomy

beneficence

nonmaleficence

informed consent

right of refusal

client's bill of rights

INTRODUCTION

For all health care practitioners, ethical business practices and professionalism are the basis of the health care system's contract with society. Ethics and professionalism demand placing the interests of clients above those of the practitioner, setting and maintaining standards of competence and integrity, and providing ethical guidance on matters of health. The principles and responsibilities of health care ethics and professionalism must be clearly understood by both the profession and society. Essential to this social contract is public confidence in practitioners, a trust that depends on the integrity of both individual practitioners and the whole profession.

Professional Accountability and Scope of Practice

Professional accountability is the state of being accountable or responsible for professional obligations, including legal liability for failure to perform as expected. Accountability in the professional context means answering to clients, professional colleagues, and other key professionals, which requires that the professional account for his or her judgments, actions, and nonactions, as defined by the nature of the professional-client relationship.

Professional organizations ensure accountability and protect public safety by certifying the competence of their members through licensing and continuing-education requirements. Accreditation and professional affiliations maintain quality control and show your accountability to clients, colleagues, and the profession as a whole. They confirm that you abide by prevailing health and safety standards, conduct yourself in accordance with relevant legislation and/or professional regulations, and possess the specialized knowledge and skills of your field. Licensing agencies and professional societies are able to maintain basic standards of quality and professional expertise in the field, and they ensure, through continuing-education requirements, that licensed individuals are keeping pace with recent developments.

Once you've successfully completed an approved training course and met state or national requirements, you are deemed "competent" to practice in a subject area. In many cases, you are also required to keep up with continuing education and professional development to maintain a current knowledge of the discipline. Credited coursework is offered in a diverse range of formats (traditional classroom attendance, correspondence courses or distance education, weekend workshops, professional seminars and conferences) that vary widely in scope, practical value, length of study, and fee. Opportunities for advanced study outside continuing education are also abundant, offering the practitioner a diverse range of possibilities in certification, titles, and credentials, all associated with varying degrees of validity. Checks and balances on this system are minimal; those that exist are fueled in great measure by the personal accountability, honesty, and integrity of individual practitioners.

Scope of practice refers to your area of competence, which is usually obtained through formal study, training, and/or professional experience and for which you've received certification or other proof of qualification. Unlike many standardized training programs or fields of study, state requirements, training, and required coursework in your field may vary significantly in curriculum and number of necessary hours of study. Some schools provide substantial training in specialized procedures, while others may only touch on these subjects, if they are discussed at all.

Your scope of practice is circumscribed, in part, by local licensing restrictions, which are sometimes very general. Within this legal parameter, practitioners have some latitude in determining what modalities will constitute their practice. Misrepresenting your educational achievements, credentials, or abilities is a crime, as well as a serious breach of responsibility that endangers client safety and reflects poorly on the profession as a whole. If a subject is outside your area of expertise, don't hesitate to say so, and direct the client to appropriate informational resources or professional services.

Choosing to provide services for which you are not appropriately trained or competent is a dangerous personal decision that undermines the profession and may carry weighty legal implications. Your personal level of discretion and ethical standards will largely determine the manner in which you advertise your services, describe your education and professional experience, and list credentials. You will have to decide for yourself not only whether you can rightfully claim substantive experience in a discipline for which you've attended a three-hour workshop or watched a series of instructional videos but also when you can properly call yourself an expert in one modality or another.

You have an additional obligation to your clients and the profession to keep pace with new developments in the field and maintain skills at a professional level. This obligation is partly fulfilled through formal continuing-education requirements, but it can be supplemented by reading industry journals and attending seminars, workshops, and conferences. Make sure any information or suggestions you pass along are supported by the professional community and recent research findings and are appropriate and safe for the client.

Use the following guidelines to avoid misrepresentation of your professional experience or credentials in promotional materials or discussions with clients and colleagues:

- List your education, training, work history, degrees, and credentials as accurately as possible in résumés and biographical statements. Include your experience in a different field of study only if it benefits or enriches your current practice and clients.

- Review licensing and regulatory standards for practitioners in your area, and keep up with legislative issues, current events, and research related to your field. Confirm that your practice adheres to current legal and regulatory requirements.

- Note your capabilities and strengths, including any modalities, techniques, special knowledge, areas of specialization, or skills you employ on a regular basis or have made a focus. Do not overstate your level of ability or training, but revise the list regularly to reflect any change in educational status or experience.

- Note among your weaknesses, unapologetically, any areas in which you've received training but have had little or no practical experience. Being realistic about your abilities and honest with your clients is the best way to ensure their health and safety. Pretending familiarity or expertise in an area is unfair to your clients, at best, and is likely to be hazardous to both your practice and their health. If you pursue new educational avenues, update your résumé to reflect current study and expected completion dates, but do not claim the academic standing or associated credentials until *after* you have written confirmation of successful completion.

- Develop relationships and referral networks with colleagues who are highly skilled in alternate areas of expertise so that you can refer your clients to them without reservation and they can do the same. Knowing other approaches to treatment can help you develop your own areas of specialization or focus and define what you do and do not want in your practice. Conferences, association meetings, or professional get-togethers are a good time to compare notes and learn about useful resources and opportunities in your own field and related disciplines.

- Don't be tempted outside your scope of practice by clients asking for an informal opinion, diagnostic guess, treatment recommendations, or any other statements you are unqualified to make, especially when there is any possibility of risk to the client. Develop a standardized response that explains your lack of formal training in the area and clarifies the credentials and experience required, and suggest a referral to a qualified professional in the area.

Safety in Bodywork

Practitioners are required to abide by industry standards of safety and hygiene. Client draping, towels, the table surface, and other relevant materials must be cleaned according to accepted standards of sanitation and must meet all legal health and safety requirements (including universal precautions relating to communicable diseases). Practitioners should know how to cover cuts and use sanitizing supplies, such as disinfectant hand wipes, effectively.

Practitioners must have the skills and knowledge to assess a client's condition and provide safe and appropriate therapy. Be attuned to verbal and nonverbal client feedback, and be alert to possible contraindications for treatment. Sometimes the decision to treat a client is less than clear-cut, requiring a bit of research or consultation with medical personnel more familiar with the client's condition. Never allow the client, the client's relatives, or even the client's doctor to pressure you to proceed if you have any doubts regarding the safety of a specific procedure for a specific client. You are ultimately responsible for any injury sustained by the client during or resulting from treatment and for the medical and legal liability associated with it—even if the client's physician specifically recommended or prescribed the bodywork.

If you have strong concerns about the client's health that are related to medication or procedures received through another source, suggest that the client have a trusted health care professional review the course of treatment. Pronouncements like this should not be made flippantly, as they could be the basis of legal action against you for practicing medicine without a license. If you believe your client has a serious medical condition or may have suffered an injury, tell the client immediately and refer him or her to the appropriate health care professional. Do not discuss the condition with the client's doctor or anyone else unless you have explicit permission from the client to do so. Be sure to document your referral and the reasons for it in the client record.

Keep scope of practice in mind when you give advice or make recommendations to clients. While listening attentively to your client is a relatively risk-free venture, sharing your opinions is not. Depending on the topic of conversation and your specific comments, you may be engaging in high-risk behavior whenever you have casual conversations with a client. Resisting requests for "advice" in any subject outside your areas of expertise is your safest option, but it is natural to be drawn into discussions with a client, especially one you've come to know well.

Advice can be a dangerous and slippery slope for practitioners in large part because they may have some knowledge and experience regarding a topic that is health-related but not strictly within their scope of practice. If you have found an effective nutritional supplement or exercise program that relieves the same symptoms your client is experiencing, you may have a strong impulse to share that information with your client. Or you may want to warn your client away from a health regimen that you consider ineffective or potentially dangerous.

When giving your point of view, make sure you delineate a professional recommendation, based on years of experience and study, from suggestions or opinions of a more personal or general nature. Help your client distinguish between subject matter in which you are, or are not, professionally qualified. If a health or medical issue is outside your scope of practice, recommend that the client see a qualified health professional regarding the matter.

Resist the appeal of being an authority on topics outside your scope of practice, and put strict limits on comments, opinions, and claims that relate to the following points:

- Never recommend that a client stop receiving treatment or medication.

- Beware of recommending medications, herbal mixtures, or nutritional supplements to the client, even if the item does not require a prescription.

- Refrain from bad-mouthing any procedures, services, or therapies that are part of your client's health regimen, and do not criticize the individual who provides them.

- Do not make psychological assessments or counsel the client regarding emotional matters or interpersonal relationships unless you have a degree in counseling and are advertising your services accordingly.

- Never impose your religious or spiritual beliefs on a client. Leave evangelical literature and discussions outside the office.

- Even if you are in great shape, resist the urge to recommend muscle strengthening or toning exercises, unless you are also qualified as a physical therapist, athletic trainer, or related-occupation professional with appropriate credentials.

Misconduct

Misconduct has been a persistent and troubling issue in health care since the early days of modern medicine. The Hippocratic Oath urged members of the medical profession to refrain from "mischief, and in particular, sexual relationships with both female and male persons." In recent years, accusations of misconduct in the health care and personal service industries have become increasingly common, due in part to formal regulation of the complaint process and greater awareness of the issue among the general public.

Misconduct takes many different forms that vary considerably in type and degree of severity. The following examples of misconduct demonstrate the need for ethical vigilance in every aspect of business practice, from organizational matters to billing to social interactions.

Misrepresentation of educational status: Identifying yourself as a craniosacral therapist after taking a two-hour course.

Financial impropriety: Charging different fees to a cash-paying client and an insurance-paying client.

Exploiting the power differential: Asking a stockbroker for financial tips during a treatment.

Misleading claims of curative abilities: Telling a client you guarantee her pain will be gone in two sessions.

Accessibility: Refusing to adapt your office (or make some reasonable accommodation) for those with physical challenges.

Bigotry: Refusing to work with someone due to race, religion, gender, size, or sexual orientation.

Inappropriate advertising: Using a provocative picture in advertising; presenting misleading qualifications.

Dual relationships: Dating a client.

Violation of laws: Practicing out of your home when doing so is not permitted by law.

Confidentiality: Name-dropping of famous clients; telling a spouse details about his or her partner's session.

Contraindications: Treating a client when you or the client are sick or infectious; ignoring signs of conditions that preclude physical contact.

Informed consent: Working on a minor without parental knowledge; treating someone's injury without permission.

Practicing beyond scope of practice: Doing spinal adjustments, massage, or counseling without appropriate training.

Sexual misconduct: Watching a client undress or hugging a client in a sexual way.

Even in cases where inappropriate behaviors are the unintended result of thoughtlessness, errors in judgment, or improper planning, they risk potentially serious repercussions for the client and heavy penalties for the practitioner. Victims may face emotional and physical scarring with lifelong implications, and allegations of misconduct—even false ones—wreak havoc with practitioners' lives and livelihoods.

Harassment

Harassment is a specific kind of misconduct or boundary violation in which an individual of equal or greater authority is inappropriately familiar with a co-worker or junior employee. Harassment can manifest itself in abusive remarks or behavior, belittling statements and actions, and discussion or commentary of an overly personal or offensive nature. Sexual harassment is abuse of power, typically exercised within the context of work, containing a sexual or gender-specific component.

Sexual harassment, like sexual misconduct, is not defined by any specific sexual interaction between two individuals. While the prototypical case involves a coercive exchange of sexual favors for job benefits or advancement, the sexual dimension in sexual harassment and misconduct can be subtle, as much a matter of sexual connotation or subtext than any one explicitly sexual act. Abuse of the power differential can manifest itself in a hostile or difficult work environment, not easily perceived by outsiders. The Equal Employment Opportunity Commission defines sexual harassment as any unwelcome advance, request, verbal statement, or physical conduct of a sexual nature, including visual displays, in which:

- Submission is made a condition of an individual's employment, either explicitly or implicitly.

- Submission forms the basis for work-related evaluations, such as decisions regarding employment benefits or advancement.

- The individual is subject to intimidating, offensive, or hostile environmental elements that interfere with the individual's ability to work effectively or productively.

Harassment may include the discussion of sexually explicit topics at a place of business, unnecessary or inappropriate references to specific body parts or functions, and visual depictions of a provocative or offensive nature, such as posters or calendars featuring photos of nude or scantily clad models. Sexual harassment can occur between men and women, women and women, men and men, or any other combination of sexual or gender identity. Sexual harassment may feel humiliating or shameful, making the victim reluctant to report the incident.

Legal liability, in cases of a hostile or oppositional work environment, requires that the plaintiff prove a pattern of inappropriate behavior or a series of incidents involving offensive language, behavior, or physical contact. In cases of sexual harassment, the plaintiff is required to prove that a random "reasonable person" would consider the incident(s) in question "sexual harassment," based on his or her understanding of the incident(s). This can be problematic in that one individual's "reasonable person" may interpret certain behavior, statements, or displays as abusive, while another might find them inappropriate, and another might consider them acceptable. Courts typically weigh the type of misconduct, its context [including factors such as the extent of deception or cover-up that accompanied the incident(s)], and its frequency of occurrence when making a determination of liability. If the accused practitioner's employer was made aware of the incident(s) in question—either at the time or after the fact— the employer's place of business may also bear legal liability for harassment.

Sexuality

Sexual misconduct, one of the most egregious examples of inappropriate behavior, refers to any sexual activity between the practitioner and the client. It includes not only obvious transgressions, such as intercourse, masturbation, fellatio, cunnilingus, anal intercourse, or oral sex, but also any direct or indirect physical contact between practitioner and client intended to sexually arouse one or both individuals. While women are less likely than men to be accused of sexual misconduct, they are not immune to such allegations.

Some practitioners employ strategies of avoidance, ignoring the issue of sexuality entirely, either consciously or unconsciously, due to their own embarrassment or discomfort with the topic. While this approach may save you an awkward moment or two, an inability or refusal to address the subject when necessary (e.g., ignoring signs of sexual arousal) may not only be inappropriate but be professionally irresponsible and a breach of ethical conduct.

Human sexual response is influenced by a complicated mixture of biological, social, and psychological forces that vary enormously from person to person. Each individual responds differently to the tactile stimulation of massage and may be more or less susceptible to changes in the human nervous system, limbic system, and parasympathetic nervous system. Physical arousal can occur unexpectedly because nerve impulses associated with massage are not confined to just the immediate area receiving tactile stimulation but radiate outward, over a more widespread area. Manipulation of the lower extremities, buttocks, and abdomen are particularly likely to produce the unintended "side effect" of sexual response because these areas of the body share the same nerve pathways as the genitals. An incident of sexual arousal during treatment is typically experienced as a momentary surge of sexual energy that dissipates almost immediately.

If physical signs of sexual arousal, such as an erection, occur but are momentary and are not associated with other signs of sexual stimulation, intervention may be a matter of moving to a part of the body less prone to sexual response, such as the upper body or head, or using different movements that encourage response in the sympathetic nervous system. Be aware of the following points:

1. Brief incidents of physical arousal are involuntary by-products or side effects of specific physiological processes activated by massage.

2. Such momentary or fleeting incidents are not abnormal or inappropriate in the context of treatment.

If the client indicates sexual interest or continues to show signs of sexual arousal after you have moved to a different region of the body, you will need to address the situation immediately. The same is true if the client verbally or tacitly expresses sexual interest, regardless of physical arousal.

Strategies for Client Safety

Ensuring your clients' safety requires more than not being sexual toward them or avoiding overt sexual behaviors with them. It means actively and consciously **"desexualizing"** the experience of treatment, that is, making something with potential sexuality no longer sexual, or deemphasizing that dimension. Desexualizing treatment is a process of deconstructing the experience into its component parts, acknowledging human sexuality as a given, and accepting the practitioner and client as sexual beings.

It is best to address the issue of sexuality and client safety early in the therapeutic relationship. Practitioners can incorporate the subject into the intake routine by providing the client a brief written statement explaining that treatment is a nonsexual experience, what constitutes appropriate conduct, and the ethical necessity of these statements or the discussion. Tackling the topic of sexuality proactively, rather than in reaction to a specific incident, can prevent or avoid potential misunderstandings and disabuse a client with ulterior motives.

Desexualizing treatment requires a substantial degree of self-awareness and honesty. Only by acknowledging one's own sexual nature can one begin to control when, how, and with whom it is expressed. The sexual component of treatment must be acknowledged and understood but channeled and expressed appropriately. Practitioners must be able to realistically appraise their own potential for sexual response during treatment and acknowledge not only how their own or their co-workers' sexual natures might affect clients but also the impact of clients' and co-workers' sexual natures on them.

Think about the way you interact with clients and colleagues and how you are perceived. Do you send out mixed messages? Are your intentions absolutely honorable? Are you a flirtatious person? Be clear about your intentions, and be aware that any attempt to pursue a sexual or romantic relationship with a client is grossly inappropriate.

Avoid ambiguity or the appearance of impropriety in your words and manner. Dress appropriately in a professional manner, avoiding any outfit that could be construed as revealing or provocative (Figure 12.1). Your demeanor should approximate that of other professional health care personnel. Use appropriate language; avoid cursing or indelicate comments. Use medical terminology when referring to physical conditions or parts of the body. Never discuss sexual topics with or in front of the client, joke about sexual matters, make sexual remarks or jokes, or use sexual innuendo.

Keep the room comfortably warm, and give clients adequate time to disrobe and dress. Make sure the client is able to change without assistance or is given the needed help, and leave the room (even if the client says it's not necessary), closing the door or curtain behind you. Always knock and/or ask the client's permission before you reenter the area.

It's common for clients to feel some degree of anxiety or insecurity related to the process of disrobing and draping. You can often minimize potential anxiety or concern in your clients by stating and/or providing written information regarding disrobing before treatment begins. Explain that a draping procedure is required for purposes of modesty and physical comfort. Describe the draping, explaining that it will cover all parts of the client's body except the specific area receiving attention.

Explain to clients what can and cannot be removed or left on without impeding your access to parts of the body; reassure the client that it is not necessary to remove any more clothing than her or his personal comfort or modesty will allow. Request that clients do not begin undressing until you have left the room. Never allow the client to dress or undress in your presence. Inform your client before you begin of the areas that will be your focus, and ask permission to proceed. Expose and work on only one area of the body at a time, and cover the exposed part before moving on to another area.

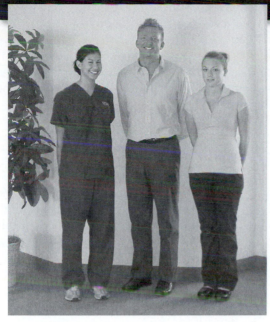

Appropriate attire for the massage professional is khakis and a polo shirt, lightweight slacks and shirt, or neatly pressed scrubs

FIGURE 12.1

Once you finish work in an area, you will re-cover it and move to the next area. Draping should cover the genitals and buttocks of all clients and the breasts of female clients. Tell clients to let you know if they have a question or concern or are uncomfortable in any way. If you encounter a client who prefers not to be draped, explain that you are unable to proceed with the session until the client agrees to this customary procedure.

Maintain a comfortable and professional environment. Avoid meeting new clients at unknown locations, at hotels, or in the client's home, where your personal safety may be at greater risk. If you meet the client on-site, set up the treatment table in a neutral location, rather than a bedroom, if possible (in some cases, such as home visits, use of the bedroom may be necessary). Encourage relaxation through your client's visual, auditory, and olfactory senses, but keep the look and smell of your environment subdued and professional. Avoid creating an overly perfumed, romantic, or sensual atmosphere. Remember that a client may be allergic to certain odors, have strong negative reactions to certain smells, or associate a given odor with an unpleasant memory or incident. Music should also be soothing and subtle and should be played only after you have asked your client about his or her preference for music or silence during the treatment.

Your business should support client and co-worker safety by:

- Developing institutionwide or companywide antiharassment policies for all employees and posting them in public locations throughout the workplace.

- Having clients read and sign a client's bill of rights (see below).

- Providing informational materials and a mandatory educational session for all employees to raise awareness about workplace harassment and misconduct and to discuss what constitutes it and how to address it.

- Establishing a protocol for reporting complaints and investigating allegations of misconduct that ensures timely and responsive follow-up and the confidentiality and safety of employees and clients.

- Establishing a formal system of checks and balances and a review process to evaluate employees and provide feedback from co-workers and clients regarding relevant skills and "table-side manner."

Reporting Misconduct

If you believe another practitioner is acting unethically or illegally, you have a responsibility to report this. Contact your state board or national licensing agency to file a complaint. Usually, after a board hearing, if the practitioner is found to have violated the law, the regulatory board will impose one or more of the following penalties: reprimand, fine, administrative cost, probation, license suspension, or license revocation. The individual making the complaint is usually notified in writing of the status of the complaint throughout the process.

Business Management and Promotion

Conducting your business in an ethical manner is largely a matter of treating people fairly and decently, using your skills and time effectively, and adhering to high standards in your work. Your promotional materials, record keeping, financial dealings, and conduct in day-to-day business matters should also be able to pass ethical scrutiny. Maintaining your practice in good standing means:

- Filing local, state, and federal taxes.
- Discussing and/or displaying fee schedules and billing practices prior to a first meeting.
- Making the client's welfare your paramount concern.
- Following generally accepted accounting practices.
- Keeping accurate financial records.
- Maintaining client confidentiality.
- Engaging in respectful and cooperative collaboration with other professionals.
- Making appropriate referrals, if necessary.

Because you are a representative of your profession, any negative perceptions of your marketing materials or advertisements tend to reflect poorly on your colleagues and the profession as a whole. Promotional materials should:

- Include your license number, place of business, and phone number.
- Refrain from using fear or guilt as motivational tactics.
- Avoid unrealistic, misleading, or sensational claims, as well as promises to cure specific conditions or ailments.
- Avoid using any wording or image that might be construed as sexual in nature.
- Adhere to truth-in-advertising standards.

Setting Fees

Setting fees is a dicey issue for many practitioners. Some people feel an essential conflict in charging for caregiving services. Remember that you have a responsibility to value your work and expect others to value it. In some cases, guilt or discomfort is associated with the abrupt change in roles that occurs at the time of payment—your transition from caregiver to financial agent. Remember that charging a fee clarifies and confirms the therapeutic nature of the session—it reinforces appropriate boundaries necessary to a healthy client-practitioner relationship. There is safety and familiarity for you and the client in the practice of exchanging a fee for services.

How much is enough? Charging for services in the "caring professions" carries unique ethical issues related to fairness. If you are independently wealthy, you may not feel the need to charge at all or to charge much. Many practitioners, however, have found that giving away services for free or providing discounts to some clients, but not others, presents its own difficulties; services are not appropriately valued by the client, or the therapeutic relationship is altered.

Fairness in fees is important. The issue is complicated considerably when you charge different fees to different clients receiving the same services. Some questions to help you determine fairness in fees include:

- Is this payment policy usual, or are you adjusting it for a particular client?
- If you are adjusting it, is this fair to your other clients and yourself? (For example, if you are changing your rate due to the client's circumstances, are you sure that no other client faces the same circumstances but simply hasn't told you about them?)
- What criteria are you using to set this rate?
- Will you resent the adjustment, or will it change the way the client perceives you or the therapeutic relationship?
- Will you feel fairly compensated for your work?
- Are you lowering your rate because you have problems saying no?

In some cases, the practitioner feels a need to "save" or "rescue" a client that stems from an unhealthy personal need. You may feel the world owes the client a break, and you are the one to provide it (perhaps he just lost his job). This impulse may be strong, but you should resist it, in favor of a business relationship in which you provide care to the client in return for a *standard* fee. If you do choose to provide discounts or sliding-scale fees, have strict rules and stick to them. The same is true for all payment policies. Apply them equally to all clients.

It is important to note that personal and professional interests are not inherently in conflict with one another; in fact, they often coincide. It is natural to want to earn money through one's professional activity, and a practitioner's personal desire to be compassionate is compatible with his or her professional obligations. That desire becomes problematic only when the personal interest in earning a livelihood interferes with one's commitments and obligations as a health care professional.

Selling Products

You may choose to sell products as part of your business. If you do, be aware of potential ethical dilemmas associated with sales. In some professions, selling adjunct products is discouraged due to the power differential that exists between you and your client. Clients may choose to purchase products for many reasons, but your agency in the decision may influence them in a way that borders on unethical to some practitioners.

Providing useful, reliable products at a good price may be perfectly honorable (the sale of products is no more inherently "unclean" than the sale of services), but you may feel discomfort if you're identified too closely with products your clients don't like. Products should always be reliable and of high quality.

Are you selling products purely to generate an income, with no concern for the client's welfare? Watch your motives to make sure that the sale isn't the only reason you're encouraging the purchase. Perhaps you really believe in these products and want the client to benefit fully from them. You are providing easy access to certain items that you feel have the potential to increase well-being—this is a useful service. How you sell those products should be ethical too: no "hard sell" or manipulation. Your client should face no penalties if he or she chooses not to purchase a product you carry: no "attitude" or "I told you so's."

You should know something about the products you choose to sell. This point raises some of its own ethical questions. Consider, for example, the sale of nutritional supplements. Selling products suggests that you condone their use. Are you qualified to determine the utility of this product, or is this outside your scope of practice? Perhaps you are very well read in nutrition and feel capable of providing direction; it is still possible to find yourself in ethical hot water.

Currently, most of these products are not regulated. Clients are free to take nutritional supplements without a doctor's prescription. However, if a client has a negative response to a particular ingredient—such as an allergic reaction (and even the most highly respected nutritional supplements provoke allergic reactions in some individuals)—you will have to face the repercussions. Always provide information about contraindications or combinations of supplements that are associated with adverse reactions. It's fine to believe in the product, but you should also believe that it may not be good for everyone.

Documentation and Records

Proper documentation and record keeping are a critical, if mundane, dimension of a successful practice. Keep notes legible and accurate. If it is ever necessary to refer to files at some time in the future (e.g., in a medical emergency or legal proceedings), the context and details of your notes should be clear. Other health care personnel will need to know the background, presenting status, actions taken, and results, along with some discussion of treatment strategies and expected objectives. Adhere to the following guidelines for preparing and maintaining records:

- Maintain accurate and truthful records. Record only factual information, observations, and actions. Don't record your opinions or conjecture about the client or his or her condition. When recording statements made by your client (e.g., regarding an injury), use quotation marks to demarcate the client's words. Keep a separate file for personal notes or any material of a speculative nature.

- Make sure the forms you use to collect client information are appropriate to your practice and cover all pertinent areas. Make sure forms are free of errors and are easy to read and understand. Questions should be stated simply. Avoid jargon or complicated medical terminology, or define terms as needed. Review forms on a regular basis, and revise or simplify confusing formatting or content.

- Take a comprehensive case history, and review it with the client before beginning treatment. It should include an overview of the client's general state of health and thorough medical history, his or her reason(s) for seeking treatment, onset and duration of problematic symptoms, medical history of family members (if appropriate), and occupational background.

- Train staff members to record client histories and other important information properly and thoroughly and to ask appropriate follow-up questions if there is any ambiguity in a response. Implement some structure or mechanism to ensure that this information is complete for every client and answers are recorded in sufficient detail. Review any personal or medical information taken by other staff members in a personal interview with the client to ensure that information was recorded properly and in adequate detail.

- Areas that do not apply to a specific client should be marked "N/A" (not applicable) rather than left blank.

- Develop a short, simple form that clients can use to note their progress (or lack of progress) at each visit.

- Document any client noncompliance with the care plan, including canceled appointments (*dnka* = did not keep appointment), refusal or failure to follow health care instructions and/or take needed medication, and activities or behaviors that pose a risk to the client's health. Communicate the rationale for your opinion, and do not proceed with any action that conflicts with your professional judgment.

- If you feel the client's disregard for professional recommendations is putting him or her at risk, have the client sign a form acknowledging that the client has been informed of the potential consequences of his or her action or inaction and is choosing to refuse recommended treatment.

- Notes should be legible as well as accurate. Pay attention to your handwriting, and use clearly written and recognized abbreviations. Remember that you and other people may need to refer to these notes years in the future. Make sure they are easy to read and understand.

- File records promptly and accurately. Establish a strict filing system and adhere to it, and be sure other staff members know the system and the importance of using it.

- The following guidelines were established for litigation purposes and should be standard practice in all health care environments:

  — Alter records as minimally as possible and only when necessary.

  — If you find something in error, do not erase. Cross out the error using a single line, so as not to conceal what is written underneath, and write the word *error* above the incorrect statement.

  — If you review your records and feel the need to clarify a point, write the date and the additional comments with the note (labeled "addendum").

  — If litigation is threatened, do not make any kind of change to the records.

Not all file contents are subject to the same retention times. Keep records for current and former clients for as long a period as is practically possible but at least the length of time specified by federal and state regulations as the legal minimum. Retain children's records after the children turn 18 for a length of time that equals the state's statute of limitations.

Confidentiality

Keep all original records in your possession. Provide copies of x-rays, notes, and records documenting client care to clients or health care facilities requiring their own copies. Share information only in cases where disclosure is required by law, court order, or another appropriate, professionally approved manner, according to legal requirements.

Impress on all staff members the importance of maintaining confidentiality and retaining original file copies. Institute the following procedures when providing copies, and make no exceptions:

- Have the client sign and date a release authorization form.

- Keep a copy of the release authorization with the client's records.

- Copy only the information requested.

- Note in the client's file the party requesting the copy, what specifically was requested, and when, to whom, and where the copy was sent.

All information and matters relating to a client's background, condition, and treatment are strictly confidential and should not be communicated to a third party (even one involved in the client's care) without the client's written consent or a court order. Treat clients with respect and dignity. Handle personal information with sensitivity, and keep the content of written records a private matter. Practitioners who can't resist telling secrets or repeating gossip in their personal lives should be aware of the heavy penalties associated with jeopardizing client confidentiality in a professional context.

During the past decade, the traditional medical ethical principle of confidentiality, that is, the health care provider's duty to protect the client's personal health information, has come into increasing conflict with a perceived need for health information databases serving administrative, planning, and research purposes. Computerization has greatly facilitated the establishment and linking of such databases and, thereby, has made breaches of confidentiality much easier. In response, many governments have adopted laws to regulate health databases. These laws have generated much controversy. Privacy advocates complain that these regulations are more about facilitating access to personal health information than protecting privacy, whereas administrators, researchers, and some medical associations criticize the bureaucratic requirements that the laws impose on routine medical and research practices.

Professional caregivers have strong reasons for preserving confidentiality. In order to receive care, clients have to reveal personal information to physicians and others who may be total strangers to them—information that they would not want anyone else to know. They must have good reason to trust their caregivers not to divulge this information. The basis of this trust is the ethical and legal standards of confidentiality that health care professionals are expected to uphold. Without an understanding that their disclosures will be kept secret, clients may withhold personal information. This can hinder caregivers in their efforts to provide effective interventions or to attain important public health goals.

However, there is also a need for practitioners' limited disclosure of their clients' health information to other health care providers to assist in the care of the clients, to insurance companies and other agencies for reimbursement of payment for health services, and to database managers for public health, health system administration, and research purposes. As a general rule, health care professionals should give priority to the client's interests over those of others. Disclosure of personal health information should protect client confidentiality as much as possible. Where confidentiality cannot be maintained, clients should be informed about how their personal health information will be used and whether the information will be identifiable or anonymous.

New Clients

It is generally a good idea to assume that a new client knows nothing about your practice. Many practitioners develop an information sheet to acquaint the client with basic treatment concepts. A sheet outlining office personnel, customary procedures, and other useful points regarding the place of business (e.g., restroom locations) and what to expect in a typical session can be distributed to clients in the waiting room before a first session. Providing basic instructions and answers to common questions in a brief information sheet can be very effective in putting new clients at ease, especially when clients are new to the experience and unfamiliar with a facility's personnel and way of conducting business.

Uncertainty tends to increase clients' feelings of vulnerability and loss of control, while familiarity, structure, and predictability tend to increase clients' feelings of security and comfort, giving them a greater sense of control. Establish a set routine and session protocol to which your clients can grow accustomed. Ideally, sessions should be held at regular intervals, at a single location, for a specific, limited amount of time. Sessions should begin and end punctually and should not be interrupted by phone calls or intrusions from staff or other clients.

Session Protocol

During the session, be sure to get consent prior to working on areas such as the abdomen or gluteals. You may want to inform the client when you are moving to these vulnerable areas or include the information in your explanation before starting the session. Keep the following general guidelines in mind:

- Assess sensitivity and tolerance, and inform the client as you progress to deeper movements.

- Perform treatment only with client permission and after you are certain the individual is adequately informed about the process.

- Take care not to startle a client in a relaxed state.

- Inform the client regarding potential treatment aftereffects, such as tenderness or soreness, and their expected duration.

- Ask the client as you near the end of the session whether any area in particular needs further attention.

- Invite feedback, and implement changes based on client comments.

While good communication is integral to the therapeutic relationship, the practitioner should never confuse or misrepresent it as their area of professional competence or specialization. Conversational topics should never venture outside your scope of practice and experience. Unless you have the appropriate training and degree, do not attempt to act or make recommendations akin to those of a psychological counselor or therapist, even if the client requests that you do.

At the end of each session, discuss the client's treatment plan and health objectives. Ask the client to assess his or her progress or lack of progress toward treatment goals. Answer any questions the client may have, and note the following information in the client's record:

- If the client feels bruised, nauseated, or light-headed (check blood pressure and monitor).

- The length of the session.

- When the client should return for another session (session intervals/frequency).

- Anything the client can do to accelerate progress toward treatment goals.

- Anything the client should do or not do between sessions.

- What results the client can expect, and when.

Practitioners who recommend that clients replenish fluids after a session may want to provide bottled water at their offices.

Terminating a Professional Relationship

If you feel it is appropriate, either because a specified, finite course of treatment with a client is concluding or because you believe your relationship with the client has become dysfunctional, unproductive, or emotionally damaging, it may be necessary to terminate your professional relationship with the client. While this can be a difficult and uncomfortable task, it is important that it not be postponed out of a desire to avoid confrontation or discomfort.

Terminating a potentially damaging relationship is an important professional obligation with specific responsibilities. A practitioner must be able to realistically assess her or his own limitations and/or the client's potential for therapeutic benefits and make a determination in the client's best interests, without feelings of failure or guilt. The practitioner must develop a plan for termination that is considerate of the client, with attention to the possibility that it will be received with emotion or distress.

Informed consent provides a framework for termination because it specifies the need for an ongoing discussion between the client and the practitioner regarding the expected goals and anticipated timeline for therapeutic benefits. Involve your client in the process so that he or she is aware of treatment objectives and can ask questions and make determinations about his or her progress toward them. Discuss obstacles to client progress as they come up so that your client is not surprised by an unexpected pronouncement or abrupt changes in your assessment of his or her condition from one session to the next. Be sure to follow customary procedures for client assessment, and document relevant information about the client's progress or lack of progress toward treatment goals.

Before terminating the client, be sure to:

- **Consult appropriate information resources and supervising personnel.**   Contact a professional colleague or supervisor about your situation with the client, post a question on a professional treatment Web site, or refer to professional organizations with which you are affiliated. You may be able to find an alternative to terminating the client or a sensitive way to present the issue to him or her. If you appeal to any of these resources, be absolutely certain that you maintain strict rules of confidentiality and privacy, ensuring that the client's name or other identifying information is never revealed.

- **Do a reality check.**   Make sure you and the client are "on the same page" by comparing your understanding of a therapeutic relationship with the client's and discussing disparities in the way you and the client perceive the relationship, including difficulties and desired objectives. This kind of clarification can help you determine the scope of the problem: whether it is the result of miscommunication or misinterpretation, something that can be remedied, or requires termination.

If it is necessary to terminate the client, be sure this is done when you have sufficient time to discuss the subject fully. Take the time to respond to any questions the client may have, and give the client sufficient time to react to the news, respond to it, and regain composure. Do your best to leave the client with positive feelings about you and your practice. Provide referrals to other practitioners or health care professionals, as appropriate.

More Concepts in Professional Ethics

Many different philosophies of ethics have emerged over the years to address different kinds of ethical dilemmas. Ethical dilemmas occur when two or more ethical principles clash. Bioethics (also called *medical ethics*) initially grew out of concerns about the disproportionate power that physicians have relative to clients in therapeutic decision making and physician research practices involving human subjects. Bioethics eventually extended the scope of ethical analysis very broadly, to include any factors that come to bear on matters of health. One of the best-known approaches to ethical dilemmas in health care is that of *principalism*, a form of bioethical analysis in which caregivers attempt to resolve ethical problems by drawing on four main principles or values: autonomy, beneficence, nonmaleficence, and justice.

Principalism was formally introduced to the general public in 1978 through the Belmont Report, produced by a congressional commission. The report identified three ethical principles: respect for persons (now referred to as *autonomy*), justice (now referred to as *fairness*), and beneficence. Belmont ethics, which came to be known as principalism, was an early framework for determining right from wrong. It is still used extensively in the health care professions, as well as many other disciplines. Although this analytical framework is limited—in some cases, there is no way to simultaneously reconcile the values of all three principles—and has been replaced over the years by more complicated systems, it is still the basic structure for much ethical analysis.

Autonomy, Beneficence, and Nonmaleficence

The principle of **autonomy** (self-rule) is based on the principle of respect for persons, which holds that individual persons have the right to make their own choices and develop their own life plans. In a health care setting, the principle of autonomy translates into the principles of informed consent and right to refuse. In order to affirm autonomy, every effort must be made to discuss treatment preferences with clients and to document them in written records.

Persons are treated in an ethical manner not only by respecting their decisions and protecting them from harm but also by making efforts to secure their well-being. Such treatment falls under the principle of beneficence. The term **beneficence** is often understood as covering acts of kindness or charity that go beyond strict obligation. In this context, beneficence is understood in a stronger sense, as an obligation. Two general rules have been formulated as complementary expressions of beneficent actions in this sense: (1) Do not harm, and (2) maximize possible benefits and minimize possible harms (beneficence and nonmaleficence).

The principle of beneficence requires us, other things being equal, to do good, that is, to do what will further the client's interest. The principle of **nonmaleficence** requires us, other things being equal, to avoid harm to the client, or not to do what would be against the client's interests. Both principles rest on the fundamental importance of holding the client's interest paramount. The first—to do good—refers to the positive requirement of furthering the client's interest. The second—to avoid harm—refers to the requirement of refraining from doing what damages the client's interest.

There is no way to use these principles to make decisions in the abstract. However, with these qualifications in mind, we can assert that the least controversial treatment is one that accords with the interest of the client, is consistent with the standard of care within the profession, is agreed to by the client, is engaged in with his or her informed consent, and satisfies the principles of both nonmaleficence and beneficence. As with all hard cases, the different claims covered by the principle of beneficence may come into conflict and force difficult choices.

Informed Consent and Right to Refuse

Informed Consent

The concept of **informed consent** came out of the "patient's rights" movement of the 1960s. Now a customary procedure both inside and outside health and medical care, informed consent refers to a patient's right to be informed about his or her health care or medical condition and participate in decisions regarding that care or condition. The patient, or patient's guardian, is required to sign a written statement acknowledging agreement to proposed treatment terms and awareness of the known risk factors associated with them.

Informed consent usually takes the form of an agreement between the practitioner and the client that states their shared objectives, the proposed treatment plan, expected outcome(s), and the anticipated time frame for results. It may also refer to the client's medical history, asserting that the client has informed the practitioner about all known physical or medical conditions and current medications and will inform the practitioner if any of these conditions change.

The notice of informed consent in treatment typically includes a statement explaining the role of treatment in pain and stress reduction or for some other specified purpose and its limitations:

- Treatment does not take the place of medical examinations, care, or treatment.

- The practitioner is not a doctor and does not diagnose medical conditions or prescribe medication.

- Clients should continue to consult their primary caregivers or other specialists for ongoing health care and medical conditions.

- Consult your primary caregiver to review health care recommendations before making significant changes in your health and exercise regimen or diet.

Informed consent should:

- Explain the client's condition and diagnosis clearly and concisely, in language he or she can understand.

- Inform the client about the treatment(s) or procedure(s) you recommend, including:
  — The name, nature, and details of the recommended treatment(s) or procedure(s).
  — Indications for the recommended course of action.
  — The likelihood of success of the recommended treatment(s) or procedure(s) for this client.

- Describe the expected benefits and known risks of the recommended treatment(s) or procedure(s).

- Describe reasonable alternatives to the recommended treatment(s) or procedure(s), including the expected benefits and known risks of each alternative.

- Identify the practitioners who will be involved in performing the treatment(s) or procedure(s).

- Advise the client if the recommended treatment(s) or procedure(s) is novel or unorthodox.

- Encourage the client to ask questions.

Right of Refusal

Both the practitioner and the client are ensured the **right of refusal**. For a client, this means the right to refuse, modify, or terminate treatment regardless of any prior agreements or statements of consent. For a practitioner, it means the right to refuse to treat any person or condition for just and reasonable cause. These rights safeguard a client's freedom to choose any practitioner and a practitioner's freedom to terminate treatment, if necessary. These rights might come into play in cases of negligence or abuse. For example, a practitioner can refuse to work with an abusive or unstable client, and a client can refuse treatment from a practitioner he or she suspects is practicing under the influence of alcohol, drugs, or any illegal substances.

Client's Bill of Rights

A **client's bill of rights** typically includes the following information:

- Name of practitioner.

- Details of practitioner's certification and list of credentials.

- Practitioner's area of expertise, philosophy, and/or approach to treatment.
- Fees and service schedule.
- Payment terms.
- Filing procedures for written complaints.
- A right-to-information statement, asserting the client's right to the following information:
  — Practitioner's assessment of the client's physical condition.
  — Recommended treatment, estimated duration of treatment, and expected results.
  — Copy of the client's health forms and records that are held by the practitioner.
- A statement of confidentiality.
- A statement of refusal, explaining the client's right to terminate a course of treatment at any time and choose a new practitioner.
- A right-to-invoke statement, explaining the client's right to invoke these rights without fear of reprisal.

As you have learned, an ethical code is a compilation of statements defining the ethical boundaries in your business. Your licensing and professional affiliations are associated with a specific set of ethical standards, legal principles to which you are committed. Think about the other ethical standards that guide your practice. What concepts of fairness, for both you and the client, play into decisions made in conducting business? If you sell products as well as services, what requirements guide your decisions to sell these products in particular? As you implement these practices in your business, remember that conducting your business in an ethical manner is not only good for you and for your clients; it's good for business.

CHECKLIST

Have you done these things yet?

☐ Have you implemented guidelines to avoid misrepresentation in your written materials?

☐ Have you developed antiharassment policies?

☐ Have you implemented ethical practices in all aspects of your business?

☐ Have you set fees at a rate that is fair for you and your clients?

☐ Have you developed an ethical code for your business?

SO WHAT DO YOU THINK?

1. You're entitled to terminate a professional relationship that you believe has become dysfunctional or unproductive. If you simply dislike a client, is that sufficient reason to terminate your relationship with him or her?

2. Do you have an ethical obligation to set fees at approximately the rate charged by other professionals with your credentials and expertise? If yes, why? If no, why not?

3. Why would you need to formulate your own formal ethical code, given that you're bound by—and should know—the ethical codes in your practice area and by the law?

4. How far must you go to ensure that your client's consent is truly informed? If you have provided the necessary forms and orally explained the proposed treatment in terms a reasonable person would understand, must you continue to explain if the client appears not to understand?

5. What factors influence your own differentiation between writing down "factual" information regarding a client's session and recording personal opinions?

6. If a client, in your personal judgment, has diminished autonomy, what steps should you take if he or she refuses to consent to a procedure that, according to the standard of care in your profession, is essential?

7. With the same client, what if the procedure in question is not essential but strongly recommended?

8. Given the principle of autonomy, what are the many factors contributing to the fact that the practitioner, not the client, bears the burden of responsibility concerning ethics and boundary issues?

Marketing Your Business

LEARNING OUTCOMES

After completing this chapter, you should be able to:

13.1 Learn who your customers are.

13.2 Find out what your customers value.

13.3 Successfully network and grow your business.

13.4 Understand what successful promotions and public relations entail.

KEY TERMS

customer referral

loyal customers

value

customer service

referral

networking

promotions

public relations

advertising

Even the best products and services need to be marketed properly for a company to be successful. Without the proper marketing techniques, a business will have trouble surviving in today's market. Marketing is a conglomerate of many different parts that need to be put together in a plan of action, which will in turn help to create a demand for your products and services.

Objective of Your Marketing Plan: Referrals and Customer Loyalty

The objective of your marketing plan is to grow your business by increasing your customer base for the least amount of money invested as possible. The oldest sales tool on record, the **customer referral**, is the least expensive way to get customers in your door. Keeping customers loyal is the best way to grow your business for many years to come because **loyal customers** who value your service refer others to you. They want their friends and co-workers to have the same positive experience that they do. This positive experience is key to your long-term success. But before you get your first referral, let's explore how you get and keep your first customer by understanding the impact of customer service.

Building a business is hard work, which can be extremely enjoyable and rewarding; it should be seen as a labor of love instead of as drudgery, for you will be given many chances to stretch yourself and grow. There are many activities outside your field of expertise that must be done and must be done well. If the statement "Build it and they will come" describes your marketing plan, you will be very lonely. Customers don't just come to your door.

We will explore how to build your marketing plan to generate and retain customers in a variety of ways, including networking, promotions, public relations, and advertising.

Know Your Customer

Customers buy what they **value**. Think about the services that you purchase. Do you return to a doctor who has a terrible bedside manner? Do you continue to see a therapist who consistently makes you wait 45 minutes? When you go to a restaurant, does bad service ruin a great meal?

Whether you are a doctor, a lawyer, a dentist, or a therapist, you are a service provider. Knowing your customer includes understanding what your customers value most and delivering that entire experience to them. It is not enough to be incredibly skilled in your craft. The very best service providers understand and act on the needs of their customers. The best businesses know that understanding their customers is an ongoing process.

Exceptional Customer Service Generates Customer Loyalty

What will make a customer react positively and be loyal to your business? The answer is exceptional **customer service**:

- Competence, which gives customers the feeling of being well taken care of.
- Courtesy.
- Consistency.
- Sincerity.
- A pleasant environment, which gives customers a feeling of well-being, a sense that your business is a nice place to be today and to return to tomorrow or in the near future.

What will make a customer react negatively and never visit your business again?

- Rudeness.
- No follow-through (things are forgotten).
- Lack of punctuality (customers are made to wait).
- Physical pain that is not met with an empathetic and caring reaction.
- Unmet commitments (you don't do what you say you are going to do).
- Ambivalence (no one really cares, and it shows).

Customers pay a dollar amount for your service. If they value the experience, they spend less time considering the price paid.

What service businesses do you visit regularly? Starbucks has built an entire industry on delivering high-quality products with exceptional service—people enjoy their coffee experience and return to purchase again and again. We buy $5 cups of coffee because Starbucks employs happy people who provide exceptional customer service in a pleasing atmosphere. It also delivers a fabulous grande, decaf, nonfat, French vanilla latte. Do you need a $5 cup of coffee? No. Do you want a $5 cup of coffee? Yes. Can you get a cheaper cup of fresh-brewed coffee elsewhere? Yes. Starbucks has proved that a vast number of people consider price less important than the product and the overall customer experience.

Customer Service and Quality

Ultimately your goal of customer loyalty and referrals is based on your ability to understand issues you have with customer service and quality and overcome them by adapting and improvising. Your profit and ultimately your existence depends on this.

Although it is seven times easier to sell more services to an existing customer than to a new one, some businesses should not focus on generating repeat sales. As a therapist, you want to relieve your customer's current pain and minimize the chance of its future recurrence. Relieving that pain may take several visits, but ultimately your goal is the health and well-being of your customers. Perhaps your customer's overall wellness program needs to address stress and bad habits. Additional services may include various products, a personal trainer, or a lifestyle coach. These are all businesses that you can refer business to, and they can refer customers back to you.

Trusted referrals will generate additional customers. So what is a referral? A **referral** occurs when a customer tells someone else that your business will be of value to that person. How likely is it that customers will refer your business? When they are satisfied, they will recommend. Consequently, customer satisfaction and high-quality service are extremely important to the success of your business.

There is only one way to know what your customers think of your customer service and the overall experience you offer, and that is to ask. Most people are flattered that you care enough about their opinion to ask. The best answer you can get is not necessarily "Everything's perfect!" The best answer you can get identifies a problem that needs to be worked on. Be inviting and easy in your questions. Make it a pleasant, open conversation. Once you've gotten some direct feedback from people, spend some time thinking about how you will change your service to satisfy their needs. Sometimes the answers will surprise you, but don't get defensive. You asked. Nothing sells a business like a business owner. But, if you are not comfortable asking the questions, hire a marketing or public relations firm to do this for you or find someone you trust to represent your business well.

Following is an example of a telephone script that you can use to solicit feedback from your customers.

"Global Resort and Spas are so dedicated to improving their customer service, they have hired [this firm] to understand your thoughts and expectations. Is now a good time? This can take as little as five minutes or as long as you like. Great, thank you for your time. Global set out to achieve exceptional customer service. Did they meet or exceed your expectations? Why or why not? I see you had a massage from Trudy. Is there anything that you can think of that would improve your overall massage and relaxation experience? Have you tried any of Global's other services? Why or why not? I see you recommended Sue Friend and Mary Lamb to Global. Would you be willing to recommend Global's services again?"

Some people may not be comfortable giving verbal feedback or feedback that isn't anonymous, while others may feel intruded on by receiving a phone call. Additionally, if you are governed by HIPAA, you have to have permission to give customer information out to a third party. Given these restrictions, you might consider having customers fill out a postcard questionnaire that they get when they see you. The questionnaire should have postage already attached and be addressed to you.

Let's look at some numbers that address the impact of customer service on willingness to recommend (see Table 13.1). Studies are done in many large industries, but they really aren't relevant to you. You need to understand your business in your community and your service level with your customers. The numbers in Table 13.1 should motivate you to take time to understand your customers. Recognize that this is an ongoing commitment, not a one-time activity.

You may be thrilled with a 75 percent "very satisfied" rating and the fact that 90 percent of those customers are willing to recommend. But when you evaluate the inverse, you find that 25 percent of customers were *not* very satisfied. Although 90 percent of very satisfied customers would definitely recommend services to others, only 25 percent of somewhat-satisfied customers would do so. This drop in commitment to recommend is something to explore. Your business depends on referrals, so you can't afford that drop.

Let's apply the percentages above to an example with 40 customers. Table 13.2 shows the results.

In this example, 29 out of 40 customers are willing to recommend your service. That means 11 out of 40 are not. You can see how this analysis would come up with completely different results if the percentage of very satisfied customers was not 75% but 50%. Table 13.3 shows the lower figures.

TABLE 13.1

Customer Satisfaction and Recommendations	
Overall Satisfaction with Service	**Definitely Recommend to Others**
Very satisfied 75%	90%
Somewhat satisfied 20%	25%
Neutral to very dissatisfied 5%	0%

ASK AND YOU WILL RECEIVE

In all of the years that I have taught business courses, the referral is one of the most asked-about items when it comes to growing a business. The most important thing about referrals is that you actually ask for them! So many businesspeople are afraid to ask for new customers. It is also very important that you do not inappropriately bother your customers about referring new customers to your business. As has been said above, a happy customer is a referring customer, so all that you have to do is remind that happy customer that you would love a new customer. (LSR)

Number of Satisfied Customers and Recommendations

TABLE 13.2

Overall Satisfaction with Service among 40 Customers	Definitely Recommend to Others
Very satisfied 75% = 30	90% of 30 = 27
Somewhat satisfied 20% = 8	25% of 8 = 2
Neutral to very dissatisfied 5% = 2	0

Number of Satisfied Customers and Recommendations: Lower Figures

TABLE 13.3

Overall Satisfaction with Service among 40 Customers	Definitely Recommend to Others
Very satisfied 50% = 20	90% of 20 = 18
Somewhat satisfied 45% = 18	25% of 18 = 4
Neutral to very dissatisfied 5% = 2	0

In this case, 22 out of 40 customers are willing to recommend your service. That means 18 out of 40 are not. A drop of 25 percent from very satisfied to somewhat satisfied generated a completely different outcome.

If you have questions about changes you see in customer satisfaction or expectations missed, ask your customers and your employees. Their insight is invaluable. Customer satisfaction and high-quality service are extremely important to the success of your business.

You are in the service business. Keep the concept of "What does my customer value in my overall service?" in your mind as we go through the process of building your marketing plan. Delivering what your customer wants and needs generates referrals and customer loyalty—key contributors to your long-term success.

Generating More Business

Now let's explore how to generate more business. We will start with the most personal and productive manner of generating referrals, networking, and then move on to reaching larger audiences with promotions, public relations, and advertising.

Networking

Networking is how people you don't know get to know you and your business. Your goal is to develop a relationship, explain your business, and get to know new people and their businesses. Networking is not a get-together of your oldest and dearest friends; it is a means of meeting people who do not know, or have had very limited exposure to, you and your business. There are two major rules to networking: You have to attend, and you have to be in the right frame of mind. Remember that you are approaching this networking opportunity as if you were approaching someone to get to know them better and for them to get to know you better, so you can grow a relationship together.

Some people have a difficult time in networking situations. This is where team members can become very useful to you. They can accompany you in marketing situations and provide you with support and an objective point of view on how you could improve your performance in these situations. Additionally, they can become spokespeople for you at such events if you are hopelessly lost and afraid to network. They can help you grow into an effective salesperson.

The Right Frame of Mind

"You can never get a second chance at a first impression." The best way to think about networking is that the next person you meet may be your new best friend. You may meet your next best customer through this encounter. A positive frame of mind is attractive and generates positive dialogue. Everyone has bad days, and some events in our lives are tough to shake. However, "I'm having a bad day" is not the first impression you want to leave with someone. Leave your personal situation at the car door. Between the car door and the front door, commit to who you are and why you are attending this event. Be happy. It is a choice. Be in a good mood.

You Have to Attend to Be Able to Network

There are thousands of networking opportunities available to you every day. Some are organized networking events, and others are opportunities to get involved and meet people in your local community. Regardless of who attends, your next best customer may be the sister, brother, cousin, tennis partner, or neighbor of the person you are speaking with. The only bad networking contact is the person who walks away with a less than favorable impression of you.

Every local newspaper prints a community calendar that identifies organized networking events. Some examples of memberships, forums, associations, and groups focused on networking are:

- Chamber of commerce.
- Toastmasters.
- Women in Business.
- Business Networking Institute (BNI).

Volunteer opportunities are very good networking events. It may make sense for you to combine a topic that interests you with your networking goals. For example:

- If you are a therapist, you can volunteer at your local marathon or triathlon event or with the American Heart Association fund-raiser (Figure 13.1).
- If you are selling jewelry in your spa, volunteer for various committees for your local art festival event.
- Or choose something that just interests you, such as your local humane society.

Your customers have a variety of interests as well. The important message is that you cannot network at your front door with the pizza delivery person. You need to get out there.

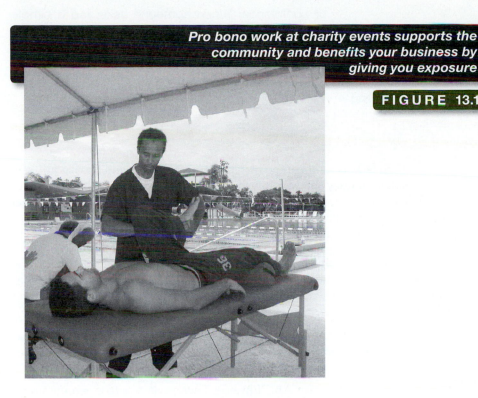

Pro bono work at charity events supports the community and benefits your business by giving you exposure

FIGURE 13.1

Seven Do's and Seven Don'ts of Networking

DO

1. **Bring current business cards.** If you don't have a logo or a business card and you don't know a qualified person to create them for you locally, look into companies like logoworks.com to create a logo and stationery packet (business cards, letterhead, and envelopes) for you. They are inexpensive, provide multiple alternatives, have a fast turnaround, and can handle the printing for you as well. Americans see 70,000 images a day. Your image is important. It does not have to be expensive.

   Make certain that your business cards are professional-looking. Do not attempt to create a business card on your own if you do not have a talent for doing so. There is nothing worse than a cheap-looking business card; it creates a cheap image in your potential customer's mind. The same goes for all other materials that are to be handed out to customers or potential customers.

2. **Be prepared.** Have a one- or two-sentence description of your business that introduces you, your company, what you do, and what you specialize in or what you do best. Below are a few written examples; personalize them, and make them your own. Practice saying your introduction out loud so that it sounds natural and not like a script from a textbook. This simple exercise will help to build your confidence.

   a. "I'm Betty Johnson and I'm a massage therapist with 12 years' experience. I specialize in everything from rejuvenating, stress-relief massages to neuromuscular massage for athletes to solutions for a better lifestyle for victims of unfortunate accidents."

   b. "I'm Joe Brown and I'm a physical therapist at ABC Physical Therapy. We have five physical therapists, two occupational therapists, and a speech therapist and provide rehabilitative services and techniques for everything from 'weekend warrior' injuries to spinal cord injuries and the effects of strokes."

PRACTICE MAKES PERFECT

I have given speeches aloud to my dog for many years. Although the dog didn't ask too many questions, the role of speaking out loud helps to generate a feeling of confidence. When someone asks you a simple question—"What do you do?"—it won't be the first time you answer the question out loud, in a clear, concise, professional speaking voice. (JHS)

c. "I'm Brenda Moss and I'm the owner of Global Resort and Spas, a full-service salon and day spa with seven locations from Anytown to Yourtown. We lead the region in repeat customers because our clients look and feel fabulous when they leave. They rely on that professional level of excellence on every occasion for every service."

Be prepared to describe the perfect referral. "My best prospect is someone who is looking for, is in need of, experienced an event like . . ." Give examples to help people understand your business and what makes you unique and interesting. Here are written examples; personalize them and practice:

a. "The perfect referral for my massage business is a person between 30 and 65 who needs therapy due to repetitive stress or athletic injury or issues from a sedentary lifestyle or an unfortunate accident."

b. "The perfect referral for ABC Physical Therapy is a person who is under doctor's care and needs guidance with the approved list of providers from his or her insurance company. During this time of stress and rehabilitation, people need to know who will provide the best care. We work with our patients to accomplish their physical goals in an environment of care, dignity, and respect."

c. "The perfect referral for Global is a woman who desires to enhance her life. She may watch the Style Network and wish for her own makeover. It's the right time in her life to let a professional stylist and makeup artist create the perfect image for her lifestyle, as well as give her the perfect massage to provide a euphoric feeling to greet the new day with confidence."

3. **Show interest in the other person.** Ask about the person's business, life, or interests. People love to talk about themselves, and this is a great way for you to ask leading questions about them, such as:

a. How did you get into this business?

b. What challenges do you face every day?

c. Economically, I would assume this is a (busy/slow) time for you. How are you managing the (increase/decrease) in demand?

d. Since you've been in business so long, has your growth been what you expected? Why or why not?

4. **Remember what you heard.** Write down pertinent words on the back of the person's business card after the event. This will help to jar your memory. People are impressed when, two months later, you ask, "How did that event you attended go?" or you mention some specific the person spoke of last time. You are developing a long-term relationship with your community. People are impressed when you remember details they shared with you.

5. **Remember the person's name.** Repeat a person's name back to her or him to help you remember it. "Very nice to meet you, Bob Johnson. How long has Johnson Enterprises been in business?"

6. ***Follow up.*** If you connect with a person, follow up with either an e-mail, phone call, or letter saying that you enjoyed meeting the person and hope to see him or her in the future. If you have an offer or a business opportunity to share, go ahead and do so. However, do not make every interaction a reason to send a brochure. If you are going to send sales material at this point, make sure there is personal interaction that goes with it. Write a personal note.

7. ***Dress appropriately and enjoy yourself.*** Never be the worst-dressed person in the room. You are not there to show off your way-cool fashion, nor should you show up in scrubs. You are there to introduce yourself; your clothes should reflect you and your business. Consider that your clothing for the event is like oregano: an accent flavor, not the main course.

DON'T

1. Spend the entire interaction talking about yourself and your business. You are there to share and learn.

2. Be a wallflower. Get up and move around. Introduce yourself. Everyone is there for the same reason.

3. Spend the entire time with people you already know or with one person (there's always one) who dominates the conversation and is not talking about business. Excuse yourself politely and move on. Use your time wisely. You will never get that hour back again.

4. Let your cell phone ring unless you are expecting an emergency call. If it rings, apologize and explain that a personal situation requires that you have your phone on (e.g., the only reason the phone is on is in case your daughter calls from school), and then check to see if that is the call. If it is, excuse yourself and take the call elsewhere. If it is not, do not take the call.

5. Say "I'm bad with names." Get good with names. Repetition is the best way to create a memory.

6. Put every person you meet on your direct-mail list. Developing a relationship that will generate long-term customers and referrals through networking is not accomplished with a three-minute business-card swap and months of direct mail. Many people are turned off by this approach and will not buy your services because of it.

7. Dress inappropriately and enjoy yourself too much.

Networking occurs to generate customers for, as well as referrals from, other businesses. As a therapist, you may have chiropractors, orthopedic doctors, podiatrists, family physicians, personal trainers, nutritionists, fitness gyms, or retail fitness equipment facilities as potential referral sources of your cards and brochures. You may distribute their business cards as well. Always be careful to know the business you are referring your customers to, and you should assume the same from your referral sources. You are competent and qualified and provide excellent customer service. Make sure you are sending your customers to businesses that have a similar style of work ethic.

Keep track of who was referred by whom. It is always a good idea to thank a customer for a referral of your new best customer.

Promotions

Promotions are one way to get your name in front of your prospective customers without paying for advertising. It's good for business to draw attention to your business, and doing so also helps the community that you are serving. To understand this concept, consider the following examples.

- A therapy center may sponsor a blood drive. For every patient who donates, the physical therapy office will donate a free minitreatment or a $10 gift card. Set up a station outside the blood donation facility, and draw some attention to your business for a good cause. Accident victims, cancer patients, and premature babies all need blood; whole blood only lasts a few short weeks. The American Red Cross is always in need of supply.

- A salon may sponsor a Locks of Love event to donate hair to be used in wigs for people who have lost their hair due to disease or illness. Contact the local Locks of Love program, and have a representative present at the event. Hire a local photographer to create a keepsake picture set of the event for those donating hair. Have your salon donate the hair that is cut in addition to any contributions.

- A single therapist may sponsor a Career Closet event for underprivileged women who need job-interview suits. Work with your customers, and ask them to donate. Ask the people in your office area to participate with you. Make it an annual event.

Choose something that matters to you. The options are endless for promoting a worthy cause and assisting your local community.

Local newspapers, community newspapers by subdivision, local twice-weekly papers, and the local sections of major newspapers are always looking for feel-good stories and local events. Most papers state how they prefer to receive event information from local businesses—via fax, e-mail, or Web site submission. If you can't find this information, call the paper and ask.

If you do not have the ability to write well, do not write a promotion piece yourself. Poor spelling and grammar, as well as bad sentence structure, can ruin a perfect opportunity for a successful promotion. Again, this is what you have team members for. Make sure that everything that is presented to the public is double- and triple-checked for accuracy of facts, spelling, and punctuation.

Ten Do's for Sponsoring a Promotion

DO

1. Write a quick overview of the event, not more than 200 words, and send it to every local newspaper you can find at least two or three weeks in advance of the event. If the event is big enough, send the write-up to local television and radio. *Note:* Invite television to the second annual event, not the first!

2. Make sure your write-up is clear and concise and includes all the details: date, time, location, event description, and benefits to those who attend. See the example in Figure 13.2.

3. Clip the announcement from the paper, frame it, and place it on your reception desk.

4. Mail copies to customers who may have missed it in the newspaper. Ask them to give their support or to bring their friends. *Note:* People take note of newspaper print more than your generated flyer. Flyers are fine to use, but if you can use newspaper print, you will get more attention.

5. Take a lot of pictures on the day of the event. Hire a photographer if you can.

6. Get contact information from everyone who attended.

7. Network with every attendee; get to know the people who are at your event. (This is why someone else needs to take the pictures!)

8. Write a quick overview of the event, and send it with several pictures to every newspaper you originally sent the announcement to. Get permission from

Example of a community announcement

FIGURE 13.2

"Locks of Love" planned in Anytown, USA

ABC Professional Photography Studios and Global Resort and Spas, 123 Main Street in Anytown, will join together Monday, August 24, from 10 a.m. to 2 p.m. to host an event to benefit Locks of Love. Hairstylists at Global Resort and Spas will donate their time by providing complimentary haircuts to those donating 10 or more inches of hair to Locks of Love.

Those who don't quite have 10 inches of hair to donate may receive a haircut for a donation of $20 to Locks of Love and a minimum donation of 6 inches of hair. After a participant receives a hairstyle, John Doe of ABC Professional Photography Studios will photograph the participant and provide her with a photomontage of this day.

Those donating 10 or more inches of hair will also receive a gift certificate for a portrait from ABC Professional Photography Studios. Bleached hair cannot be used, but dyed or permed hair can be. For more information, call 123.123.1234.

Example of a community announcement

FIGURE 13.2

An example of a press acknowledgment of a public event

FIGURE 13.3

A hair-raising fund-raiser

ABC Professional Photography Studios recently joined forces with Global Resort and Spas in Anytown, USA, on August 24 to collect both hair donations and financial contributions to benefit Locks of Love. A total of 130 inches of hair was donated by 12 people, along with $115 in cash donations. Hairstylists Tom Smith and Sally Jones, along with the salon owner, Jane Doe (below), gave up their day to create amazing hairstyles for each donor. The last ponytail donated, measuring 18 inches, was the longest ponytail donated. Among the donors were Donor 1 (above left), shown before and after her donation with stylist Tom Smith; Donor 2 (above), before and after with stylist Sally Jones; and Donor 3 (left), of Anytown.

Note: There were seven photos printed with the above text by local press. This was all submitted by business owners.

every person in the pictures to use her or his photo in the newspaper. Get permission from parents for pictures of children under 18.

9. Send the event overview and pictures to newspapers and other sources you forgot to send the initial announcement to. They may print it anyway.

10. Once the follow-up is printed, mail copies to everyone on your contact list, all of your networking contacts and customers, sharing the good news of the event you sponsored. Figure 13.3 is an example of the resulting half-page press generated by the Locks of Love follow-up.

Promotions like this are great conversation starters. People are pleased with your community action and will frequent your business because you made an effort. But unless you are committed to doing the 10 steps above, don't bother with the event. You are sponsoring an event to help a good cause and generate positive buzz and customers for your business. Follow through with all 10 steps, and you will reap the rewards.

Promotions work to generate buzz, good press, and customers for your business.

Public Relations

Grand openings, openings of second offices, awards, presentations, speaking events, new hires with credentials, and major promotions are all examples of **public relations** events (Figure 13.4). Use the same methods as described in promotions to

Corporate chair massage is a great marketing tool, as well as a vehicle through which you can work outside the normal confines of your clinic or center

FIGURE 13.4

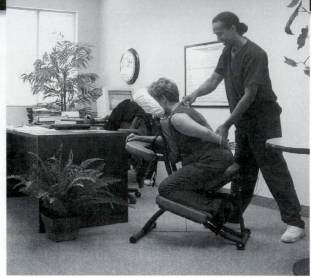

access the media. Don't be shy, but don't think communication with the media is a sales brochure. The media are not interested in selling your latest product or service for you. Don't write text like "We are always number 1 in customer satisfaction" or "Serving our customers is what we do best." You are not writing to your customers. The media are interested in providing news that is of interest to their readers, not printing ad copy for you for free. Keep your text short and to the point; write facts that describe your business and the topic you feel should be noted by the general readership. Send a photo of yourself, preferably a professional press photo, and make sure that the photo is relatively recent.

Figure 13.5 is an example of a public relations announcement, but read your local paper carefully for more examples.

Now that you are getting familiar with how to work with the media, let's have a little fun with it and step "out of the box."

You are a subject-matter expert. You know more about your field of expertise than anyone; it's now time for your target customers to know that.

Media sources love top-10 lists. A top-10 list is a good way to get a point across. Sit down, pour your favorite beverage, and creatively think and write on one of these topics:

- Top-10 reasons to get a treatment twice a month.

- Top-10 exercises to solve back pain.

- Top-10 repetitive movements that cause pain. (Include the solutions.)

- Top-10 qualities to look for when choosing a therapist.

- Top-10 questions to ask your therapist.

Set your list aside and look at it next week. Be prepared to change it. Ask your team members for their opinions. Call a marketing or public relations firm or someone whose opinion you value highly and get feedback. Place the top-10 list with the media, and see what happens. In the worst case, it won't be printed, and you can use it as a sales tool on a flyer or brochure for your prospective customers. In the best case, it will be printed, and you will get a one-line description of your business and contact information in the local press for the price of a little imagination.

People believe what they read. Public relations and press are great ways to make people aware of your business through means that your competitors are not using.

Example of media coverage

Global Resort and Spas buys neighboring ABC Salon

Global Resort and Spas announced that it is expanding its Anytown, USA, facilities with the purchase of ABC Salon, located at 123 Main Street. The purchase of the Salon will expand Global's facilities to 3 in XYZ County, with 27 employees providing luxurious spa treatments, hairstyles, manicures, and massages. Owner Jane Doe states, "The commitment to customer service displayed by ABC Salon made it a natural fit in our growing network of Global Resorts and Spas."

FIGURE 13.5

Advertising

The **advertising** landscape has changed. It's more complex than ever because we have more avenues to deliver messages: network stations, premium channels, cable channels, infomercials, radio, satellite radio, HD radio, trade magazines, a variety of newspapers, direct mail, e-mail blasts, Internet advertising, Web-page hits, billboards, coupons, signage, and so on.

The most important piece of advertising that you will use is the business card. No matter what other advertising you use and no matter what your advertising budget is, the business card is a must. You should be handing out business cards to anyone that you meet, and you should think it appropriate to do so. Your business card is a tool that will draw attention to you and your business.

Consumers are inundated with 70,000 images a day. How will you get your prospective customers to hear your message at a cost that makes sense for your business?

You will need a great image and a well-defined use of your advertising dollars. (See Figures 13.6 and 13.7.) You are not in the business of advertising. You are in your line of business, and advertising is a way to generate awareness and business. Your goal is to generate business for the least amount of dollar investment possible. Be prepared to try different avenues for a period of time. If they don't work, try another.

How do you make your message stand out? A logo is the graphic representation of your company, and it should be professionally done. Customers see professional, crisp color images every second of the day. Your 9-year-old's drawing may generate an emotional bond for you, but it can't compete in today's image-centric marketplace to grab the attention of your customers and create a positive memory.

When working with a graphic artist, expect the following questions:

- Who is your target audience—by age, gender, income level?

- What are you selling?

- What feeling are you trying to convey to your audience (e.g., one of strength, endurance, and toughness or one of feminine beauty and an aura of indulgence)?

Sample business card

FIGURE 13.6

Sample brochure

FIGURE 13.7

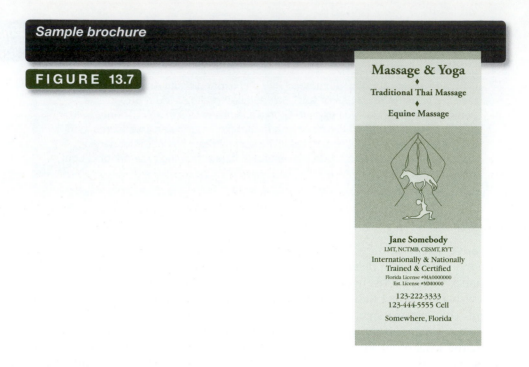

Massage & Yoga
◆
Traditional Thai Massage
◆
Equine Massage

Jane Somebody
LMT, NCTMB, CESMT, RYT
Internationally & Nationally
Trained & Certified
Florida License #MA0000000
Est. License #MM0000

123-222-3333
123-444-5555 Cell

Somewhere, Florida

- Describe your industry.
- What do your competitors' logos look like?
- What colors have they chosen?

Your marketing message must be clear and crisp and express your business. Additionally, it must conform to your business plan, goals, and mission statement. Your company name and logo must build a positive memory in your audience's mind. The goals of your logo and company name are to:

- Get attention.
- Develop interest.
- Influence a buying decision.

Keep signage in mind while you create your logo and company name.

Some companies use a tagline, a few words that describe the business. The goals of a tagline are to:

- Get attention.
- Develop interest.
- Influence a buying decision.

As well as:

- Show the value of your product and service in the eyes of the customer.
- Build and maintain credibility.

It is difficult to develop a great tagline. We are all familiar with some of the great taglines of our time: Nike's "Just Do It," Allstate's "You're in Good Hands," and Apple Computers' "Think Different," which were all generated by advertising agencies.

Start with a name and a logo, and either never create a tagline (and don't worry about it—many successful businesses have never had a tagline!) or come back for a tagline later. The authors of this book suggest you use the help of a professional to create a phrase that accomplishes the five goals above.

Note: Most of the time, a logo is altered to fit with tiny print on a business card and with large-scale signage. Very few logos can handle both extremes. Make your logo work in print first, usually a stationery pack of letterhead, envelopes, and business cards. A reputable sign company will help you alter the logo (e.g., thicken a line, reduce a shadow) to create great signage while maintaining the integrity of your brand.

Signage

Every service business that is not a home-based business requires signage of some kind. You have chosen your location well, and now you need to choose signage. This is the most visible and one of the most costly investments you will make. Before you talk to a reputable sign company, speak with your landlord. Review your lease, and understand all limitations with signage. Look at the signage of surrounding businesses. Take into consideration the quality of the sign material and structure in regard to the weather conditions in your area. Your sign blowing down and hitting a pedestrian is not the story you want to see about your business on the news.

Aspect ratio is the height-to-width dimension of a logo. Look at the sign dimensions, and make sure that your logo or company name can be seen from a distance. Don't have the letters so small, with so many words, that the sign can't be read. The easiest way to understand aspect ratio and color is to go to a professional or minor league baseball field and look at the signs on the outfield fence. From your seat, which sign stands out as readable? Which sign stands out as eye-catching? What is the height-to-width ratio and color combination of the sign that gets your attention?

Choose a reputable, knowledgeable sign company that will assist you with your decision.

Advertorials

An *advertorial* is a paid-for advertisement disguised as an article. It is entertaining and informative, provides information that has a high utility for the readers (i.e., readers can use the information immediately), and is self-promoting. Freelance writers, marketing firms, or public relations firms can write advertorials for you. Choose a magazine or newspaper that you think reaches your target audience, those whom you want to have as your customers. There are several advertorial newspapers that focus on health care and are direct-mailed to homes. Explore the cost of writing an advertorial and placing it in this type of forum. Most newspapers and magazines have areas for advertorials. Look around, and you will be able to see options that are available to you in your local community.

Think about your target customers. Where do they drive? What age are they? What magazines do they read?

Direct Mail, Coupons, Radio Ads, Billboards, Television

All types of advertising are available to you at different costs and returns on investment.

Every market is different as well. Determine first whether you need advertising, as many businesses can operate exceedingly well on referrals only. When you look at the number of companies advertising, you need to make sure that your message is heard louder than your competitors'.

Quality

"How good is 99.9 percent?" is asked by authors Edward Scannell, John Newstrom, and Carolyn Nilson in their book *The Complete Games Trainers Play,* Volume II (McGraw-Hill). This question is asked to generate thoughts about the impact of mind-sets like "That's good enough for me" or "The customer doesn't expect any more than that."

THE COUPON

The one single thing that made our business a success, with regard to promotional materials, was the coupon (Figure 13.8). We used all different shapes and sizes (from business cards to full-page certificates and everything in between). We gave anything from 20 percent off to half price to free treatments. We got these coupons to potential customers through current customers. We were, in effect, able to use current customers as salespeople. This was particularly successful, so much so that even today we use the same technique. The important thing to remember is that the salespeople do not feel as if they are salespeople. The benefit that they receive is a happy friend whom they did something nice for; you received a good lead; and the new customer got a free or reduced-price service. Be careful not to do too much of this, and do not use people in such a way that they feel uncomfortable. Pick the right opportunities. A significant portion of our business has come from a select number of referral sources. If they are nurtured properly, they will grow exponentially and fast! (LSR)

What quality is good enough? What quality level is acceptable for your business? Is it 95 percent? 96? 97? 98? 99? If 99.9 percent is good enough, then:

- 12 newborns will be given to the wrong parents daily.
- 114,500 mismatched pairs of shoes will be shipped per year.
- 18,322 pieces of mail will be mishandled per hour.

If quality drops .1 percent, to 99.8 percent, then:

- 2 million documents will be lost by the IRS this year.
- 2.5 million books will be shipped with the wrong covers.
- Two planes landing at Chicago's O'Hare airport will be unsafe every day.

Customers suffer:

- 315 entries in *Webster's* dictionary will be misspelled.
- 20,000 incorrect drug prescriptions will be written this year.
- 880,000 credit cards in circulation will turn out to have incorrect cardholder information on their magnetic strips.

Massage coupon sample

FIGURE 13.8

- 103,260 income tax returns will be processed incorrectly during the year.
- 5.5 million cases of soft drinks produced will be flat.
- 291 pacemaker operations will be performed incorrectly.
- 3,056 copies of tomorrow's *Wall Street Journal* will be missing one of the three sections.

When your quality drops, how do your customers suffer?

The examples above are to make you think. No one is perfect, but everyone can certainly make efforts to improve his or her business every day. Below are some examples of ways to improve your customer service. Every day, you can do one of them better than you did it the day before.

- Return phone calls immediately.
- Honor your commitments to your work schedule.
- Don't reschedule clients due to personal issues that have arisen.
- Don't favor clients.
- Be honest.
- Admit mistakes and take responsibility.

There is only one way to know what your customer thinks about your quality and customer service, and that is to ask. Once you've gotten some direct feedback from people, spend some time thinking about how you will build your business to satisfy their needs.

Ultimately, the goal of your marketing plan is customer loyalty and referrals because a repeat customer or a referral involves the least amount of money spent on marketing and sales and thus equals more profit for you. Spend your time focusing on quality and customer service. Use networking, promotions, public relations, and advertising to generate awareness and a referral network. With these tools, you will create a long-term business that will generate the results you desire.

CHECKLIST

Have you done these things yet?

☐ Have you created your business card?

☐ Have you created other promotional materials, such as brochures, gift certificates, and letterhead?

☐ Have you identified your customers?

☐ Have you identified what your customers value in your business? List the top five factors:

1. _____

2. _____

3. _____

4. _____

5. _____

☐ Have you explored possible networking opportunities? List the top five:

  1. _____
  2. _____
  3. _____
  4. _____
  5. _____

☐ Have you thought of five ways that you can promote your business? List them (be creative):

  1. _____
  2. _____
  3. _____
  4. _____
  5. _____

☐ Have you done your top-10 lists?   _____

SO WHAT DO YOU THINK?

1. How much money do you think you should spend on advertising?

2. What would make advertising successful? What is the amount of return that you want for every dollar that you spend on advertising?

3. What are the most important elements of a marketing plan? Why?

4. What are the most important elements of customer service for your customers? Why?

5. What kind of fund-raisers and promotions are the best for your business? What makes them good, as compared to others?

6. Realistically, what can you do to improve your business every day?

Financial Policies

CHAPTER FOURTEEN

LEARNING OUTCOMES

After completing this chapter, you should be able to:

14.1 Understand the concept of policies and their importance in business.

14.2 Write financial policies that will help your business run smoothly.

14.3 Understand the various methods of payment.

14.4 Recognize insurance filing procedures for payment.

KEY TERMS

policy

satisfied customer

essential (necessity) approach

market approach

payment for services

gratuity

tip

insurance reimbursement

INTRODUCTION

The parameters of your business are determined by the policies for the business. One of the most important considerations when developing the policies is to make sure that your policies line up with your mission statement and goals (Chapters 2 and 3). If the policies do not help you achieve your goals and fulfill your mission statement, they are not the appropriate policies for your business. Policies should be documented for both employees and customers. For example, an employee handbook that describes each person's duties and responsibilities will prevent misunderstandings among employees and between employees and management. A printed brochure outlining elements such as fees based on treatments and cancellation policies will help to prevent disagreements between customer and business owner.

What Is a Policy?

A **policy** is a rule. It is a specific way to tell your employees, customers, and all who are involved in your business what the rules are. Why is it important to have rules, and why is it important to have them documented? Won't rules or policies get in the way and make life more complicated? The answer is no. Simply put, your customers will not be satisfied with the service they receive if their expectations are not met. However, if your customers have a good idea of what they are going to experience and if their experiences are close to or match their expectations, they will most likely become repeat customers. An example is treatment time and fee: Let's say your published price is $75 for a 50-minute treatment. You work on a customer for 50 minutes and he pays the $75 at the conclusion of the treatment. If you work only 30 minutes but still request the full fee, he will not be satisfied with the service and will be unlikely to return as a customer. If he is happy with the treatment that he received, he will be a **satisfied customer** and will likely return again.

Setting Fees

How much money are you going to charge for your services? This can be both the easiest and the most difficult question you will face when starting a new business. There are two approaches to determining the correct fee for services. The first approach is the **essential (necessity) approach**. This approach is simply based on the amount of money you need to make during a given period of time. If it is essential that you earn $1,000 per week to meet living expenses, there are many ways to get to that number. Table 14.1 shows different ways to earn the $1,000.

How did we determine that $1,000 per week was the amount that was needed? It is simply the amount of expenses that you have per week for your business plus the amount of money that you want to earn for yourself per week.

TABLE 14.1

Options for Earning $1,000	
Price Charged	**Number of Treatments per Week**
$ 25	40
40	25
50	20
100	10
200	5

NOT SO FAST

A friend of mine who was very successful in running his own service-oriented business once told me, "You cannot raise your prices in fewer than two years. Every two years is acceptable to the customer." I have always used this piece of advice as a guide, and it has served me well, as it did him. (JLS)

As you can see, you can work eight times as much to make the same amount of money, but why would you do that if you can make the same amount of money for much less work? Remember the old adage: "Work smarter, not harder or longer."

The second approach is the **market approach**. The market approach is based on the amount of money that people are willing to pay for your services. This amount is often what the market will bear. In other words, there is a point at which people will not be willing to pay for your services. As you charge more for your services, there are fewer people who are willing, or able, to pay for those services. Having fewer customers may not necessarily be a negative circumstance. Fees are usually determined by socioeconomic factors. Some markets may allow you to charge $200 per treatment, whereas other markets may only allow a $25 charge. How do you determine this? Make some phone calls to existing businesses in the area you plan on covering for outcalls or in which you intend to physically locate your office. You also can ask friends, relatives, and colleagues what they pay for similar services to help determine how much you should be charging. However, remember to compare "apples to apples" and "oranges to oranges" not "apples to oranges." You should not charge the same price for a different type of treatment that may require specific knowledge, equipment, or training. An example of this is charging the same amount for a Swedish massage and a hot-stone massage, when the equipment, time, and cost of training are far greater for hot-stone massage than for Swedish massage.

You will find that the prices of a single treatment in any given market will fall on a curve and appear bell-shaped. Table 14.2 is an example of what the numbers for a bell curve look like for 100 therapists' prices (in $5 increments).

> **TIDBIT**
>
> One of the most difficult things to do is to raise prices. People tend to object if you raise prices too much at one time or too often, so be careful to set your prices properly so that you do not have to raise them too quickly.

Therapists' Prices

TABLE 14.2

Price Charged	Number of People Charging This Amount
$ 25	2
30	1
35	0
40	4
45	3
50	10
55	4
60	8
65	9
70	17
75	14
80	13
85	4
90	5
95	2
100	2
Others	2

REALITY CHECK

MAKE SURE THAT IT MAKES SENSE

After hearing from a couple of customers that they would like to pay for services with a credit card, I decided to sign up with a merchant services company to accomplish this. I elected to use the same company a friend used for her business. However, as soon as I signed up and started paying a monthly fee for the machine rental and a percentage to the credit card companies, only one of my customers made use of this amenity. That meant half of my fee for that customer's massage went to the cost of the machine and the monthly service fee. My first mistake was not doing enough research into costs, and my second mistake was not recognizing what a small percentage of my business would actually warrant this service. With a year's contract, my only route out was to find another new business that was willing to take over the equipment and contract. I was able to do this but not without a lot of hard work. It was a hard lesson learned. (JLS)

Without going into complicated statistical measurements, you can see that the majority of people charge between $60 and $80. Recognizing the median fee within the bell-shaped curve, you will not charge more than what is accepted at the risk of pricing yourself out of this market. You will want to charge $70 per treatment, acknowledging that you will need to do 15 treatments to make approximately $1,000 (actually $1,050).

Payment for Services

It is a good idea to let people know in advance what forms of payment you accept, especially if you do not accept credit cards.

How are you going to accept **payment for services**? Are you going to accept credit cards, and which ones are you going to accept? (See Figure 14.1). Will you take personal checks or just cash? A lot has to do with the type of business you are running; if you conduct a sizable business, it is smart to accept credit cards. It also behooves you to do a little research here. Find out whether your client base wants to pay by credit card or by cash, check, or barter.

If you are involved in a mobile business, you can use credit cards in a very easy manner. You can keep a credit card terminal at your house or establishment and manually input the credit card information at the end of each day, after getting the information at your customer's home. Another option is to purchase a mobile credit card terminal and use it at your customer's home directly. You can carry a receipt book and handwrite a receipt for the customer, or you can print out a receipt later and bring it at the time of your next visit. If you want to use technology to a greater degree, you can also e-mail a receipt to your customer. One thing that is important for you to do is to get a signature for the charge that you are processing.

Credit Card Companies

If you have only an occasional need for accepting a credit card payment, using PayPal is an option, albeit a bit of an involved process.

There are many options with regard to taking credit cards. The best advice is to keep this as simple as possible, particularly if you are just starting to take credit cards as a form of payment. When looking at credit card processing companies, you should shop around and have several sets of eyes look at the offers and the contracts that are involved in credit card processing. Typically there are three things that the credit card company charges for:

- *Monthly charge.* This is typically a minimum fee that the credit card company charges each month.

If your volume of treatments or product sales is quite large, it makes sense to accept credit cards as payment

FIGURE 14.1

- **Swipe charge.** This fee is charged to you every time you swipe a credit card through your machine. The amount can range from 5 to 20 cents per swipe. If you manually input the card information, there may be an additional charge per item.

- **Percentage charge.** This is the amount of money that the processing company charges as a percentage of the sale. For instance, if you sell $100 worth of services and the rate for your processing company is 2 percent, you will pay the company $2 as the percentage charge.

So, if you have a sale of $100, you will have up to $2.20 subtracted from that amount, and the money will be deposited directly into the account that you specify within a specific period of time (usually 2 to 3 business days).

Accepting credit cards can be an expensive proposition, but it is a major convenience for your customers and they will be very happy that you have the ability to accept credit cards. If you have an establishment in which you receive customers, you are almost obliged to accept credit cards. Without that option, your customers may find it more convenient to go to another establishment that does accept credit cards. The best thing to do is to take the cost of the credit card charges into account when you are determining what you will charge for your treatments.

Gratuities and Tips

Gratuity and **tip** are two words that are interchangeable and can be either very important or inconsequential to you depending on your type of establishment. If the establishment is a medical setting, gratuities should not be depended on and possibly should even be discouraged. The reason for this is that accepting gratuities would change the customer's perception of the treatment from a medically oriented treatment to a non-medically oriented treatment. If the treatment is more of a personal service treatment, which would include home visits, gratuities should be accepted happily *and taken with gratitude.*

TIDBIT

The best place to start looking for credit card information is the bank at which you currently do business. This is just a start.

A CONVENIENT FORM OF PAYMENT

We did not accept credit cards until about 2001. For the first few years, credit cards were used for less than 10 percent of our business. In the past few years, that percentage has grown to over 60 percent. Credit cards are a convenience for our customers and also for us. Many customers keep their card numbers on file for us to charge them, and we do this service for them gladly. We are able to process credit payments on the same day without having to make a lot of trips to the bank to deposit them, which is a big convenience for us. (LSR)

Tips and gratuities can play an important part in your financial well-being, yet please remember that tips are optional and not something you should depend on. If you do depend on them, you may develop a bad attitude if you do not receive a tip that you think you deserve. If you don't receive a tip, you should look for the reason. Please look in the mirror before you look elsewhere if you are not satisfied with how a customer treats you financially. If the situation becomes more common than not, it is time to recognize what you may be doing wrong. If you don't, you may be losing customers as well as tips.

The way that your customers treat you, both financially and otherwise, is a good measure of their satisfaction with your treatment and how they have been served. Remember to put yourself in the shoes of your customers, and you may see a different side to your treatment to them and your treatment of them. If the treatment that you provide is fantastic, but the customer service that you provide to them is not good, then the overall effect will be negative.

All payments should be made at the time that the services are provided. You should not have any accounts receivable in your business unless you accept insurance payments. If you do accept insurance payments, you must collect any co-pay from your customers at the time that services are rendered.

Insurance Reimbursement

Are you going to accept **insurance reimbursement** for your services? When it comes to insurance payments, nothing is guaranteed. It is important that you have an understanding with your customer that if your services are not paid for by the insurance company, then your customer is responsible for the balance due unless his or her contract specifies that the individual is responsible for only a specific fixed co-payment.

The most important thing you must do when it comes to insurance reimbursement is to get all the information up front and verify all coverage prior to the first visit of your customer (Figure 14.2). You need to follow the procedures outlined below to minimize nonpayment by insurance companies. Please refer to the insurance verification form in Chapter 16 and Appendix E, and complete the form by calling the insurance company and verifying the following:

1. Is your customer insured by the insurance company?

2. Does your customer's insurance company reimburse for the treatments that you provide?

3. Does your customer's insurance company pay you for the treatments that you provide? Are you an approved provider for these services?

4. Are there any special restrictions to the treatment that you are providing, such as the amount of time spent per session and the number of sessions allowed per diagnosis, week, month, or year?

Insurance companies are sticklers for detail, so make sure all paperwork is filled out properly whether it is filed by hand or electronically

FIGURE 14.2

5. What amount of money is allowed for the treatment, and what amount of money will be paid for the treatment?

6. Are there any other special requirements for the reimbursement of the treatment?

7. Are there any documents, other than a physician's prescription, that are required for reimbursement? Are SOAP notes required for reimbursement?

8. What is the customer's financial obligation with reference to co-payment or in the case of nonpayment by the insurance company?

Referrals from Medical Professionals

When a chiropractor or medical doctor sends a patient to you for treatment, this is called a *physician referral* or *doctor referral*. Such referrals can be very important to you because they lend a high amount of credibility to your work. Referrals can also open a door to liaisons or partnerships with referring physicians who can continually contribute to your customer base. But you need to remember that physicians and other health care practitioners require a medically acceptable range of care and handling of paperwork or they will not use your services.

These requirements stem from three reasons: Physicians are under strict codes of ethical and moral practice and can be charged with malpractice if they refer inappropriately; customers referred out will not return to the physician if they are unhappy with the referred care; and insurance companies will not pay the physicians for their customers' care if you do not keep adequate and clinically legal and clear documentation.

Most medical insurance companies, rehabilitation agents, and workers' compensation agencies require detailed SOAP notes (see pages 173–176 or Appendix E). They may also require a written narrative.

TIDBIT

It is important to acknowledge referrals not only from health care providers but also from your current customers who refer new customers to your business.

Bartering and Exchange of Services

Bartering occurs when you trade your goods or services for someone else's goods or services. Unless you and the other person are totally clear about each other's expectations before the exchange, there is no chance that the barter will be successful. We recommend that any barter or exchange-for-services agreement be put in writing. Even with the transaction documented, one person often ends up "on the short end of the stick." Make sure that you review the success of the situation on a very regular basis and that all parties are happy with the results of the bartering. Be cautious of creating special deals; they can be back-breakers. Remember, all income derived from bartering is taxable.

CHECKLIST

Have you done these things yet?

☐ Have you done enough research to decide what your fees will be?

☐ What amount do you need to make to meet expenses?

☐ What is the going rate for similar services in the area?

☐ How many treatments do you need to do?

☐ What forms of payment will you accept?

☐ Will you accept insurance?

SO WHAT DO YOU THINK?

1. If you are a sole proprietor, is it really important to write out policies? After all, you are the only one making decisions, right?

2. Is it really important for you to figure out how many treatments per week you need to do, or can you just work as much and make as much as you can? What are the advantages and disadvantages of working each way?

3. Is it worth your while to accept credit cards or insurance reimbursement for payment of services?

Additional Business Policies

CHAPTER FIFTEEN

LEARNING OUTCOMES

After completing this chapter, you should be able to:

15.1 Accurately determine the most advantageous hours of operation for you.

15.2 Identify your focus.

15.3 Recognize good customer service.

15.4 Integrate all aspects of appropriate professional relationships into your practice.

KEY TERMS

micro view of hours

macro view of hours

treatment

customer interaction

dual relationship

In addition to requiring financial policies, your business will depend on policies in many other areas of operation. These policies will help you keep your business in line with what you want to, and need to, accomplish. The policies outlined in this chapter pertain to your relationship and interaction with your customers.

Hours of Operation

What are the times that your establishment should be open for business? In order to determine hours of operation, you first need to determine the hours your customers will be available and most likely will be requesting your services. Do not assume you know availability; ask potential customers what their optimal hours for your services would be. Ask the neighboring businesses what their hours of operation are so that you can accommodate their employees as customers, as well as their customers (if you are opening a physical office); a percentage of your business may consist of people within the local area. In addition, you can call other establishments that provide similar services and set your hours by their example, especially if they have been operating for a number of years and appear to know the customers in the area well. Take into consideration the demographics of your potential customers, such as working women with children. For these potential customers, child care and school hours may be an issue. Combine all the information you have gathered from this research, and blend it with your personal needs to determine the hours of operation for your business.

This is not, however, a cut-and-dried matter. Although there are no hard-and-fast rules that say when an establishment should be open, common sense should prevail. When looking at your hours of operation, you can use them as a marketing advantage for your potential customers. If you operate your business during hours that nobody else is open, you may have a distinct advantage over other similar businesses. However, if you notice that people are not able to take advantage of your services at those times, the unusual hours may not be an advantage after all. You should strive to maximize the number of treatments or sessions you can perform, but the hours of operation must be convenient for your customers.

Charting Hours

It is smart to keep track of the busiest days and the busiest times of day that your business experiences. This is not a quick process; it must be charted over a period of time. There is both a micro and a macro view of the hours needed to be open.

The **micro view of hours** consists of the busiest hours of the day and the busiest days of the week. The micro view can be tracked very easily by looking at your schedule book over a period of weeks. Simply mark the hours of the day and the days of the week that are filled with treatments. Noting the number of treatments over a 10-week period by hour is one way to keep track of the micro view of the busiest hours. Figure 15.1 shows an example of how to keep track of your micro hours per week.

By keeping track of the number of treatments for each hour on a regular basis, you will be able to track your busiest days and your busiest times of the day. This will help you to not only adjust your business hours but also plan for any adjustments that you may need to make within your schedule. These adjustments may include adding additional staff for busier times or reducing staff during leaner periods in each week. Please remember that your customers get used to your business hours very quickly, so changing them often is not recommended. As you can see from the data in Figure 15.1, the establishment does not have to be open before 9 a.m., and it would be possible to reduce the end-of-the-day hours on certain days of the week. Additionally, if it is required to have a set lunch hour, it would make sense to make that lunch hour

FIGURE 15.1

Example of a week of treatments

Hour	Monday	Tuesday	Wednesday	Thursday	Friday	Saturday	Sunday
8:00 AM	0	0	0	0	0	0	0
9:00 AM	3	2	2	3	4	2	0
10:00 AM	3	2	2	4	3	5	0
11:00 AM	4	3	3	4	4	6	0
12:00 PM	5	6	5	5	6	4	0
1:00 PM	6	6	6	5	5	3	0
2:00 PM	3	2	2	1	1	1	0
3:00 PM	3	3	2	2	3	4	0
4:00 PM	4	5	4	3	4	6	0
5:00 PM	6	7	5	6	6	7	0
6:00 PM	6	6	6	7	7	3	0
7:00 PM	5	6	4	4	3	2	0
8:00 PM	2	3	2	2	1	0	0

coincide with a slower time of day, if at all possible. In Figure 15.1, a lunchtime of 2 p.m. would make much more sense than a lunchtime of either 12 or 1 p.m.

The **macro view of hours** consists of the busiest times of the month and year. More specifically, it shows the busiest times during seasonal periods and holidays, beyond just the normal variations of a business week. The ability to make adjustments is crucial to businesses operating in "seasonal" areas. Figure 15.2 shows how to track your yearly treatments to figure out your macro hours.

The intent here is not only to see the number of treatments performed but also to understand how well your time and your employees time were managed. This information can be extremely valuable. Looking at Figure 15.2, you can see that if you want to cut back on the number of days worked, you would maximize the number of treatments in a week if you cut Thursday from your schedule because Thursdays have had the least number of treatments historically. Another thing that you can look at is the variation in the number of treatments at different times of the year. After a relatively short time, you will be able to "predict" the number of treatments that you will be performing during a certain week. This is helpful in planning vacations, employee schedules, and, most importantly, your hours of operation.

Treatment Types

Which types of **treatment** you will provide in your establishment depends on many different factors, including, but not limited to, space, education, experience, licensing, finances, demand, and staffing. If you are a sole practitioner, the services offered will be limited, which may or may not be a bad thing; in fact, it can and should be used to your advantage. If you have a specialty treatment that you are particularly good at, that is what you should be offering your customers. It is not a wise choice to attempt to perform a treatment or modality that you are not proficient at. Your customer is unlikely to be satisfied with less than optimal service. That is not to say you have to be a master of all modalities; simply learn to capitalize on what you do best.

REALITY CHECK

PAY ATTENTION TO YOUR SEASONS

South Florida is a seasonal area, and the first year that I was in practice, I didn't realize how much my business was going to drop off. It was a lean off-season, to say the least. Only then did I realize the importance of planning for the lean times during the better times. (LSR)

How do you become proficient in a technique? The first thing that you must do is learn from someone who is good at the technique that you want to learn. The next step is to practice what you have learned for at least 100 hours. During that time it would be ideal to practice on the person who taught you, if at all possible. Additionally, it would be very good if you practiced on others who have used the same or similar techniques for a period of time.

It is very difficult, if not impossible, to do more than one or two types of therapy well and be proficient at them. It is far better to be good at one or two types of treatment than to be not as good at several types of treatments. This is not to say that a therapist cannot perform more than one type of service, but it is a warning not to try to be all things for all people. This is where a group of practitioners can work together to provide a wider variety of services for your customers. This group can consist of an informal system of referrals, a group of therapists sharing office space, or an actual partnership. The important point is to provide your customers with services in a professional manner that they are happy with.

FIGURE 15.2

Example of yearly treatments

Week	Monday	Tuesday	Wednesday	Thursday	Friday	Saturday	Sunday	Total Week	Total Year
1	6	7	5	4	5	7	0	34	34
2	5	6	6	3	6	7	0	33	67
3	7	6	5	3	7	6	0	34	101
4	6	7	4	5	7	7	0	36	137
5	7	6	5	5	6	6	0	35	172
6	5	6	5	5	8	5	0	34	206
7	8	7	4	4	7	8	0	38	244
8	7	8	4	4	7	6	0	36	280
9	6	6	5	5	8	8	0	38	318
10	7	7	6	4	8	7	0	39	357
43	8	6	6	4	7	5	2	38	395
44	7	6	7	4	7	7	0	38	433
45	7	7	5	4	8	8	0	39	472
46	8	7	7	5	8	7	0	42	514
47	7	8	6	4	7	7	0	39	553
48	7	6	6	3	6	7	0	35	588
49	6	8	5	5	7	6	3	40	628
50	8	7	6	5	7	7	0	40	668
51	7	7	6	4	8	7	0	39	707
52	8	6	5	5	8	7	0	39	746
Total	137	134	108	85	142	135	5	746	746

DO WHAT FITS

My massage training was mostly based on neuromuscular and sports massage. From that base, I added the unique art of Thai massage to create what I refer to as an eclectic blend of therapeutic massage. My proficiency at that particular blend is my version of being good at one or two modalities. The proof is in the clients, who come from all across the country for "season" for this particular massage. For all other work, I refer out. (JLS)

If you are a sole practitioner specializing in one type of treatment or modality, keep on hand business cards of therapists who work in different modalities whom you can refer customers to. This practice earns respect from customers, and you will find those customers are more likely to return as customers when they need the particular therapy you perform.

If you are planning an organization that has multiple therapists in a shared office space, the same quality-of-service principles apply. Each therapist should offer work according to her or his strengths for better customer satisfaction. If your organization is focusing on a specific type of therapy, such as sports-related injuries, all the people in the organization should have an understanding of, and focus on, sports-related therapies.

When there is no focus, or identity, for the organization, the business will not achieve its goals and the success or very existence of the business may be in jeopardy. Here are some questions to ask yourself: What is the focus of the business? Why is the focus of the business so important? How do we find out whether or not the business is following the right track and is focusing on the correct things? For answers to the last question, look back at your mission statement and your goals. Are you fulfilling them? Are you headed in the right direction? If not, why? Is it because you have lost sight of your goals, or is it because you have found that your mission statement and goals have changed? If you have lost your way, it is time to get back on track by reviewing why you are off track and how you got there. If your mission statement and goals have changed, it is time to go back to the beginning and make revisions, if necessary. Goals are not carved in stone; they are always evolving along with your life experiences. Before you abandon your mission statement and goals, consult with all of your advisers.

Customer Interaction

Customer interaction comes in two forms. The first is professional interaction during treatments, office visits, and home visits. The second is all other interaction that takes place under all other circumstances.

Professional interaction should be just that: professional. What does *professional* mean? What is not professional? This seems to be a very easy subject on the surface, yet the term *professional* can take on many different meanings depending on the individual circumstances. One simple example is attire. In some venues, shorts can be proper attire as part of a uniform, whereas in a medical office setting the wearing of shorts would be inappropriate. Attire may not seem like customer interaction, yet it is precisely your appearance that a patient sees. If you are not dressed in a professional manner, you will not be seen as a professional in the eyes of your customers.

Professional dress is different in different places and for different reasons, but there certainly is dress that is unprofessional. What that consists of is something that the customer notices that is not normal. Something that your customer sees as inappropriate *is* inappropriate. As stated before, there are some instances where shorts and a short-sleeve shirt are completely appropriate for the treatment that you are providing, and sometimes they are inappropriate. The individual circumstances are the telling factor in what is appropriate or not.

SAYING NO MAY MEAN MORE BUSINESS

A customer called to say that he was having a particular problem and he wanted to make an appointment with me. I suggested that instead of making an appointment for therapy, he should go to a local health food store and tell the staff what he had just told me. When he asked me why, I explained to him that they may be able to help him with supplements for his problem, and if they couldn't help him or the supplements didn't work, then he should call me right away. He called two days later and said that his problem was gone, and he thanked me for saving him the travel time to my establishment and the cost of at least one treatment, which most likely would not have helped. In the following week or so, he referred three new customers to me, telling them that they could trust me because he knew that I was honest. (LSR)

Here is the bottom line on what is important about the way that you, as a professional, dress: If something that you wear, or don't wear, is inappropriate, you will lose customers, jobs, and, potentially, your livelihood. Nobody is really going to care more about that than you. Making a statement with what you are wearing is far less important than making a living at what you are doing.

So how you look is very important to professional interaction. In fact, people will determine a lot about you by the way you look even before you begin to speak. They will have their minds made up, and it may be very difficult for you to change their first impressions of you.

Once you have your professional look down, it is time to understand what professional speech is. It is easy to speak in a professional manner; unfortunately, it is much easier to speak unprofessionally. There are certain things that are inappropriate no matter what, including cursing, off-color comments or jokes, and personal remarks that are not specifically related to the customer's condition or treatment.

There are a number of circumstances in which the line gets very fuzzy when therapists are speaking with people about their conditions. Certain personal activities may affect a person's physical condition, and it is imperative that you know what is happening in the life of your customer for you to treat him or her. The line will be determined by you and the customer. It should be one that is agreed on with respect and openness, particularly toward the customer's desires. You should also be very aware that none of your customers should cross the line of your comfort zone. Nobody should feel uncomfortable, including you, during interactions.

Additionally, your personal business should be just that, personal and yours. It need not be shared with any of your customers. If a topic is something that does not belong in the newspaper, it does not belong in a conversation between you and your customer. No matter how personal a customer's conversation is with you, you should not reciprocate with the customer. This is particularly important when things are not going all that well in your personal life. Nobody wants to hear your sad story about how things are going badly in your marriage, relationship, family, or business ventures. People also don't want to hear how well things are going for you and how great your relationships are and that your sex life couldn't be better. The list goes on and on. The whole point is that the conversation between you and your customer should be about professional matters and not much else. See Chapter 11 for further discussion on this topic.

This does not mean that some personal conversation cannot occur. For example, it would behoove you to ask a customer how his or her family is, and if there is someone who is sick, it would be a great idea to ask specifically how that person is doing. You can also offer some general information about your life, such as family members. This doesn't mean that you have permission to tell your customers all the details of your life, but you can let them know that you do have a life.

IT IS HOW YOU SAY IT

One of the toughest things for students to grasp is that they cannot talk with clients in the same way they talk with friends while "hanging out." In the classroom I constantly have to emphasize this point through proper grammar, pronunciation, enunciation, and use of medical terminology.

For those not in a classroom any longer, it may be a difficult task to break bad habits. Such habits include all mannerisms, or "reactions," that have become habitual, such as a sigh or overuse of colloquialisms or catchphrases. (JLS)

There are innumerable options for both professional and unprofessional client interaction between the professional and the customer. This is a very tricky subject, and one that can be argued in regard to what degree of interaction is appropriate between a customer and a professional. What is acceptable and what is not acceptable must be determined on a case-by-case basis.

One thing that does not have to be determined on a case-by-case basis is the point at which an interaction between a customer and a professional crosses the legal line of acceptance. There are laws that prohibit a sexual relationship between a professional and a customer in certain professions, no matter what circumstances it occurs under.

But what about relationships that are clearly not illegal yet are very social in nature? This is where the line gets blurred and difficulties crop up fast. Having a social or business relationship in addition to a therapist-customer relationship is called a **dual relationship**. This occurs when you and your customer have more than one role in your interaction with each other. This can be successful at times, or it can create friction; it can also lose you a friend, customer, or business associate.

How can that be? Well, let's say you and a long-time customer have shared many good times together, as well as tough times, as therapist and customer. Then one day the two of you go out and have dinner on a social basis. The dynamics of the relationship have just changed: Your customer is now also your friend. Does the relationship in the treatment room change? If you say no, you are just kidding yourself. Some of the things that you say to your customer will be heard by her as your friend, and that friend will take what you say in a different way than would be the case if she were just your customer.

How about if a long-term customer invests in your business and therefore becomes a business partner. This person, who has seen you for a long time, continues to want to see you, but now he expects different treatment because he is your partner—a special case who should have special treatment. Don't you see the same thing with your family and close friends? They expect special treatment because of their special relationship with you. You are not going to treat your friends or family the same as everybody else when it comes to business.

The circumstances do not matter; what matters is how you are to deal with the potential problems that can result from dual relationships. In a perfect world, you would not have to worry about this potential problem, but none of us lives in a perfect world. People will take advantage; people will have hurt feelings; people do want to feel special; and people do want to be treated specially. It would be easy to say that you can stay away from dual relationships and you can keep your private and business life out of the treatment room, but it would be foolish to believe this completely. We are human beings and we react in a way that is relational to others, and that can cause problems such as dual relationships.

Given all the problems that can occur, where should the line be drawn and who should draw it? The safest line should be as close to the more conservative choices of you and your customer. This is very difficult to determine, but the successful businessperson will be able to judge where the line is and hopefully stay very clear of that line. Listed below are some examples of where the line can be drawn; each is explained after the list. Please see how easily the line can be crossed and how easily trouble can occur as each line is crossed.

1. **Professional relationship only.** There is no contact of any sort outside the professional setting. There is cursory knowledge of each other's personal life, yet there is no knowledge of intimate details of each other's lives.

2. **Professional relationship with personal interaction in the professional setting.** There is still contact only within the professional setting, yet the parties (one or both) share intimate details of their lives.

3. **Professional relationship with personal interaction outside the professional setting.** There is contact both inside and outside the professional setting, along with a sharing of intimate details of one party's or both parties' lives.

Example 1

There should be no issues with dual relationships whatsoever. There should not be any problems with interactions beyond those of the therapist-customer relationship. The roles that each party plays in the relationship are clearly defined and should not have any negative impact on the relationship.

Example 2

There are three possible combinations in this type of relationship: The first is that the customer relates intimate personal details to the therapist; the second is that the therapist relates intimate personal details to the customer; and the last is that each party relates intimate personal details to the other party.

The first scenario is very common and most likely does not pose a problem in the relationship, for much of the time the customer is looking for a professional whom he or she can trust. The only caveat here is that you must not practice any kind of treatment beyond the scope of practice of your license. If you are not a mental health care professional, you cannot give advice as one. You can, however, be a good listener and be supportive of your customer.

The second scenario is unfortunately also all too common. There are no circumstances that would dictate that you give intimate personal details to a customer. Even if a customer is going through a crisis that you went through, you should simply state that you can empathize with her or him because you went through a similar situation in your life—no further details need be shared. It may feel good to be getting this off your chest, but it is not good for the customer to be hearing any of the details.

The third scenario can cause many problems also. It allows the communication to become far too personal, and there then becomes no separation between the therapist and the customer. They can become too dependent on each other's listening, and the therapist and customer can and will trade places in the relationship, which is not what a therapist-customer relationship should be. This is unhealthy for the relationship, and it will eventually cause problems between the two parties.

Example 3

You will begin to see many more problems crop up as the relationship drifts further and further away from a strictly therapist-customer relationship. As the line of the relationship begins to blur, the authority, or expertise, of the therapist will come to be questioned by the customer, simply because the customer will perceive the therapist more as a friend than as a therapist. The way a friend listens to another friend is completely different from the way a customer listens to a therapist. What would you, as a therapist, do if a customer disobeyed a direct instruction regarding her care between visits? You would explain to the customer why it is imperative that she follow your directions for her well-being, and you would tell her that if she does not follow the directions you give in the future, you will have no choice but to drop her as a customer because of noncompliance. If a customer has a personal relationship with you outside the professional setting, she will be less likely to follow your instructions and, when confronted, will tend to be adamant about not following your instructions. At this point, you have lost the person as a compliant customer and also as a friend, because you will begin to resent the fact that your customer is not taking you as seriously as she should and the customer will begin to resent you for trying to pull rank on her.

If your relationship goes further than casual friendship and becomes a sexual relationship, you have crossed a line into an area that most likely will lead to official problems, whether from a licensing board, the police, or possibly a civil action against you by your former customer–love interest. There are very specific rules with regard to this.

Customer interaction is one of the most difficult balancing acts that you will face in a professional setting. How you set up your policy on this subject will greatly reduce the possibility of any problems. You must draw the line of demarcation and stay on the right side of that line as much as you can. Under certain circumstances you will cross that line from time to time. Before you do so, it is imperative that you review why you are crossing the line, how far you will be crossing the line, and what the potential for problems is if you cross the line.

Customer Service

Customer service has been touched on in several places in this book, yet there should be policies set for customer service. The bottom line in customer service is to provide excellent customer service that will win you more customers. The areas that are of most importance to any customer are time, convenience, honesty, safety, and satisfaction. Though these seem like the same old catchwords, they are important and they will make or break a business.

Top Tips of Success

Along with adhering to the standards and ethics of your profession, follow the "tidbits," or highlights, listed below to ensure a healthy and successful career (Figure 15.3).

1. ***Communication is the key.*** Whether you are discussing your session length, fees, or cancellation policy, clarity is appreciated by clients. It gives them a sense of security in your professionalism. Further, you must stay in contact with clients if you are unavoidably stuck in traffic, caught with a flat tire, or too ill to work.

2. ***Recognize your pivotal person, and appreciate him or her.*** There will be at least one, and often more than one, pivotal person during the course of your career. This is a person from whom many other clients will manifest through direct or related contact. Appreciate this person by treating him or her well. This does not mean you should give your pivotal person better service than anyone else; it means you should extend your gratitude for his or her support with a simple "thank you" or perhaps gift certificates or the like. Your pivotal person is also the client you always work into your schedule no matter how tight it is.

> *Hard work and careful planning lead to success, and success is a great feeling*

FIGURE 15.3

3. ***Always be professional in your demeanor and attire.*** If you are working out of your own space, be it your home or office, it can be a great temptation to have a more relaxed attitude. However, approach every appointment as if you were in a professional office located outside your space. In many companies, employees spend certain days a week working from home. Much is made of these people sitting in their pajamas at the computer and phone. Although you certainly wouldn't greet a client in your pajamas, you also do not want to be so relaxed in your attire that it exudes laziness. Clients will read this as indifference toward them and your work.

4. ***Punctuality is of utmost importance.*** You must be on time, if not a few minutes early, for all appointments. Clients will allow themselves to be late getting home (for a home visit) or be delayed in getting off the phone, but tardiness from the therapist will put you in disfavor. Clients will simply choose to work with another therapist if you are repeatedly or inexcusably late. In addition, you must refrain from changing appointments for personal reasons. A note here: Often when you start tinkering with your schedule (moving clients around to "accommodate" changes), the whole thing falls apart and you may find yourself with many canceled appointments or missed opportunities for work.

5. ***Never handle personal business while working on a client.*** A friend dropped her regular therapist because he started answering his cell phone while working on her. In this case, the therapist took the client for granted after a long working relationship by mistakenly believing she would not mind if he picked up the phone when his stockbroker called. Do not let familiarity breed contempt.

6. ***Always be upbeat even if you are not feeling well or are a little "down."*** As much as it is a cliché to answer "Fine" when someone asks "How are you?" this is a good principle to follow. Clients will feel bad if you are not feeling well, are too tired from all the work, or are having some sort of difficulty.

7. ***Always be honest.*** If you can't be trusted, you won't last long in any business. You have to be honest in your financial dealings, as well as in your treatments. Your policy should show that you have your customer's welfare ahead of your

REALITY CHECK

BALANCING AVAILABILITY AND CONVENIENCE

When we opened our office, I continued to do a limited number of home visits. As I continued to build my practice, I reduced the number of home visits and today do just a few. This is not convenient for many of my customers who would love for me to go to their homes, yet I could not possibly see the number of customers in a day that I currently do if I was traveling to their homes. For these customers, the inconvenience of having to come to my office is countered by their ability to get an appointment at all. (LSR)

own financial gains. This means that you won't treat a customer when treatment isn't needed or will be ineffective. You won't charge for services that you did not perform, and you have the financial well-being of your customer in mind when you plan for her or his care.

8. *Think of convenience for your customer first.* Are you asking your customers to inconvenience themselves without good reason? Are you asking them to do something that takes away from the experience that you are providing them? An example of this is giving a customer a treatment while construction is going on in the next room. The noise and commotion are a definite problem if the customer wants to relax during the treatment. Your policy should allow for the highest amount of convenience for all of your customers as a whole.

CHECKLIST

Have you done these things yet?

☐ Have you charted hours of operation to determine the optimal hours for you to be open?

☐ Have you established a clear focus of the type of service you will be providing?

☐ Have you developed a clear understanding of the professional relationship?

☐ Have you listed at least five ways to increase your chances of success?

☐ Have you determined whether they fit with your personality, or will you have to change some things?

SO WHAT DO YOU THINK?

1. How important is it to have clearly defined customer and service provider roles? What are the pitfalls of not having clearly defined boundaries?

2. What are some words that should not be used when speaking with customers, and what are the proper alternatives?

3. What are examples of professional and unprofessional dress in your situation?

Medical Documentation

CHAPTER SIXTEEN

LEARNING OUTCOMES

After completing this chapter, you should be able to:

16.1 Determine how to set up a proper patient file.

16.2 Create client intake/history forms for your type of business.

16.3 Write proper SOAP notes.

16.4 Identify what documents are needed to file for insurance.

16.5 Understand the Health Insurance Portability and Accountability Act.

KEY TERMS

client intake/history form

SOAP notes

health insurance claim

preauthorization

carrier

carrier identification number

coding

deductible

co-pay

coinsurance

Health Insurance Portability and Accountability Act (HIPAA)

INTRODUCTION

Running a business requires handling an enormous amount of paperwork (Figure 16.1). You may be able to navigate through it yourself, but if you are not an organized person by nature, you may want to hire someone to set up a system that you can work with. Being lost in a sea of paperwork can be debilitating and put an end to what is an otherwise healthy business. Set aside a few minutes each day, week, or month to properly fill out and file all paperwork to stay current and compliant with the law.

Patient/Customer Paperwork

There are many forms that fall into the category of patient paperwork. The type of establishment that you are running will determine some of the paperwork that you will be using on a day-to-day basis. The first form that is needed is the **client intake/history form**, which should consist of personal information, such as name, address, phone numbers, and medical information required for specific types of treatment. The amount of detail will be greater for a treatment given in conjunction with other medical procedures than for simpler treatments such as spa work. This is not to imply that therapists who do relaxation work do not need to have medical information, but it does mean that there may be more complications in the treatment process for customers who have had medical procedures. If you are operating a well-ness center where there is an acupuncturist or naturopathic physician on board, the client intake will need to be more extensive.

In all cases, the minimum of information required is:

- **Name.** Include the first, middle, and last.
- **Address.** Include street (and apartment number), city, state, and zip code.
- **Phone numbers.** Include home phone, cell phone, and business phone.
- **Age (birth date), sex, and marital status.** (*Note:* The Social Security number is not necessary; in fact, if you are not billing insurance, it would be better if you do not include the Social Security number. With the increase in identity theft, people are becoming more hesitant to give out that information.)
- **Employer's name and address.** This serves several purposes. First, it may give you insight into the possible causation of the customer's condition. If a customer works in an office setting, you may be able to deduce the reason for

Don't get lost in that sea of paperwork

FIGURE 16.1

the right shoulder pain that he or she is experiencing. Second, the employer's business may be a great place to market your practice, though you must keep in mind your customer's privacy.

- **Basic medical questions.** Include questions on headaches, fainting, dizziness, tingling, weakness or swelling in any of the extremities, chest pains, blood pressure issues, heart conditions, diabetes, and pregnancy. This list is not all-inclusive, but it is a basic start. It is important that the intake form matches the type of treatments that are being performed and thus the amount of information that is needed by the therapist. If a customer is looking for a relaxing treatment, she or he surely does not want to fill out a 10-page health questionnaire, yet if the proper information is not recorded on the health questionnaire, the treatment requested may not be appropriate given the condition of the customer.

- **Physicians' names, past treatments, and medication.** Include the names of the customer's primary physician and of any other physician who is currently treating the person. Also ask if there is any medical condition that the customer has been treated for in the past year, and have your customer list all the medications and supplements that he or she is taking. This is very important, because many people tend to forget whether they have a medical condition and what medicine they are taking for it. The list of medications can serve as a double-check of the customer's condition.

- **Accident question.** Ask whether or not the visit is a result of an accident (either work-related, auto, or other).

- **Reason for the customer's visit.** If the customer is looking for a treatment to relax, you need to know that fact. If your customer wants a treatment that accomplishes something such as an increase in the range of motion of the right shoulder, you should be planning your treatment to accomplish that. It is imperative that you pay attention to the type of treatment that is requested by the customer. Not only will this information enable you to better serve your customer, but it will give you an opportunity to inform your customer about what your plan of treatment will be and how it will accomplish your customer's goals.

- **Past therapy treatments.** Ask whether or not your customer has had a similar treatment in the past; if the answer is yes, ask for more specifics, such as what treatment and how often. It is important that you know the experiences of your customers and what those experiences were like for them. Knowing any of their preferences will be helpful in determining your treatment approach.

- **Customer signature and date.** This is important because it provides a start date for your treatment.

Client intake/history forms must be updated every six months. If there are no changes, have the patient sign off on that.

If a customer is coming to you as a result of an auto accident or a work-related accident, or if a customer wants to use health insurance to cover your services, you will have to do quite a bit more paperwork and verification of information. This verification includes checking that your customer has coverage, what the coverage consists of, and what the customer's responsibility is regarding any co-pay or payment that must be provided at the time that the services are rendered.

Examples of Client Intake/History Forms

Client intake forms come in many varieties. Figure 16.2 shows a basic intake form used by a massage-specific business. The information form in Figure 16.3 is used by a wellness business (acupuncture, herbalist, etc.). Both forms are suitable for any type of customer.

TIDBIT

If a new customer tells you that every time she received a treatment in the past, she was sore and bruised, you should take that as a clue to use a lighter touch than you normally would for her first treatment. Explain that everyone responds to a therapist's touch differently and that you will work lighter at first and then gradually increase the pressure.

FIGURE 16.2

CLIENT INTAKE FORM

NAME _____ DATE _____

Address _____

Phone _____ Cell phone/pager _____

E-mail _____

Occupation _____

Referred by _____

Physician _____

Are you currently being treated? _____

Are you taking any medications? If so, what? _____

HAVE YOU HAD ANY OF THE FOLLOWING DURING THE PAST YEAR?

__SEVERE HEADACHE __ FAINTING __ DIZZINESS __ CHEST PAINS __ HEART PROBLEMS
__NUMBNESS/TINGLING OR SWELLING IN HANDS/FEET __ HIGH/LOW BLOOD PRESSURE
__PREGNANT__HERNIATED DISCS __ OTHER

Is this a result of an auto accident or work-related? _____

I AM SEEKING TREATMENT FOR: _____

Have you ever had a massage before? _____

How often? _____

I hereby request and consent to massage therapy and any other therapies that are included within the scope of the professional treating me. I understand I will be receiving massage for therapeutic reasons and understand there are some risks to treatment including—but not limited to—soreness, bruises, and inflammatory pain. I do not expect the therapist to be able to anticipate or explain all risks and complications, and wish to rely on the therapist to exercise reasonable skill during the course of treatment.

I understand that massage therapy may involve some undressing. I understand that at all times the therapist will abide by my wishes with regards to my comfort level of undress. I also understand that I can request an area not to be treated or exposed.

I have read, or have had read to me, the above consent. I have also had the opportunity to ask questions regarding its content, and by signing below I agree to the above-named procedures. I intend this consent form to cover treatment for my present as well as all future conditions (and will notify therapist of such).

PATIENT'S SIGNATURE _____

TIDBIT

New practitioners are always concerned that clients may not disclose all their conditions or medications. You are not a mind reader. You can only go on what they tell you. Take all other signs and symptoms into consideration, and make your best judgment.

Depending on the type of establishment that you are running, some of the questions in these forms may or may not be necessary or even appropriate for your purposes. The questions that should be used are determined by your policy. Some customers may not want to divulge certain information to you. If you deem such information necessary for your treatment, you should explain to your customer why it is important that he or she provide you with the information that was requested. This situation happens quite a lot with alternative health care providers, and it offers the perfect opportunity to raise the value of your treatments in the eyes of the customer.

A client information form

FIGURE 16.3

Wellness Center

Please note that all information is strictly confidential

First name: _____   Last name: _____

Address: _____   City/postal code: _____

E-mail address: _____   Cell phone: _____

Home phone: _____   Work phone: _____

Date of birth: _____   Age: _____

Marital status: _____   No. of children: _____

Occupation: _____   Primary physician: _____

Emergency contact: _____   Phone #: _____

Whom should we thank for referring you to this office? _____

Have you received acupuncture before, and if so, when? _____

Reason for today's visit: _____

_____

_____

How, when, and where did this condition begin? _____

_____

_____

What types of treatments have you tried, if any? _____

_____

What makes it better? _____

What makes it worse? _____

Please list any other health problems you would like to address, in order of importance: _____

_____

_____

Your Medical History:

Surgeries, major illnesses, hospitalizations, major accidents (include dates): _____

_____

_____

_____

_____

Current medications, supplements, and vitamins (and what they are for): _____

_____

_____

_____

Continued

Do you currently have or have you ever had any of the following?

Anemia   Epilepsy   Fibromyalgia   Arthritis   Diabetes   Multiple sclerosis

Emotional disorder   Drug problem   Digestive disorders   Heart problem

Pacemaker   Tuberculosis   Cancer   Hepatitis   HIV   Allergies

High blood pressure   Kidney disease   Osteoporosis   Asthma   Stroke

Ulcers   Thyroid problem   Kidney stones   Gallstones   Alcoholism   AIDS

Do you have any drug allergies? _____

Lifestyle:

How do you feel about your diet? _____

Exercise?   Yes   No   How often? _____ Type? _____

Sleep: Hours per night _____ Rested in AM? _____

Trouble falling asleep? _____ Trouble staying asleep? _____

Do you get up to urinate more than once? _____

Work: Enjoy work?   Yes   No   Hours per week working _____

Please indicate the use and frequency of the following:

	Yes	No	How Much		Yes	No	How Much
Coffee -				Water -			
Tobacco -				Marijuana -			
Alcohol -				Soda pop -			

Symptom Survey (please check all that apply)

0 = never   1 = rarely   2 = occasionally   3 = frequently   4 = always

0 1 2 3 4 low appetite	0 1 2 3 4 ravenous appetite
0 1 2 3 4 loose stools	0 1 2 3 4 heartburn/acid reflux
0 1 2 3 4 gas/abdominal bloating	0 1 2 3 4 mouth sores
0 1 2 3 4 fatigue after eating	0 1 2 3 4 belching or vomiting
0 1 2 3 4 organ prolapses	0 1 2 3 4 gums bleeding/swollen
0 1 2 3 4 bruise easily	0 1 2 3 4 thirst

0 1 2 3 4 spontaneous sweat	0 1 2 3 4 fatigue
0 1 2 3 4 allergies	0 1 2 3 4 catch colds easily
0 1 2 3 4 asthma	0 1 2 3 4 tired after exercise
0 1 2 3 4 shortness of breath	0 1 2 3 4 general weakness
0 1 2 3 4 cough	0 1 2 3 4 nasal discharge
0 1 2 3 4 dry nose/mouth/skin/throat	0 1 2 3 4 sinus congestion

0 1 2 3 4 sore, cold, or weak knees	0 1 2 3 4 feel cold often
0 1 2 3 4 low-back pain	0 1 2 3 4 edema
0 1 2 3 4 frequent urination	0 1 2 3 4 impaired memory
0 1 2 3 4 urinary incontinence	0 1 2 3 4 hair loss
0 1 2 3 4 ear/hearing problems	0 1 2 3 4 infertility
0 1 2 3 4 early morning diarrhea	low normal high libido

Continued

A client information form (Continued)

FIGURE 16.3

0 1 2 3 4   irritable   0 1 2 3 4   muscle spasms/twitches
0 1 2 3 4   feel better after exercise   0 1 2 3 4   numb extremities
0 1 2 3 4   tight feeling in chest   0 1 2 3 4   dry, irritated eyes
0 1 2 3 4   alternating diarrhea/constipation   0 1 2 3 4   ear ringing
0 1 2 3 4   symptoms worse with stress   0 1 2 3 4   anger easily
0 1 2 3 4   neck/shoulder tension   0 1 2 3 4   red eyes

_____

0 1 2 3 4   feel heart beating   0 1 2 3 4   chest pain
0 1 2 3 4   insomnia   0 1 2 3 4   disturbing dreams
0 1 2 3 4   sores on tip of tongue   0 1 2 3 4   headaches
0 1 2 3 4   anxiety   0 1 2 3 4   palpitations
0 1 2 3 4   restlessness

_____

0 1 2 3 4   dizzy upon standing   0 1 2 3 4   feeling of heaviness
0 1 2 3 4   see floaters in eyes   0 1 2 3 4   nausea
0 1 2 3 4   heat in palms or soles   0 1 2 3 4   foggy thinking
0 1 2 3 4   afternoon fever   0 1 2 3 4   enlarged lymph nodes
0 1 2 3 4   night sweats   0 1 2 3 4   cloudy urine
0 1 2 3 4   frequently flushed face

_____

Urination: (Circle all that apply)   Burning   Urgent   Scanty

    Difficulty   Profuse   Dribbling   More than 1x a night

Bowel Movements: Frequency _____

Consistency (circle):   well-formed   hard   loose   alternates between formed and loose

Do you ever notice any undigested food, blood, or mucous? _____

Are you thirsty?   Yes   No   If so, do you crave warm or cold drinks? _____

Do you find that you "run" particularly hot or cold? _____

How is your energy in general? _____

Do you often get headaches or migraines?   Yes   No

How do you feel emotionally right now? _____

_____

Women Only:

Are you currently pregnant? _____ Are you on the birth control pill? _____

# of pregnancies _____ # of live births _____   # of miscarriages _____   # of abortions _____

Have you experienced menopause?   Yes   No   When? _____

If you are experiencing menopausal symptoms, please describe: _____

_____

Is your period regular?_____# of days from the start of one period to the start of the next _____

Continued

Average number of days of flow: _____   Flow is: Light   Normal   Heavy

Color is: Pale   Normal   Dark   Bright   Red   Brown   Purple

Blood clots?   Yes   No

Do you get pain or cramps?   Yes   No   Severe?   Yes   No

Nature of pain (circle):   Sharp   Dull   Constant   Intermittent   Burning   Aching

Do you experience any of the following before or during your menstrual period?

Water retention   Breast tenderness/swelling   Depression   Irritability   Migraines

Insomnia   Diarrhea   Constipation   Nausea   Hot flashes   Night sweats

Men Only:

Date of last prostate checkup: _____   Results: _____

Circle all that apply: Groin pain   Decreased libido   Testicular pain   Impotence

Painful urination   Difficult urination   Dribbling urination   Incontinence   Premature ejaculation

Nocturnal emissions   Increased libido   Other: _____

_____

I am committed to your health and well-being. While Chinese medicine is a very thorough health care system, it is not a replacement for Western medical treatment, including regular checkups with your primary care physician. I recommend that you consult a physician regarding any condition for which you are seeking acupuncture treatment. We, the undersigned, do affirm that _____ _____ (print patient name) has been advised by William Stikim A.P. to consult a physician regarding the conditions for which such patient seeks acupuncture treatment.

Patient Signature: _____ **Date:**_____

Licensed Practitioner: _____ **Date:**_____

I consent to acupuncture treatment and other procedures associated with Traditional Oriental Medicine by _____. I have discussed the nature of my treatment with _____.
I understand that methods of treatment may include but are not limited to: acupuncture, massage, moxibustion, gua sha, cupping, electric stimulation, and Chinese herbal medicine.
I have been informed that acupuncture is a safe method of treatment, but that it may have side effects including bruising, numbness, or tingling near the needling sites that may last a few days, and dizziness or fainting. Bruising is a common side effect of cupping and gua sha. Unusual risks of acupuncture include pneumothorax and organ puncture. Slight superficial burns are a possible side effect of moxibustion.

I acknowledge that if I do not give 24 hours notice for cancellation of an appointment, I will be charged a full fee for the missed appointment.

Patient Signature: _____ **Date:** _____

Figure 16.4 is an example of a working intake form for a massage therapy clinic. This clinic does not accept insurance reimbursement, so the form does not contain too much legal information. Some of the things that can be left out are Social Security number, customer license information, and all insurance information.

This intake form is short and to the point. Any additional questions or observations that you may have with regard to the customer can be written on the back of the form. The beauty of this form is that it is not overwhelming for your customer. If there are any additional questions that you feel are necessary for all customers, they can be added to the form.

REALITY CHECK

AN OPPORTUNITY TO EDUCATE

When one of my customers didn't fill out the medications section of my intake form, I asked if he was taking any medication, and he responded that it didn't really matter with regard to the treatment that he was going to receive. I explained to him the physiologic changes that can occur during a treatment, and I explained that the medication can have an effect on the outcome of the treatment. I made my point, and the customer realized that the treatment was valid and effective and that it justified serious thought with regard to his medications. (LSR)

A working intake form

FIGURE 16.4

REHAB & THERAPY, INC.
437 West Main Street
West Palm Beach, FL 33415
(000) 000-0000   Fax (000) 000-0000

NAME _____ DATE _____

ADDRESS _____ PHONE _____
_____ CELL PHONE _____

BIRTH DATE _____ / _____ / _____ SEX _____ MARITAL _____ E-MAIL _____

EMPLOYER _____ EMPLOYER'S PHONE_____

EMPLOYER'S ADDRESS _____

I WAS REFERRED TO REHAB & THERAPY BY _____

HAVE YOU HAD ANY OF THE FOLLOWING DURING THE PAST YEAR:

SEVERE HEADACHES	Y	N	TINGLING/WEAKNESS IN HANDS	Y	N	HAND SWELLING	Y	N
FAINTING	Y	N	TINGLING/WEAKNESS IN FEET	Y	N	FOOT SWELLING	Y	N
DIZZINESS	Y	N	BLOOD PRESSURE/ HEART	Y	N	CHEST PAINS	Y	N
PREGNANCY	Y	N						

NAME OF PRIMARY/FAMILY PHYSICIAN _____

ARE YOU BEING TREATED BY A PHYSICIAN? _____ FOR WHAT?_____

ARE YOU CURRENTLY TAKING ANY DRUGS? _____ PLEASE LIST _____

HAVE YOU BEEN TREATED FOR ANY OTHER MEDICAL CONDITIONS IN THE LAST YEAR?_____

HAVE YOU HAD MASSAGE THERAPY BEFORE?_____ HOW OFTEN DO YOU RECEIVE MASSAGE?_____

IS THIS VISIT A RESULT OF A WORK-RELATED ACCIDENT?_____ IF SO, DATE OF ACCIDENT_____

IS THIS VISIT A RESULT OF AN AUTOMOBILE ACCIDENT?_____ IF SO, DATE OF ACCIDENT_____

I AM SEEKING TREATMENT FOR:_____

PATIENT SIGNATURE _____ DATE _____ / _____ / _____

Logo and license number if required by state law

SOAP Notes

SOAP notes serve several purposes: They allow other practitioners to assume treatment of the client if you are not available; they keep physicians informed of a client's progress; and they are legal documents that may be used in a court of law. The letters in the acronym *SOAP* have the following meanings:

>   *S (subjective)* is what the client tells you (e.g., "My right shoulder hurts.").
>
>   *O (objective)* is what you observe. Take into account everything you notice about the client, from gestures to posture. Remember to make a notation in this section of your notes for every finding: anything found during palpation ("right supraspinatus palpates as hypertonic"), any observations of gait (how the client walks), any change in range of motion ("right shoulder has decreased or limited range of motion"), and anything found during muscle testing ("right supraspinatus and middle deltoid test weak on abduction").
>
>   *A (assessment/action)* is the combination of "S" and "O," or your deductive reasoning of the facts in front of you. If this is the second or subsequent time you have seen this client, "A" can also represent the action you took last session.
>
>   *P (plan)* is the treatment plan you have formulated for a specified amount of time. The plan can also be dictated by a referring physician. The plan is determined by the prescription given to your customer.

As with client intake/history forms, there are a variety of SOAP note formats. In addition to those shown in this chapter, formats are available in various medical software programs. SOAP notes written on an out-call basis are legally acceptable if they are in a spiral-bound notebook; notes in a loose-leaf binder or on single sheets are not acceptable in a court of law.

Making Corrections

Many states have specific policies for handling medical errors and have required forms of notation for legal documents. It is essential that you keep clear and accurate records. Use appropriate medical abbreviations (refer to a good medical dictionary or text for a listing), and properly correct any mistakes that you may make in SOAP notes. Mistakes, such as a misspelling, should have a one-line strike-through and be initialed, and your initials should be circled. Use of "white-out" or correction tape is absolutely forbidden.

Examples of SOAP Notes

SOAP notes are shown in Figures 16.5 through 16.7. All three forms are used by massage-specific businesses.

The form in Figure 16.7 is advantageous simply because it reduces the amount of time and writing required. It can be used for any customer, whether or not you are billing an insurance company for reimbursement. You can take any or all of Figure 16.7 and customize it for your particular needs.

Posttreatment Assessment

A good treatment plan also involves a thorough posttreatment assessment. Take the time to review all SOAP notes from previous sessions. Decide what worked and what did not; make appropriate changes. These changes may involve referring out if the desired result is not being reached, making a change in modality

This client intake form includes SOAP notes

FIGURE 16.5

CLIENT HISTORY FORM WITH SOAP NOTES

Client Name:_____ Date:_____

Address:_____

_____

Date of Birth:_____

Referred by:_____

Physician Name:_____

S: CHIEF COMPLAINT:

    ONSET

    DURATION

    PAIN LEVEL (Scale 1–10)

      WHAT INCR/DECR PAIN

      PAST MEDICAL HX (that may have an impact on chief complaint)

      FAMILY MEDICAL HX (that may have an impact on chief complaint)

      ACTIVITIES OF DAILY LIVING (ADLs)

O: ROM

    STRENGTH

    GAIT

A: ASSESSMENT/ACTION

P: PLAN/TREATMENT

    MODALITIES

    EDUCATION

    FREQUENCY

for a different approach, or making a change in the frequency of treatment for maximum results.

Understanding Insurance

Health care facilities across our nation accept the responsibility of filing insurance claims. With some insurance companies, customers with specific needs for treatment can use their insurance benefits to pay for treatments from an individual therapist not affiliated with a medical facility and not doing treatment from a physician referral. However, the companies that pay individual therapists are still very few.

FIGURE 16.6

Medications should be listed on the client's intake form, and questions should be asked of the client to give the massage therapist a broader understanding of the medications

EVERYDAY GOODFEELING MASSAGE CLINIC
CLIENT INFORMATION/INTAKE FORM

Name: _____   Birth date: _____

Address: _____   Home phone: _____

_____   Cell phone: _____

Occupation: _____   Work phone: _____

General health condition: _____   Usual blood pressure: _____

Have you had any serious or chronic illnesses, operations, infections, or trauma?

_____

_____

_____

Are you in recovery for addictions, emotional issues, or abuse? _____

Are you under a doctor's, chiropractor's, or other health practitioner's care? _____

If so, for what conditions? _____

Please list any medications, vitamins/minerals, or herbal supplements you may be taking, and what each is for.

_____

_____

_____

_____

Do you have any allergies? _____

Do I have permission to contact your doctor/practitioner/therapist? _____

Names of doctors/practitioners/therapists:

_____ Phone # _____

_____ Phone # _____

Why did you come in for our service? _____

What results would you like to achieve? _____

Is this your first massage/treatment? _____

How did you find out about our services? _____

In case of emergency, notify _____ Phone # _____

I have completed this information form to the best of my knowledge. I understand the massage services are designed to be a health aid and are in no way to take the place of a doctor's care when it is indicated. Information exchanged during any massage session is educational in nature and is intended to help me become more familiar and conscious of my own health status and is to be used at my own discretion. I agree to notify this clinic 24 hours in advance of any cancellation.

Date: _____   Signature: _____

Patient Name_____ Date_____

Subjective Information: **Other Information:**

       PAIN ⇩ ROM

_____ Cervical _____   _____

_____ Shoulder _____   _____

_____ Thoracic _____   _____

_____ Lumbar _____   _____

_____ Arm/Hand _____   _____

_____ Leg/Foot _____   _____

_____ Headache_____   _____ None _____ Occasional _____ Frequent _____ Constant

Objective Findings:

           L   R

S TP P T N _____ / _____ Occipital/Splenius

S TP P T N_____ / _____ SCM/Scalenes

S TP P T N_____ / _____ Levator/U. Trapezius

S TP P T N_____ / _____ Rhomboid/M. Trapezius

S TP P T N_____ / _____ Latissimus/L. Trapezius

S TP P T N_____ / _____ Thoracic Paravertebrals

S TP P T N_____ / _____ SITS Group

S TP P T N_____ / _____ Pectoralis Group

S TP P T N_____ / _____ Serratus Anterior

S TP P T N_____ / _____ Lumbar Paravertebrals

S TP P T N_____ / _____ Quadratus Lumborum

S TP P T N_____ / _____ Iliopsoas Group

S TP P T N_____ / _____ Hip Rotators

S TP P T N_____ / _____ Hamstrings/TFL

S TP P T N_____ / _____ Quad Group

S TP P T N_____ / _____ Gastroc/Soleus

S TP P T N_____ / _____ Tibialis Anterior

S TP P T N ___ O ___   S-Spasm   1-Mild   **Response to Treatment:**

S TP P T N ___ T ___   TP-Trigger Point   2   _____ Excellent

S TP P T N ___ H ___   P-Pain   3 ↕   _____ Good

S TP P T N ___ E ___   T-Tenderness   4   _____ Fair

S TP P T N ___ R ___   N-Numbness/Tingling 5-Severe _____ Poor

Treatment:

_____Therapeutic Massage   97124   _____Neuromuscular Reeducation   97112

_____Hot/Cold Pack   97010   _____Manual Therapy Techniques   97140

Other_____   Other_____

                                           _____

                                           Therapist's Signature

Rehab & Therapy, Inc.

437 West Main Street

West Palm Beach, FL 33415

PH. (000)000-0000 Fax (000)000-0000

One of the benefits of filing for insurance is that the client might have more dollars to spend on treatments than would be the case if all the money came from his or her own pocket. Also, some people believe that if the insurance company will pay, then the service must be a viable and professional one.

The downside of insurance payments is the paperwork or computer filing load, the insurance company's control of how much you can charge, and the fact that even if you follow all the rules, you may not receive payment and may have to go to litigation to collect. If you are paid, you may wait 45 to 180 days in some cases for payment. It can be quite exasperating to pay utilities, rent, and other items while waiting for a payment from an insurance carrier. If you are not willing to wait or cannot afford to wait for your money, insurance work is not what you want to focus on in your practice.

Hopefully, you will be able to have someone in your business to tackle the task of collecting your money. The following information will enable you to understand what that person is doing for you, and it will also give you the knowledge needed to file insurance on your own.

Insurance Terms

All insurance companies use terms that are specific to the industry. The first term to know is **health insurance claim**. This term refers to the documentation and forms you submit to an insurance plan requesting payment for the service you, the therapist, have provided. Specific claim forms used are the CMS-1500 for private practice and the UB-92 form for hospital charges, such as massage in a cardiac rehabilitation setting. These are the universally accepted forms, and most health care insurance companies will not accept a claim or pay it if another form is used. The exception to this rule is that an accident insurance group, such as an auto insurance company, may use its own forms or method of filing. Verify which forms are to be used by calling the company's benefits information number, located on the insurance card. Ask the benefits representative directly. Always check for yourself whether the customer's insurance company will reimburse. The customer may not know the extent of benefits covered, and you need to be sure so that you will be paid.

In some cases you may need to get preauthorization for treatment. **Preauthorization** is the process of getting permission from the insurance company prior to the start of treatment for the services for which it will pay. A number of insurance companies require that you call to "precert," or get permission before treatment starts. You may want to get the information from the customer when the appointment is made and call before the customer comes in so that she or he will not be waiting while you get permission. Make sure you call in a private room; it is a breach of confidentiality to let any other persons hear the information you relay to the insurance personnel about the customer (see the section below on HIPAA).

When you request a preauthorization, the insurance company representative will tell you what information you must send, what type of treatment the company will pay for, how many times the customer can come for treatment, and how to send the claim for payment. If you begin treatment or a session before permission is given, you will not be paid for the services. Under the hold-harmless clause, a customer does not have to pay you if you file the insurance claim inappropriately and fail to get paid.

When you receive a referral or make an appointment for a new customer, you need to make a copy of the back and front of the customer's insurance card, ask whether the customer is covered by more than one insurance company, and make a copy of his or her driver's license. Include the copies in the customer's chart, on the left-hand side, after the customer intake information and personal data. You will need this information when speaking with the insurance company.

The insurance company is referred to as the **carrier**. That simply means that it carries the plan for the insurance program. The customer will have a **carrier identification number**, usually displayed as an insurance ID number. It may be the customer's Social Security number or a number assigned by the insurance company. If the customer's ID number is a Medicare number, it may be a Social Security number with a letter such as "A," "B," or "D" after it. Always include the letter when listing this type of number.

After the insurance information is clear and both you and the customer understand the payment arrangements, you must have the customer sign and date an assignment-of-benefits claim form, such as the one found in Appendix E . This form includes a release for records as well as a request for the payment to be mailed to the therapist. If the assignment-of-benefits form is not signed, the check may go to the customer and he or she may fail to pay you.

Remember that records cannot be released, even to the customer's attorney or insurance company, without the customer's written consent. If a physician gives you a copy of a test or diagnosis, you do not have the right to pass it on. If it originally came from another person or facility, permission must come from the originator.

Coding

After the customer intake forms have been filled out and signed, the chart has been started, and treatment has been given, the claim is ready to be filled out and sent. All insurance claims use a standardized method of **coding**, set by the World Health Organization of the United Nations, that consists of alphanumeric groupings that can be read quickly by a computer. The codes for all diagnoses are found in the *International Classification of Diseases, Ninth Revision, Clinical Modification* (ICD9-CM). The codes used for the type of service performed are found in *Current Procedural Terminology* (CPT). If a claim is filed that does not use the accepted coding, the claim will not be processed. If a claim is not processed, it will not be paid.

It is very important that you attend an insurance billing course, purchase an insurance billing book, or work with someone who has experience billing insurance. If you do not bill properly, you will spin your wheels, waste time, and lose money in the process.

Deductibles, Co-pays, and Coinsurance

There are many forms of insurance policies. Many of the policies require that the customer pay a **deductible**, which is a fixed dollar amount that must be paid or met once a year before the insurance company will cover the charges. The customer may also have to pay a **co-pay**, which is a small fee that should be collected at the beginning of each visit. If the customer does not have the co-payment type of insurance, he or she may be required to pay **coinsurance**. With a coinsurance plan, the customer pays a percentage, usually 20 percent, of the charges; the insurance company pays the remaining amount, usually 80 percent, but this amount is based on only the charges that the insurance company approves.

Besides dealing with the above-mentioned health care plans, you may have customers with disability insurance, accident coverage insurance, liability insurance, vocational rehabilitation, and many other types of coverage. It can be very confusing, but by obtaining the correct insurance or payment information and making a call to the payer, you can easily get the guidelines you need in order to file a claim and receive payment for your services.

TIDBIT

Be aware of insurance courses or books that promise an overly large amount of reimbursement for your services. Look for information that seems reasonable to you.

TIDBIT

It is important that you properly code the diagnosis and treatment on the basis of the physician prescription and your licensure and ability. Do not attempt to creatively code to increase the reimbursement amount or probability of reimbursement.

Health Insurance Portability and Accountability Act of 1996

On April 14, 2003, the first federal privacy protection standard was put into law. This law, the **Health Insurance Portability and Accountability Act**, or **HIPAA** for short, was designed to protect the privacy of customers and confidentiality of health records created by insurance companies, doctors, hospitals, and other health care providers. As a therapist, you will document information about a customer's past medical history, current health status, and prescription use, as well as any other information regarding the health of your customer, and all this information is subject to HIPAA.

The HIPAA regulations were developed by the Department of Health and Human Services (HHS) and are linked to the Department of Justice. They represent a uniform federal privacy standard across the United States. Individual state laws that provide additional protections to consumers are not affected by HIPAA.

This act protects identifiable health information, whether in a computer, on paper, or communicated orally. Some of the key provisions affecting health care professionals are as follows:

- *Access to medical records.* Customers should be able to see and obtain copies of their medical records and request corrections if they identify an error. The health care provider has only 30 days in which to turn over records. You must always keep the original record, but the cost of making copies can be charged to the customer.

- *Limits on use of personal records.* The customer must be provided with a release-of-information form to sign, designating what part of the records that have been requested by another health provider can be shared. For example, if a customer has weekly treatments for a back injury, and the orthopedic surgeon wants a copy of the customer's progress notes, you would not send her history form, which might include information about an abortion or a drinking problem.

- *Prohibition on marketing.* There are new rulings regarding the selling of customer information (such as addresses and phone numbers) to companies involved in marketing. You may not sell a photograph or image of a customer using your facility, or include it in your own marketing brochures, unless you have the written permission of the customer.

- *State laws.* For certain issues, such as reporting a communicable disease or possible crime information concerning a customer, the state laws covering such matters override the federal HIPAA regulations.

- *Confidential communications.* Under the privacy rule, customers can request that you do not call their homes to confirm appointments or pass information about your visits to family, co-workers, or friends.

- *Complaints.* Customers may file a formal complaint regarding privacy practices to the HHS Office for Civil Rights (OCR).

- *Health care insurance.* If you file insurance for procedures, you may be responsible not only for the medical HIPAA regulations but also the non-medical practice rules and regulations.

- *Civil and criminal penalties.* Complaints are investigated by the Department of Justice. Penalties for civil violations, *including honest mistakes*, are up to $100 per violation, up to $25,000 per year, for each rule violated. Criminal penalties can range up to $50,000 and 1 year in prison; if the offense is classified as "false pretenses," penalties can go up to $100,000 and 5 years in prison; and if the offense is committed to take advantage of a customer or achieve personal gain with intent to harm, penalties can increase to $250,000 and 10 years in prison.

Clinic Checklist for HIPAA

1. Do staff members discuss confidential patient information (CPI) among themselves or with customers or family in public areas?

2. Is CPI ever announced over intercoms, pagers, or cell phones?

3. Are progress and SOAP notes completed in a private area?

4. Are computer monitors positioned away from public areas?

5. Are all paper records and client charts stored in a private area—inaccessible to visitors, customers, and staff?

6. Is paper CPI shredded?

7. Are answering services and answering machines accessible only to staff with a "need to know"?

8. Are computer records—financial and others—protected with a password so that unauthorized personnel, customers, and visitors cannot access the data?

9. Are fax machines monitored to ensure that material with CPI is not left unattended?

Correct Chart Order

As well as being careful to include the previously mentioned items in the customer chart, you must also be aware of the order of the material. Insurance companies and government agencies will periodically review physician referral charts and will not pay for services, or possibly will fine you, if you have not followed the regulations. If you always treat referrals in a clinically effective manner, such a review will cause you no trouble and contribute to referrals from many health care professionals. The correct order for material contained in charts is as follows:

1. Outside of chart should have customer name.

2. Inside on the left side, chart should contain personal information, doctor referral form, and financial and payment data. Phone messages and letters from the customer are also filed here.

3. Inside on the right side, chart should contain history, assessment, all clinical and therapeutic documentation (such as SOAP notes and diagrams).

4. All charts must be free of "sticky notes," correction fluid, and informally scrawled notes. They must be filed in a "confidential," secure area away from noninvolved staff members and from customers. If a mistake is made, a single line is drawn through the mistake, the change is initialed, and the initials are circled. If the document is a medical referral, it must be dated in the following manner: 04/06/2008; a one-number day or month and a two-number year are not acceptable (4/6/08).

CHECKLIST

Have you done these things yet?

- [ ] Have you identified all the necessary forms appropriate for your business?

- [ ] Have you set up clearly organized files for customers/patients or had someone do this for you?

- [ ] Have you discussed with any employees (or other therapists working for you as independent contractors) what forms they are responsible for?

- [ ] Have you scheduled and written in your calendar the days or dates on which to review all paperwork?

SO WHAT DO YOU THINK?

1. What are the advantages and disadvantages of keeping customer SOAP notes?

2. Does your client intake form need to be detailed for the business you are running?

3. Is it better to struggle with paperwork yourself or hire someone else to do it?

4. Do you think it is important to follow HIPAA regulations even in a small or one-person office?

5. What could be some of the ramifications of not following HIPAA? Construct scenarios of all possibilities, and examine your attitude toward them.

Accounting

CHAPTER SEVENTEEN

LEARNING OUTCOMES

After completing this chapter, you should be able to:

17.1 Identify and use different financial indicators.

17.2 Identify the various accounting forms needed in business.

17.3 Recognize tax forms to be filed.

KEY TERMS

income statement

income

expenses

balance sheet

assets

liabilities

owner's equity

federal 1040 form

1040-ES form

1099 form

INTRODUCTION

The financial success of a business is based on a product, marketing, and organization. A large part of organization are the accounting processes of a business, no matter how big or small the business is (Figure 17.1). For anyone who is not accustomed to accounting, this can be the most frightful part of running a business. It does not have to be that way, and in fact accounting can be fun once the fear is gone and you better understand what is going on.

Financial Indicators

Income Statement

The **income statement** is a record of the amount of money that you made during a specific period of time. For purposes of this discussion, there are only two other terms that have to be remembered: The first is **income**, which is the money that you earn from all aspects of your business. An example of income is money received for a treatment or the sale of a product. The second term is **expense**, which is the money that you spend in the normal course of your business. Examples of expenses are rent and the cost of a product that you sell. These are the terms that you need to know to determine your total income. In fact, if you have done a budget, as outlined in Chapter 6, then you have already done a type of income statement.

Balance Sheet

The **balance sheet** shows the value of your company at a given point in time. It is a snapshot of your company's financial status. This snapshot includes three components: The first is **assets**, which are the items owned by the business. Examples of assets are a treatment table and a car that is used for business. The second is **liabilities**, which are the debts owed by the business. Examples of liabilities are the money that is owed on the car that you use or the money that you owe the government for

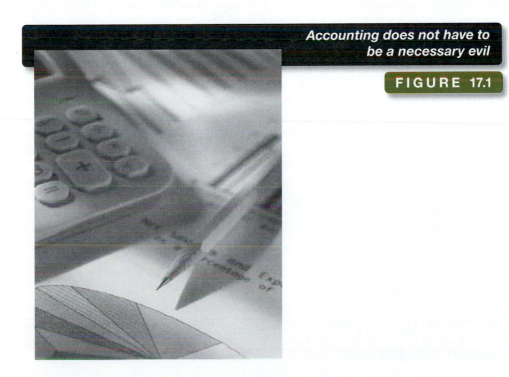

Accounting does not have to be a necessary evil

FIGURE 17.1

taxes. The final component is **owner's equity**, which is the value of the company when you subtract the liabilities from the assets; for example:

Assets	$ 25,000
Liabilities	– 20,000
Equity	$ 5,000

As simple as the example above is, the same equation holds true no matter how complicated the business becomes. Though there can be more subcategories than the ones listed, they all amount to assets minus liabilities equals owner's equity.

Determining Financial Indicators

Now that you know the two primary financial indicators for your business, the income statement and the balance sheet, the next question is how can you format and make them? The best answer is that you don't have to. Any number of accounting software programs include these statements. Quicken is the most widely used business program, and it can accomplish what you need to accomplish.

The information in the program can be set up for you by someone else, or you can set the information up using the tutorials that are supplied with the program. If you set the information up, it might be wise to have someone double-check it for you. The information that you will be entering will be your expenses, income, assets, and liabilities. The program comes preset with general categories, but you will want to make changes specific to your needs.

When you write checks (which the program will do for you), you enter the check data into your computer and then the information is automatically put in the right place in your income statement and balance sheet. It is that easy. There are many additional functions in accounting programs, including budgeting and payroll. You can expand your reports for sales, purchases, cash flows, and just about anything else that you may want to include. Before purchasing a program, make a list of the functions that you need it to perform and make sure that the program you select can do them.

The cost of accounting programs can range from well under $100 to several hundred dollars. Which program is right for you depends not just on cost, however, but also on the program's completeness in terms of what you will be using it for. The more functions that you want to accomplish with the program, the more expensive it will be. This is where a team member or your accountant will be invaluable to you.

Once you purchase a program, use it for a while without having to depend on it. If you are starting to use it in the beginning of a year, input information from a previous time frame to get used to the program and work out any bugs. If you are starting to use the program in the middle of a year, input information from the beginning of the year for practice (this will also allow you to have accurate financial figures for the whole year in one place).

Using Financial Indicators

All is well and good now that you know something about what the financial indicators are and how you can create them, but why do you need to do all that record keeping anyway? What does all that work accomplish? There are many things that financial information can accomplish:

WHAT'S THE REAL COST?

One of the ways that you should look at the cost of having someone else do the paperwork that needs to be done is by determining the amount of time that you save by not doing the work and multiplying that by the amount that you charge per hour for your services. Say, for example, that you charge $75 per hour for your treatment and it takes you six hours to file your financial paperwork each quarter. That amounts to $450 per quarter that you potentially lose in business because you have to spend that time doing paperwork instead of treating customers. Because of their expertise, professional accountants can most likely do the same amount of work in quite a bit less time, so even if your accountant charges more per hour than you do, you may save money. (LSR)

- It provides information that will help you make decisions such as whether or not you can purchase a new asset given your current profit picture.

- It shows you whether or not your business is going in the right direction. Are you making a profit, or are you losing money?

- It shows you where you may be spending too much money and where you may not be making any money in your business.

- It gives you a consistent format for comparing what you are doing from one period of time to another. This will help you to see whether you are making good financial decisions or not.

- It provides the information needed by institutions such as banks and the government.

Tax Accounting Paperwork

Approaching accounting forms, electronic or paper, can be a very daunting task. Add to that the possibility of the Internal Revenue Service or a state agency discovering that the numbers don't quite add up, and you may be experiencing some frightening consequences. A good option is to outsource this function to an accountant. He or she will know the information that needs to be submitted to the proper authorities. The downside to this arrangement is that it can be expensive, but it is not nearly as expensive as the cost you will incur if your paperwork is not filed or is filed improperly. Remember, however, that when you hire an accountant, you are depending on that person to do her or his job correctly. Even if you have an accountant file the paperwork for you, it is imperative that you at least know what paperwork needs to be filed and when it should be filed. When it comes to financial reporting, you are ultimately responsible for ensuring that everything is filed in a proper manner and at the proper time.

Each state has its own filing requirements; check with your state's department of business regulation. Generally speaking, the states require the same information that the federal government requires. (A great Web site for all of your tax questions is www.IRS.gov.) Here are the federal forms and the requirements for each:

- The **federal 1040 form** is the form that you will file to report your personal income. There are also variances to this form, such as the 1040-EZ, which is a simpler form and can be used under certain circumstances. The 1040 form is to be sent to the IRS by the 15th of April, along with payment for any taxes due. You can also file for an extension, which allows you to file your 1040 at a later date; a six-month extension is the usual time allowed. You must still pay all the taxes that are due by the 15th of April, even if you do not file your 1040. The bottom line is that you are responsible for paying your taxes by the 15th of April.

- Another 1040 form that you most likely will encounter is the **1040-ES form**, which is the form that you use to make your quarterly estimated tax payments. The amount of the quarterly tax payments includes your self-employment tax and your withholding tax. Self-employment tax is the same as Social Security tax and Medicare tax. The amount of the tax for these items is 12.4 percent for Social Security and 2.9 percent for Medicare. The withholding tax is your income tax, which is based on the amount of money that you earn less your expenses. The estimated payments are due on the 15th of April, June, September, and January for the current year's income. These payments must amount to 90 percent of your overall tax due that is not withheld from your pay. If you do not pay at least 90 percent of the amount that is due for your taxes, you will be assessed a penalty and interest on the amount that is not paid.

- If you are working for someone as an independent contractor, he or she will give you a **1099 form** at the end of the year. You are obligated to pay taxes on the amount that was paid to you and reported on the 1099 by the person or company that paid you the money. You are obligated to pay quarterly on the money that you receive during the year, even though you will not receive the 1099 form until after the end of the year. There are two ways to determine how much you should pay on a quarterly basis: The first is to divide the amount of taxes paid in the previous year by 4. This method is best if your income is consistent throughout the year and your income is steady from year to year. The second method is best if your income is not as steady. You multiply your effective tax rate (taken from the previous year) by the amount of money earned in the quarter. You are supposed to receive your 1099 by February 28th. Not receiving the form does not relieve you of the obligation to pay the taxes.

It is imperative that you pay taxes on all the money that you receive for your services. It is an obligation for you to do so. Income includes any bartering or exchange for services. If you do not pay taxes on the money that you earned, you could face severe prosecution. Instead of trying to cheat the government out of money, thus putting yourself in potential harm's way, you can offset income with expenses that are allowed by the government. You will get in a lot of trouble if you hide income, but you will not get in trouble if you spend money on your business and deduct it, as long as the expense is legitimate. Further, you will not be able to maintain a good credit record without reported income. Income and a good credit record are necessary to obtain a car loan or home mortgage.

Depending on the structure of your business, which was discussed in Chapter 3, you may have to file additional forms with the IRS. If you are a sole proprietor, you will be filing forms with your 1040 that allow for business deductions. If you are part of a partnership, LLC, or S corporation, that entity has to file income and expense forms, which show the amount of income that is allocated to each partner or principal, and you, in turn, have to report that income on your 1040 form. If you are a part of a C corporation, that corporation will send you a 1099 form showing the amount of dividends that you received. If you have not thought about retaining an accountant, hopefully this discussion will help you to consider doing so.

The corporate forms that you will have to file can be many and varied. In addition to filing the forms explained above, you will have to file forms for income, expenses, and, possibly, assets:

- Income for a business is reported on an 1120 form. If you are a C corporation, the form is 1120-C; if you are a subchapter S corporation, the form is 1120 S. Other types of business report income on forms such as schedule K, C, or SE.

- Expenses can be reported on many forms, such as 2106 for employee business expenses and 8829 for home business expenses.

- Asset acquisition can be reported on form 8594, and the depreciation for assets can be reported on form 4562.

Though this is far from an exhaustive discussion of accounting and taxes, it should have given you a few tools to take into your everyday business life. It should also have cleared up any questions that you had about hiring an accountant, purchasing a business software program, and handling the financial aspects of your business.

CHECKLIST

Have you done these things yet?

☐ Have you identified all the accounting and tax forms needed for your business?

☐ Have you discussed with your accountant who is responsible for what?

☐ Have you written the due dates for taxes in your calendar?

☐ Have you established a system for filing sales tax and making payments for products sold in your business (common in spas)?

SO WHAT DO YOU THINK?

1. Do you think what the IRS doesn't know won't hurt it?

2. Is it better to struggle with paperwork yourself or hire someone else to do it?

3. How much are you willing to spend to have your financial paperwork done?

Enjoying the Fruits of Your Labor

Enjoying the Fruits of Your Labor

LEARNING OUTCOMES

After completing this chapter, you should be able to:

18.1 Understand the financial benefits that come as a result of your hard work.

18.2 Recognize how to enjoy the personal rewards in your life.

18.3 Use the freedom of success responsibly.

18.4 Acknowledge the great feeling of satisfaction that success brings you.

KEY TERMS

individual retirement account (IRA)

traditional IRA

Roth IRA

SIMPLE IRA

simplified employee plan (SEP)

profit-sharing plan

individual 401(k)

401(k) with or without Roth

defined-benefit plan

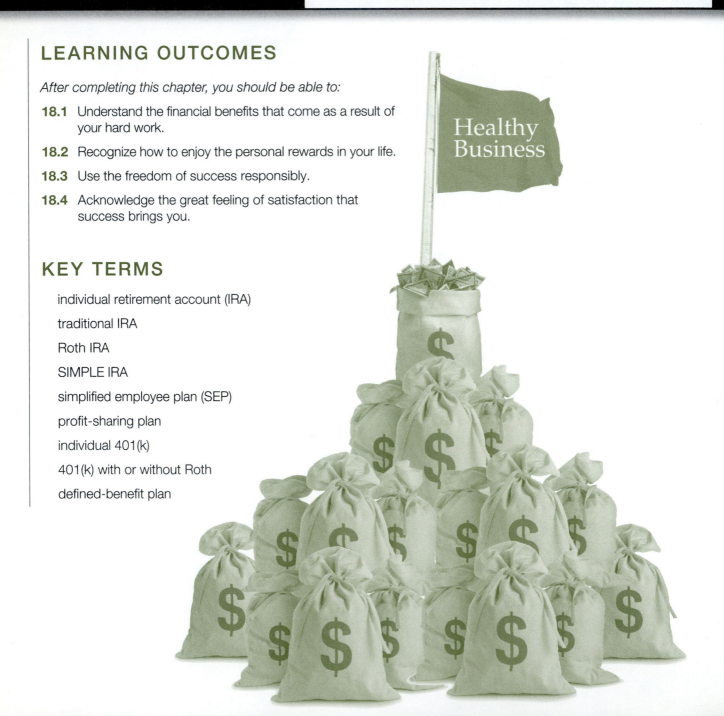

Healthy Business

INTRODUCTION

Now is the time to start to see the fruits of your labor. This is the point at which you should be able to look back and take advantage of some of the opportunities that your hard work has provided you. These fruits will present themselves to you in different ways—financial rewards, personal comfort, freedom, and satisfaction.

Financial Rewards

The initial financial rewards are obvious; you can begin to pay your bills! This can be a great relief, to say the least. After this initial phase, you will be able to reward yourself financially in other ways. You can begin to pay yourself a greater salary, which will allow you to achieve the next two fruits that were presented in the introduction above. But one of the greatest financial gifts that you can give yourself is financial security. This is accomplished by starting to think about your retirement.

This may sound premature, but it is true that you should plan for your future as soon as you can, because before you know it, your future will be here. The following are different types of retirement benefits:

- *Individual retirement account (IRA).* An IRA, whether it's a traditional or Roth type, is an individually funded plan that is not company-sponsored. There are no formal plan documents required and no required reporting to the IRS or Department of Labor (DOL) other than the entries on your personal tax return. By comparison, all company-sponsored plans must have formal documentation establishing the plan and must follow IRS and DOL rules. In addition, many require annual reports to the DOL on form 5500.

- *Traditional IRA.* Any individual under age 70½ with earned income can contribute to a traditional IRA. The annual limit in 2008* was 100 percent of earned income up to $5,000. An additional catch-up contribution of $1,000 may be made by individuals age 50 and older. The contribution is tax-deductible and must be made by April 15 of the year following the taxable year for which the contribution is being made.

- *Roth IRA.* Roth IRAs are funded with nondeductible contributions. Qualified distributions from a Roth IRA are not subject to income tax at the time of distribution. This means that both the contributions and all subsequent earnings are tax-free. To be "qualified," the Roth account must have been established for at least five years and the distribution must occur after age 59½ or at the time of death, disability, or a first-home purchase. As with a traditional IRA, the annual limit is $5,000, although the limit is reduced if the annual income exceeds specific amounts. In 2008, a single taxpayer's limit was reduced when adjusted gross income (AGI) exceeded $101,000, and it was zero when AGI exceeded $116,000. For married taxpayers filing jointly, the annual limit was reduced when AGI exceeded $159,000 and was zero when AGI exceeded $169,000. For married taxpayers filing separately, special rules apply. Please consult your tax adviser.

- *SIMPLE IRA.* An employer with no more than 100 employees who earned $5,000 or more during the preceding calendar year is eligible to establish a SIMPLE IRA plan. All employees who earned $5,000 in any two preceding calendar years and are expected to earn $5,000 in the current year are eligible to contribute to the plan. Employees may make tax-deductible contributions of 100 percent of earned income up to $10,500. Additional SIMPLE

---

* The annual limits listed above pertain to the 2008 taxable year. Please consult with your tax adviser to determine the applicable limits after 2008.

catch-up contributions of $2,500 can be made by employees age 50 and older. The employer must contribute either a dollar-for-dollar matching contribution up to 3 percent of pay or a flat 2 percent of pay for all eligible employees. Employer contributions are fully vested when made. SIMPLE IRAs are not subject to nondiscrimination testing, and there is no annual 5500 filing requirement.

- ***Simplified employee plan (SEP).*** An SEP is essentially a simplified profit-sharing plan. All employees who are at least 21 and have worked at least three of the last five years for the company must be included. In addition, if the company is part of a controlled group of companies (overlapping ownership that meets specific IRS rules), all companies must be included in the plan. The employer may contribute a discretionary percentage, up to 25 percent, of eligible compensation to the plan. The percentage of compensation must be the same for all employees eligible for the plan. The employer contribution is tax-deductible to the company and is fully vested when made. SEPs have no annual 5500 filing requirements.

The plans listed below—profit-sharing plans, 401(k) plans, and defined-benefit plans—are more complex and have more testing and reporting requirements than IRAs and SEPs. It is strongly recommended that you seek advice from a competent retirement plan professional. The American Society of Pension Professionals and Actuaries (www.asppa.org) is an excellent resource that can help you find credentialed individuals who will assist you with establishing and maintaining qualified retirement plans.

- ***Profit-sharing plan.*** Profit-sharing plans differ from SEPs by allowing flexibility in eligibility criteria, formulas for allocating contributions, and vesting of contributions. Eligibility requirements can be established that limit participation to only employees who have worked more than 1,000 hours in the year. Special contribution formulas can be established that create greater contributions for highly compensated employees, owners, and/or older employees. Employer contributions are tax-deductible up to 25 percent of eligible payroll. The allocation of contributions to individual participants is limited to the lesser of 100 percent of compensation or $46,000. Profit-sharing plans are subject to annual nondiscrimination tests and must file annual 5500s with the DOL.

- ***Individual 401(k).*** An individual 401(k) plan is a 401(k) plan that covers only the business owner and his or her spouse. Eligible employees can contribute tax-deductible contributions of $15,500 (plus $5,000 catch-up for those 50 and older) each calendar year. In addition, the employer can contribute up to 25 percent of all eligible compensation, although the amount allocated to any individual is limited to the lesser of 100 percent of compensation or $46,000. If you have employees, even independent contractors, that you pay through 1099s, seek advice before establishing this type of plan. Failure to include employees who meet the eligibility criteria can result in significant expense to correct the plan's qualified status. Annual 5500 filing requirements vary depending on the total assets contained in the plan.

- ***401(k) with or without Roth.*** A 401(k) allows the most flexibility of all the defined-contribution plan structures. The plan can be designed with the eligibility, matching, profit-sharing, and vesting features that best meet your needs. It can include contributions to a Roth 401(k) account, but unlike the Roth IRA, it has no income limitations. Eligible employees can contribute combined tax-deductible or Roth contributions of $15,500 (plus $5,000 catch-up for those 50 and older) each calendar year. In addition, the employer can contribute up to 25 percent of all eligible compensation, although the amount allocated to any individual is limited to the lesser of 100 percent of compensation or $46,000. The employer contribution can be in the form of a matching contribution or a profit-sharing allocation, with the same flexibility as that in the profit-sharing plan, described above. Although 401(k) plans are typically subject to annual nondiscrimination tests, "safe harbor" plan designs can be employed that make the plan exempt from the tests. Form 5500 must be filed each year, and, based on plan design features, annual notices to participants may be required.

- **Defined-benefit plan.** A defined-benefit plan is fundamentally different from all the plans previously discussed. With all the previous plans, either the employee or the employer makes a cash contribution to the plan. The cash is invested, and at retirement the employee will have an account balance that reflects the amount invested and the investment results. The employee bears the investment risk. If the investments do well, the employee will have more money at retirement than she or he will if the investments do poorly. In a defined-benefit plan, the employer promises a specific benefit payment at retirement age. The benefit can be based on several criteria, including years of service and average pay, or it can be simply a flat dollar amount, such as $3,000 per month for life. Thus, in a defined-benefit plan, the employer bears the investment risk. Since the employer is promising an income stream at retirement, poor investment performance will require the employer to contribute more to ensure that the benefit can be paid. A defined-benefit plan allows an owner who has not saved adequately for retirement to make significant contributions in the last several years of his or her career because service prior to the establishment of the plan can be used in the benefit formula. A defined-benefit plan requires the services of an actuary, annual nondiscrimination testing, and filing of form 5500 annually.

There are a lot of different options that you can choose from, and it is advisable that you talk to a professional when making decisions about your financial future. You must measure the risks and rewards of your investments when putting together your financial plans. You may be saying, "Wait a minute, I can't even plan for my next car payment; why should I be planning for my retirement?" The simple truth of the matter is that you have a certain amount of money to put into the pot, which will pay your bills, your entertainment, your other current needs, and your future needs. Realizing that your future needs have to be taken into account right away gets you used to the idea that you have to do something about it. Even if you put $50 a month away for your retirement, you need to do this the proper way.

Personal Comfort

Personal comfort comes with the additional money that you earn. This comfort stems from having the things that you did without while you were building your business up. It may be something as simple as a larger apartment to live in or a newer mode of transportation. It could be indulging yourself by going out to dinner or going out to dinner more often. Whatever it may be, personal comfort comes to those who work hard and can reward themselves in simple ways. Remember that you have one pie to choose from, so the amount that you invest in personal comfort takes away from your ultimate financial freedom.

This does not mean that you should forsake the personal comforts that you want now for the future possibilities, but you should not ignore those future possibilities. Instead of investing foolishly in a vehicle that you don't have to invest in, maybe a compromise vehicle will do for now. Delayed gratification is far sweeter and longer-lasting than immediate gratification that turns into guilt and even remorse.

DO IT SMARTER

This is the truest reality check that I can convey to you. On April 17, 2004, I suffered a massive heart attack at the age of 42. This brought what I needed to do in my life into focus. I realized that I had been given a chance to change the things that I needed to change and keep the things that were really working for me. I cut back my overhead, took time to relax, and started over. I now work just as hard as I did before the heart attack (maybe even a bit harder), yet I am doing it smarter, with enough changes in my personal and professional habits to keep myself healthy and successful. (LSR)

By all means, celebrate your success with greater personal comfort, but do not go to the point where personal comforts become a weight around your neck. You do not want to have to work even more just to pay for those personal comforts; they should be a reward for a job well done.

Freedom

There is so much to be said about freedom. The freedoms that a successful business brings you are manyfold. The most important is that you do not have to answer to anybody. This allows you to do your own thing and grow without impediment. The one caveat is that you should continue to do the things that made you successful. Do not think for one instant that success can permanently change your life. You can lose everything a lot quicker than you got it with a stupid mistake or bad decisions.

With freedom comes responsibility. That responsibility is to your family, friends, customers, and anyone else who helped you get to where you are now. You did not do it on your own, and you should not forget that.

The final word on freedom is that you have earned it. Use it to your best advantage, and you will gain more advantages for your business and personal life than you have ever imagined possible. Be aware, though, that freedom can be problematic if you do not use it wisely.

Satisfaction

There is no feeling in the business world that is better than the feeling of a job well done. This feeling will last longer than the money that you earned from the job. When a person invents something that changes the world, that person is not nearly as proud of the money made from the invention as she or he is of having invented something so significant. The money is just a result of the work, whereas the work itself is something that is a part of the inventor and is the inventor's alone.

You can be very satisfied about a job well done. What makes this feeling even better is looking at what you did, and at the results of what you did, and seeing how you can improve on it. A job does not end until you walk away. The satisfaction from a job well done is permanent, but the job itself changes, as do your needs, skills, abilities, and desires, so you must constantly strive to improve at your job to continue to feel satisfaction.

Time Off

One of the things that you will earn as you become more successful is the ability to walk away from your business, at least a little bit more at a time. When you can, please take time away from your business so that you can recharge. Taking a day or

RECOGNIZE YOUR LIMITS

When I first became a massage therapist, I was going through a divorce. Consequently, I worked as many hours as possible seven days a week during the season. It was three months before I took half a day off; by this time I was exhausted both mentally and physically from doing massage on the show horses—no small task—and their riders. I did recover mentally, but I believe I did irreparable damage to my joints.

The need for an income when no other money was coming in was a strong driving force. I have since learned that you only hurt yourself by not taking the time to recharge. The same holds true for learning to recognize your limits. Be realistic about how much you can safely do, and learn to say no to people who ask you to step outside the limits you have set as reasonable. (JLS)

a week to do this can sometimes mean the difference between being effective and being ineffective in your business.

Take Care of Yourself

It is imperative that you take care of yourself physically. You must determine what it is you require personally, and do it. The reason for this is twofold: First, you have to be in healthy condition to function optimally; and, second, if you do not use the services that you are providing, what kind of example are you giving to your customers? You can be the best advertising for your services! Consider exchanging services with former classmates or peers, for example.

Along with freedom as previously mentioned, once you reach a certain point in the success cycle you will have the freedom to begin to take care of yourself better. You should take time off to do this; you should take care of yourself physically so that you can continue to do the things that you do to make money.

If you don't devote time and effort to taking care of yourself, you will not last too long taking care of other people's needs. Do not feel guilty about taking care of yourself; do not neglect yourself; do not ignore signs indicating that you should be taking better care of yourself. Figures 18.1, 18.2, and 18.3 show ways of taking care of yourself.

Yoga is an excellent practice for balancing the body, mind, and spirit

FIGURE 18.1

Meditation can simply be a part of sitting still and focusing inward

FIGURE 18.2

Vacations are important to your overall well-being, whether they are frequent long weekends or every-so-often extended stays

FIGURE 18.3

Expand Yourself

Something else that you can do is increase your knowledge base. If you go to school or take classes to better yourself, your business can pay for your education if the courses are related to the business. Even if your state does not require continuing education units (CEUs) for license renewal, it behooves you to stay current with your profession and add new techniques. You may ultimately be paying for this education yourself, but it will be fully deductible.

CHECKLIST

Have you done these things yet?

☐ Have you looked at some potential financial instruments for your retirement?

☐ Have you determined which personal-comfort items are necessary and which ones are not?

☐ Have you considered what things are the most important as part of your freedom?

SO WHAT DO YOU THINK?

1. Do you think that a successful businessperson is ever completely satisfied?

2. Are there any things that are more important than business success?

3. What are you willing to compromise, and what are you not willing to compromise, to achieve business success?

State-by-State Resource Guide

Whether you are opening a massage therapy establishment, an acupuncture clinic, or a wellness center offering various services, you will need to check your state's requirements for operating such a facility. Below are Web sites for each state that will help you begin your research on achieving compliance. (*Tip:* If you type in the state's name followed by the ".gov" ending, that state's Web site will usually come up and you can navigate through the site for the information.)

Alabama

www.boards.alabama.gov

search: Boards & Commissions

Alaska

www.alaska.gov

click: Business tab/Occupations Requiring Licenses/Of Interest Healthcare Jobs/Alaska Occupational Information Healthcare Fields

Arizona

www.azdhs.gov

type in a search term

Arkansas

www.state.ar.us

click: State Directory: type: board

California

www.californiahealthfreedom.com

click: Practitioner Resources

Colorado

www.colorado.gov

click: Doing Business tab/Getting Licenses & Permits/Getting Professional or Occupational Licenses

Connecticut

www.dph.state.ct.us

click: Boards and Commissions

Delaware

http://dpr.delaware.gov

District of Columbia

www.doh.dc.gov

click: Health Regulations & Licensing/Health Professional Licensing/
Professional Licensing Boards & Registrations

Florida

www.doh.state.fl.us/mqa

click: Boards or Councils

Georgia

www.sos.ga.gov

click: Professional Licenses/Licensing Boards

Hawaii

www.hawaii.gov/dcca/areas/pvl/boards

Idaho

www.idaho.gov

type in a search term

Illinois

www.ildpr.com

Indiana

www.indiana.gov

click: Healthcare Professions & Licenses

Iowa

www.idph.state.ia.us

click: Licensure

Kansas

www.ksbha.org

Kentucky

www.finance.ky.gov
click: KY Agencies

Louisiana

www.louisiana.gov
Agencies, Boards & Commissions
click: Boards & Commissions box/list of all Boards

Maine

www.maineprofessionalreg.org
click: Professions and Occupations

Maryland

www.dhmh.state.md.us

click: Licensed Practitioners/Business and Healthcare Provider Section/
Professional License & Permits/Health Professions Licensing Boards

Massachusetts

www.ma.gov

click: Businesses tab/ Licenses, Permitting & Regulations/Occupational &
Business Licenses/Professional Licenses/Division of Professional Licensing

Michigan

www.michigan.gov

Minnesota

www.health.state.mn.us
type in a search term

Mississippi

www.mississippi.gov
click: State Agencies tab

Missouri

www.pr.mo.gov

Montana

www.mt.gov

type in a search term

Nebraska

www.hhs.state.ne.us

click: Licensing and Registrations/Professions and Occupations

Nevada

www.nv.gov

type in a search term

New Hampshire

www.dhhs.nh.gov

click: Programs & Services/Licensing & Regulative Services

New Jersey

www.state.nj.us

type in a search term

New Mexico

www.rld.state.nm.us

click: Boards & Commissions

New York

www.op.nysed.gov

search: List of Professions

North Carolina

www.nc.gov

click: NC Agencies & Websites/Boards & Commissions

North Dakota

www.governor.state.nd.us/boards

Ohio

www.state.oh.us/med or www.med.ohio.gov

Oklahoma

www.ok.gov

search: Boards & Commissions

Oregon

www.oregon.gov

type in a search term

Pennsylvania

www.dos.state.pa.us

click: Licensing/Health Related Boards/Professional Licensing Boards & Commissions

Rhode Island

www.health.state.ri.us

click: Licensing Boards & Professions

South Carolina

www.myscgov.com

click: Business/Licensing, Permits & Regulations/Licensing Boards

South Dakota

www.sd.gov

click: Useful Links tab/Licensing/Occupations

Tennessee

www.state.tn.us

click: Business & Records tab/ Health Professionals Licensing Boards

Texas

www.dshs.state.tx.us

click: Certifications, Licenses & Permits/Occupations/Professional Licensing & Certifications

Utah

www.commerce.state.ut.us

click: Occupational and Professional Licensing

Vermont

www.vt.gov

click: Business/Licenses & Permits/Health & Safety/Professional Licenses

Virginia

www.dhp.virginia.gov

click: Health Regulatory Boards/Health Professions or Nursing/Professions Regulated by Board

Washington

www.doh.wa.gov

click: Licensing/Certification

West Virginia

www.state.wv.us

click: Business in WV tab/Licensing

Wisconsin

www.state.wi.us

click: Licensing & Permits; type in a search term under Search by State Agency/Department of Regulations and Licensing

Wyoming

www.wyoming.gov

click: Business; type in a search term

Web Reference Guide

Budgeting

Business Budgeting Information
www.financialplan.about.com/msubbudg.htm

Personal Budgeting Information
www.kiplinger.com/tools/budget/

Employees

Hiring Employees
www.inc.com/guides/hr/20710.html

Employee Compensation
www.managementhelp.org/pay_ben/pay_ben.htm

Ethics

Business Ethics
www.managementhelp.org/ethics/ethics.htm

Finding Customers

Methods of Finding Customers
www.entrepreneur.com/startingabusiness/findingcustomers/
index115938.html

Goals and Mission Statements

Creating Mission Statements and Goals
www.businessplans.org

HIPAA

General Information and Answers
www.hhs.gov/ocr/hipaa

Income Tax and Payroll Information

Internal Revenue Service
www.irs.gov

Layout, Equipment, etc.

Spa

www.salonspasolution.com/salon-spa-floor-layouts.php

Legal

Common Questions Answered

www.sba.gov/smallbusinessplanner/manage/handlelegalconcerns/
index.html

Business Types

www.uwrf.edu/sbdc/leglasp7403A.html

Planning Business Services, Tools, and Resources

Small Business Administration

www.sba.gov

Score

www.score.org

Score Form Templates

www.score.org/template_gallery.html

Policies

Business

www.allbusiness.com/human-resources/workforce-management-employee/
3779025-1.html

Human Resources, etc.

www.humanresources.about.com/od/policiesandsamples1/a/
how_to_policy.htm

Retirement Planning

www.aarp.org/financial

www.mymoney.gov/retirement.shtml

Business Plan

A business plan can be used for many purposes, but the bottom line is that it is used to give people an idea of what your business is about so that they can invest in, buy, or become a part of your business. However, the business plan is not just for others but for you as well: As discussed throughout this text, it is important for you to have concrete evidence of your dreams and aspirations, and your business plan is a key piece of that evidence.

It is important that your business plan look professional and contain complete and accurate information. The main components are described below.

Components of a Business Plan

1. Executive summary
2. Company description
3. Listing of services and products provided
4. Marketing information
5. Daily operational functions
6. Implementation of goals and objectives
7. Team structure
8. Financial analysis
9. Additional information

Executive Summary
Though this is the first component of the business plan, it should be written after the rest of the business plan is formulated. It should contain the highlights of each of the other components listed above.

Company Description
This should contain the type of business structure and a list of any of the principals in the company (Chapters 5 and 9), the mission statement (Chapter 2), and the basic history of the company and the start-up plans (Chapters 6, 7, and 8).

Listing of Services and Products Provided
What services and/or products are you selling, and what differentiates them from those of your competitors? What are the competitive advantages of your products or services (Chapters 7 and 15)?

Marketing Information

This explains the who, what, where, and why of your marketing, including customers, location, and plans for growing your business (Chapters 7 and 13).

Daily Operational Functions

This identifies the type and location of the facilities, lists the equipment, and outlines the company policy of your business (Chapters 7, 8, 11, 12, and 13). This shows how the operation will actually run.

Implementation of Goals and Objectives

This lists what your goals and objectives are, how you are going to implement them, and who is going to implement them (Chapters 1, 3, 4, 5, 6, and 10).

Team Structure

Who are the team members, what are their responsibilities, and where do they fit in the company (Chapters 5, 9, and 10)? The list can include any persons (with their permission) who may be uncompensated team members.

Financial Analysis

This includes start-up costs, budgets, and profit-and-loss statements (Chapters 3, 6, and 17). This information should be prepared in a format that will allow potential investors to make an accurate judgment of the company.

Additional Information

Other items that should be included in a business plan are a cover sheet, résumés, any contracts that the company has entered into, corporate documents, and any other legal documents that may be of material interest.

References and Resources

Publications

Alternative Therapies: *Journal of Alternative Therapies in Health and Medicine*

American Massage Therapy Association, *Massage* (definition of massage, AMTA Code of Ethics) (Evanston, IL: American Massage Therapy Association, 2003).

Ashton, Joseph, and Cassel, Duke, *Review for Therapeutic Massage and Bodywork Certification* (Baltimore: Lippincott, Williams & Wilkins, 2002).

Associated Bodywork and Massage Professionals, *About Massage, Bodywork, and Somatic Therapies* (ABMP Professional Code of Ethics), 2003.

Beck, Mark F., *Milady's Theory and Practice of Therapeutic Massage*, 3rd ed. (Albany, NY: Milady Publishing, 1999).

Benjamin, Ben E., and Sohnen-Moe, Cherie, *The Ethics of Touch* (Tucson, AZ: SMA, 2003).

Boldt, Laurence G., *Zen and the Art of Making a Living* (New York: Penguin/Arkana, 1991).

Burnum, J. F., "Preventability of Adverse Drug Reactions," *Archives of Internal Medicine* 85, no. 1 (1976), pp. 80–81.

Calvert, Robert Noah, *The History of Massage* (Rochester, VT: Healing Arts Press, 2002).

Cohen-Horwitz, B., "The Nurse as Defendant," *Trial Lawyer* 14, no. 8 (1991), pp. 39–47.

Commonwealth Department of Human Services and Health, "Review of Professional Indemnity Arrangements for Health Care Professionals," in *Compensation and Professional Indemnity in Health Care: A Final Report* (Canberra: Australian Government Publishing Service, November 1995).

"Consumer Survey Fact Sheet, 2003: Massage Therapy," report commissioned by the American Massage Therapy Association (survey conducted August 2003), www.amta.massage.org.

Cox, Kathleen, *The Power of Vastu Living* (New York: Fireside, Simon and Schuster, 2002).

Crellin, John, and Ania, Fernando, *Professionalism and Ethics in Complementary and Alternative Medicine* (New York: Haworth Integrative Healing Press, 2002).

Dispenza, Joe, *Evolve Your Brain* (Deerfield Beach, FL: Health Communications, 2007).

Doyle, Derek, Hanke, Geoffrey, and MacDonald, Neil, eds., *Oxford Textbook of Palliative Medicine*, 2nd ed. (New York: Oxford University Press, 1999).

Dyer, Wayne W., *Manifest Your Destiny* (New York: HarperCollins, 1997).

Fritz, Sandy, *Mosby's Fundamentals of Therapeutic Massage,* 2nd ed. (St. Louis, MO: Mosby, 2000).

Fritz, S. C., Groenbach, M. J., and Paholsky, K., "Informed Consent," *Massage Magazine,* July–August 1997.

Fritz, S. C., Groenbach, M. J., and Paholsky, K., "Scope of Practice," *Massage Magazine,* March–April 1997.

Gawain, Shakti. *Creative Visualization* (Novato, CA: New World Library, 1978).

Greenman, Philip E., *Principles of Manual Medicine,* 3rd ed. (Philadelphia, PA: Lippincott, Williams & Wilkins, 2003).

Griffith, Brenda L., "Massage Therapy Has a Role in Pain Management," *Practical Pain Management Magazine,* January–February 2003.

Hicks, Esther, and Hicks, Jerry. *The Astonishing Power of Emotions* (Carlsbad, CA: Hay House, 2007).

Hill, Napoleon, *Think and Grow Rich* (New York: Fawcett Columbine, 1937).

Johnson, Mary Lynne, and Grant, John, *Blake's Poetry and Designs* (New York and London: Norton, 1979).

McConnellogue, Kieran, "The Courage of Touch," *Massage & Bodwork Magazine,* December–January 2000.

McIntosh, Nina, *The Educated Heart: Professional Guidelines for Massage Therapists, Bodyworkers, and Movement Teachers* (Memphis, TN: Decatur Bainbridge Press, 1999).

Millenson M. L., *Demanding Medical Excellence* (Chicago: University of Chicago Press, 1997).

National Certification Board for Therapeutic Massage and Bodywork (NCBTMB), Code of Ethics and Standards of Practice, 2003.

National Certification Board for Therapeutic Massage and Bodywork (NCBTMB), *Consumers Guide to Therapeutic Massage and Bodywork* (online guide at http://www.ncbtmb.org/pdf/consumers_guide_brochure.pdf).

National Institutes of Health, *Alternative Medicine: Expanding Medical Horizons: A Report to the National Institutes of Health and Alternative Medical Systems and Practices in the United States,* NIH Publication Number 94-066, 1994.

Pegrum, Juliet, *The Vastu Home* (Berkeley, CA: Ulysses Press, 2002).

Polseno, Diane, "Say It Ethically: Responding to Sexual Misconduct," *Massage Therapy Journal,* Fall 2003.

Prabhavana, Swami, and Isherwood, Christopher, *How to Know God* (Hollywood, CA: Vedanta Press, 1983).

Reilly, E., "Nurses and the Law," *New Hampshire Bar Journal* 26, no. 1 (1984), pp. 7–23.

Ruiz, Don Miguel, *The Mastery of Love* (White Plains, NY: Peter Pauper Press, 2004).

Salvo, Susan G., *Massage Therapy Principles and Practice* (Cotati, CA: Massage, Inc., 1999).

Schneider, Steven L. [Agency for Healthcare Research and Quality (AHRQ)], "Illnesses & Conditions: Work in Partnership with Your Doctor to Prevent Medical Errors," www.LaurusHealth.com.

Sroboda, Robert E. *Prakruti* (Albuquerque, NM: Geocom., 1989).

Tappan, Frances M. *Healing Massage Techniques—Holistic, Classic, and Emerging Methods,* 2nd ed. (New York: Appleton & Lang, 1988).

Thiroux, Jacques, *Ethics: Theory and Practice* (Englewood Cliffs, NJ: Prentice Hall, 1995).

Thompson, Diana L., *Hands Heal* (Baltimore: Lippincott, Williams & Wilkins, 2002).

Woods, Diana Lynn, and Dimond, Margaret, "The Effect of Therapeutic Touch on Agitated Behavior and Cortisol in Persons with Alzheimer's Disease" *Biological Research for Nursing* 4, no. 2 (October 2002), pp. 104–114.

Web Sites

www.acsu.buffalo.edu/~drstall/karnofsky.html

www.AmericanMedicalMassage.com

www.cancer.org ("Complementary and Alternative Methods: Types of Bodywork")

www.cdc.gov/ncidod/hip/sterile/sterilgp.htm

www.doh.state.fl.us/mqa/massage/ma_home.html (State of Florida Department of Health)

www.geocities.com/everwild7/noharm.html

www.Holisticonline.com ("Massage Therapy")

www.nccam.nih.gov

www.qwl.com/mtwc/articles/hiv.html

www.thebodyworker.com (Julie Onofrio)

Sample Forms

New Business (Project) Start-Up Budget

New Business (Project) Start-Up Budget:

Basic Expenses:	Budgeted	Actual	Difference
Automobile	$_____	$_____	$_____
Banking	$_____	$_____	$_____
Decorating (new office)	$_____	$_____	$_____
Deposits (phone, utilities, equipment)	$_____	$_____	$_____
Insurance	$_____	$_____	$_____
Licenses/fees	$_____	$_____	$_____
Treatment equipment	$_____	$_____	$_____
Treatment supplies	$_____	$_____	$_____
Membership dues	$_____	$_____	$_____
Music player, CDs, tapes, iPod	$_____	$_____	$_____
Office equipment	$_____	$_____	$_____
Office supplies	$_____	$_____	$_____
Professional fees	$_____	$_____	$_____
Rent (first, last, security)	$_____	$_____	$_____
Telephone	$_____	$_____	$_____
Other expenses	$_____	$_____	$_____

Other Expenses:

Equipment:

Refrigerator, fax,	$_____	$_____	$_____

Hydrocollator, electric heating pads, washer/dryer

Supplies:

Miscellaneous office supplies	$_____	$_____	$_____

Total Start-Up Expenses	$_____	$_____	$_____

Expense Budget

Expense Budget

Period: _____ to _____

	Budgeted	Actual	Difference
Automobile	$_____	$_____	$_____
Advertising	$_____	$_____	$_____
Associations	$_____	$_____	$_____
Banking	$_____	$_____	$_____
Education	$_____	$_____	$_____
Entertainment	$_____	$_____	$_____
Estimated taxes	$_____	$_____	$_____
Income distribution	$_____	$_____	$_____
Insurance	$_____	$_____	$_____
Interest	$_____	$_____	$_____
Licenses/fees/taxes	$_____	$_____	$_____
Treatment equipment	$_____	$_____	$_____
Treatment supplies	$_____	$_____	$_____
Office equipment	$_____	$_____	$_____
Office supplies	$_____	$_____	$_____
Payroll	$_____	$_____	$_____
Payroll taxes	$_____	$_____	$_____
Postage	$_____	$_____	$_____
Professional fees	$_____	$_____	$_____
Rent	$_____	$_____	$_____
Repairs/maintenance	$_____	$_____	$_____
Telephone	$_____	$_____	$_____
Utilities	$_____	$_____	$_____
Other expenses:			
_____	$_____	$_____	$_____
_____	$_____	$_____	$_____
_____	$_____	$_____	$_____
_____	$_____	$_____	$_____
_____	$_____	$_____	$_____
Total Expenses	$_____	$_____	$_____

Monthly Income Projections vs. Actual

Monthly Income Projections vs. Actual

Month _____

	Number of Treatments per Day		Money Collected per Day	
	Estimated	Actual	Budgeted	Actual
Day 1	_____	_____	_____	_____
Day 2	_____	_____	_____	_____
Day 3	_____	_____	_____	_____
Day 4	_____	_____	_____	_____
Day 5	_____	_____	_____	_____
Day 6	_____	_____	_____	_____
Day 7	_____	_____	_____	_____
Day 8	_____	_____	_____	_____
Day 9	_____	_____	_____	_____
Day 10	_____	_____	_____	_____
Day 11	_____	_____	_____	_____
Day 12	_____	_____	_____	_____
Day 13	_____	_____	_____	_____
Day 14	_____	_____	_____	_____
Day 15	_____	_____	_____	_____
Day 16	_____	_____	_____	_____
Day 17	_____	_____	_____	_____
Day 18	_____	_____	_____	_____
Day 19	_____	_____	_____	_____
Day 20	_____	_____	_____	_____
Day 21	_____	_____	_____	_____
Day 22	_____	_____	_____	_____
Day 23	_____	_____	_____	_____
Day 24	_____	_____	_____	_____
Day 25	_____	_____	_____	_____
Day 26	_____	_____	_____	_____
Day 27	_____	_____	_____	_____
Day 28	_____	_____	_____	_____
Day 29	_____	_____	_____	_____
Day 30	_____	_____	_____	_____
Day 31	_____	_____	_____	_____
Total	_____	_____	_____	_____

Yearly Tracking of Treatments

Week	Monday	Tuesday	Wednesday	Thursday	Friday	Saturday	Sunday	Total Week	Total Year
1									
2									
3									
4									
5									
6									
7									
8									
9									
10									
11									
12									
13									
14									
15									
16									
17									
18									
19									
20									
21									
22									
23									
24									
25									
26									
27									
28									
29									
30									
31									
32									
33									
34									
35									
36									
37									
38									
39									
40									

Continued

41								
42								
43								
44								
45								
46								
47								
48								
49								
50								
51								
52								
Total								

Weekly Tracking of Treatments

Hour	Monday	Tuesday	Wednesday	Thursday	Friday	Saturday	Sunday
8:00 AM							
9:00 AM							
10:00 AM							
11:00 AM							
12:00 PM							
1:00 PM							
2:00 PM							
3:00 PM							
4:00 PM							
5:00 PM							
6:00 PM							
7:00 PM							
8:00 PM							

Client Information Form

Wellness Center

Please note that all information is strictly confidential

First name: _____   Last name: _____

Address: _____   City/postal code: _____

E-mail address: _____   Cell phone: _____

Home phone: _____   Work phone: _____

Date of birth: _____   Age: _____

Marital status: _____   No. of children: _____

Occupation: _____   Primary physician: _____

Emergency contact: _____   Phone #: _____

Whom should we thank for referring you to this office? _____

Have you received acupuncture before, and if so, when? _____

Reason for today's visit: _____

_____

_____

How, when, and where did this condition begin? _____

_____

_____

What types of treatments have you tried, if any? _____

_____

What makes it better? _____

What makes it worse? _____

Please list any other health problems you would like to address, in order of importance: _____

_____

_____

Your Medical History:

Surgeries, major illnesses, hospitalizations, major accidents (include dates): _____

_____

_____

_____

_____

Current medications, supplements, and vitamins (and what they are for): _____

_____

_____

_____

_____

Continued

Do you currently have or have you ever had any of the following?

Anemia   Epilepsy   Fibromyalgia   Arthritis   Diabetes   Multiple sclerosis

Emotional disorder   Drug problem   Digestive disorders   Heart problem

Pacemaker   Tuberculosis   Cancer   Hepatitis   HIV   Allergies

High blood pressure   Kidney disease   Osteoporosis   Asthma   Stroke

Ulcers   Thyroid problem   Kidney stones   Gallstones   Alcoholism   AIDS

Do you have any drug allergies? _____

Lifestyle:

How do you feel about your diet? _____

Exercise?   Yes   No   How often? _____ Type? _____

Sleep: Hours per night _____ Rested in AM? _____

Trouble falling asleep? _____ Trouble staying asleep? _____

Do you get up to urinate more than once? _____

Work: Enjoy work?   Yes   No   Hours per week working _____

Please indicate the use and frequency of the following:

	Yes	No	How Much		Yes	No	How Much
Coffee -				Water -			
Tobacco -				Marijuana -			
Alcohol -				Soda pop -			

Symptom Survey (please check all that apply)

0 = never   1 = rarely   2 = occasionally   3 = frequently   4 = always

0 1 2 3 4 low appetite	0 1 2 3 4 ravenous appetite
0 1 2 3 4 loose stools	0 1 2 3 4 heartburn/acid reflux
0 1 2 3 4 gas/abdominal bloating	0 1 2 3 4 mouth sores
0 1 2 3 4 fatigue after eating	0 1 2 3 4 belching or vomiting
0 1 2 3 4 organ prolapses	0 1 2 3 4 gums bleeding/swollen
0 1 2 3 4 bruise easily	0 1 2 3 4 thirst

0 1 2 3 4 spontaneous sweat	0 1 2 3 4 fatigue
0 1 2 3 4 allergies	0 1 2 3 4 catch colds easily
0 1 2 3 4 asthma	0 1 2 3 4 tired after exercise
0 1 2 3 4 shortness of breath	0 1 2 3 4 general weakness
0 1 2 3 4 cough	0 1 2 3 4 nasal discharge
0 1 2 3 4 dry nose/mouth/skin/throat	0 1 2 3 4 sinus congestion

0 1 2 3 4 sore, cold, or weak knees	0 1 2 3 4 feel cold often
0 1 2 3 4 low-back pain	0 1 2 3 4 edema
0 1 2 3 4 frequent urination	0 1 2 3 4 impaired memory
0 1 2 3 4 urinary incontinence	0 1 2 3 4 hair loss
0 1 2 3 4 ear/hearing problems	0 1 2 3 4 infertility
0 1 2 3 4 early morning diarrhea	low normal high libido

Continued

0 1 2 3 4   irritable   0 1 2 3 4   muscle spasms/twitches

0 1 2 3 4   feel better after exercise   0 1 2 3 4   numb extremities

0 1 2 3 4   tight feeling in chest   0 1 2 3 4   dry, irritated eyes

0 1 2 3 4   alternating diarrhea/constipation 0 1 2 3 4   ear ringing

0 1 2 3 4   symptoms worse with stress   0 1 2 3 4   anger easily

0 1 2 3 4   neck/shoulder tension   0 1 2 3 4   red eyes

---

0 1 2 3 4   feel heart beating   0 1 2 3 4   chest pain

0 1 2 3 4   insomnia   0 1 2 3 4   disturbing dreams

0 1 2 3 4   sores on tip of tongue   0 1 2 3 4   headaches

0 1 2 3 4   anxiety   0 1 2 3 4   palpitations

0 1 2 3 4   restlessness

---

0 1 2 3 4   dizzy upon standing   0 1 2 3 4   feeling of heaviness

0 1 2 3 4   see floaters in eyes   0 1 2 3 4   nausea

0 1 2 3 4   heat in palms or soles   0 1 2 3 4   foggy thinking

0 1 2 3 4   afternoon fever   0 1 2 3 4   enlarged lymph nodes

0 1 2 3 4   night sweats   0 1 2 3 4   cloudy urine

0 1 2 3 4   frequently flushed face

<u>Urination</u>: (Circle all that apply)   Burning   Urgent   Scanty

Difficulty   Profuse   Dribbling   More than 1x a night

<u>Bowel Movements:</u>   Frequency _____

Consistency (circle):   well-formed   hard   loose   alternates between formed and loose

Do you ever notice any undigested food, blood, or mucous? _____

Are you thirsty?   Yes   No   If so, do you crave warm or cold drinks? _____

Do you find that you "run" particularly hot or cold? _____

How is your energy in general? _____

Do you often get headaches or migraines?   Yes   No

How do you feel emotionally right now? _____

_____

Women Only:

Are you currently pregnant? _____ Are you on the birth control pill? _____

# of pregnancies _____ # of live births _____ # of miscarriages _____ # of abortions _____

Have you experienced menopause?   Yes   No   When? _____

If you are experiencing menopausal symptoms, please describe: _____

_____

Is your period regular? _____# of days from the start of one period to the start of the next _____

Average number of days of flow: _____   Flow is: Light   Normal   Heavy

Color is: Pale   Normal   Dark   Bright   Red   Brown   Purple

Continued

Blood clots?   Yes   No

Do you get pain or cramps?   Yes   No   Severe?   Yes   No

Nature of pain (circle):   Sharp   Dull   Constant   Intermittent   Burning   Aching

Do you experience any of the following before or during your menstrual period?

Water retention   Breast tenderness/swelling   Depression   Irritability   Migraines

Insomnia   Diarrhea   Constipation   Nausea   Hot flashes   Night sweats

_____

Men Only:

Date of last prostate checkup: _____ Results: _____

Circle all that apply: Groin pain   Decreased libido   Testicular pain   Impotence

Painful urination   Difficult urination   Dribbling urination   Incontinence   Premature ejaculation

Nocturnal emissions   Increased libido   Other: _____

_____

I am committed to your health and well-being. While Chinese medicine is a very thorough health care system, it is not a replacement for Western medical treatment, including regular checkups with your primary care physician. I recommend that you consult a physician regarding any condition for which you are seeking acupuncture treatment. We, the undersigned, do affirm that _____ _____ (print patient name) has been advised by William Stikim A.P. to consult a physician regarding the conditions for which such patient seeks acupuncture treatment.

Patient Signature: _____ **Date:**_____

Licensed Practitioner: _____ **Date:**_____

I consent to acupuncture treatment and other procedures associated with Traditional Oriental Medicine by _____. I have discussed the nature of my treatment with _____ .
I understand that methods of treatment may include but are not limited to: acupuncture, massage, moxibustion, gua sha, cupping, electric stimulation, and Chinese herbal medicine.
I have been informed that acupuncture is a safe method of treatment, but that it may have side effects including bruising, numbness, or tingling near the needling sites that may last a few days, and dizziness or fainting. Bruising is a common side effect of cupping and gua sha. Unusual risks of acupuncture include pneumothorax and organ puncture. Slight superficial burns are a possible side effect of moxibustion.

I acknowledge that if I do not give 24 hours notice for cancellation of an appointment, I will be charged a full fee for the missed appointment.

Patient Signature: _____ **Date:** _____

Working Intake Form

REHAB & THERAPY, INC.
437 West Main Street
West Palm Beach, FL 33415
(000) 000-0000   Fax (000) 000-0000

NAME _____ DATE _____

ADDRESS _____ PHONE _____
_____ CELL PHONE _____

BIRTH DATE ____ / ____ / ____ SEX _____ MARITAL _____ E-MAIL _____

EMPLOYER _____ EMPLOYER'S PHONE_____

EMPLOYER'S ADDRESS _____

I WAS REFERRED TO REHAB & THERAPY BY _____

HAVE YOU HAD ANY OF THE FOLLOWING DURING THE PAST YEAR:

SEVERE HEADACHES	Y	N	**TINGLING/WEAKNESS IN HANDS**	Y	N	**HAND SWELLING**	Y	N
FAINTING	Y	N	**TINGLING/WEAKNESS IN FEET**	Y	N	**FOOT SWELLING**	Y	N
DIZZINESS	Y	N	**BLOOD PRESSURE/ HEART**	Y	N	**CHEST PAINS**	Y	N
PREGNANCY	Y	N						

NAME OF PRIMARY/FAMILY PHYSICIAN _____

ARE YOU BEING TREATED BY A PHYSICIAN? _____ FOR WHAT?_____

ARE YOU CURRENTLY TAKING ANY DRUGS? _____ PLEASE LIST _____

HAVE YOU BEEN TREATED FOR ANY OTHER MEDICAL CONDITIONS IN THE LAST YEAR?_____

HAVE YOU HAD MASSAGE THERAPY BEFORE?_____ HOW OFTEN DO YOU RECEIVE MASSAGE?_____

IS THIS VISIT A RESULT OF A WORK-RELATED ACCIDENT?_____ IF SO, DATE OF ACCIDENT_____

IS THIS VISIT A RESULT OF AN AUTOMOBILE ACCIDENT?_____ IF SO, DATE OF ACCIDENT_____

I AM SEEKING TREATMENT FOR:_____

PATIENT SIGNATURE _____ DATE ____ / ____ / ____

Logo and license number if required by state law

Quick Intake Form

Patient Name_____ Date_____

Subjective Information:

PAIN ⇩ ROM

_____ Cervical _____
_____ Shoulder _____
_____ Thoracic _____
_____ Lumbar _____
_____ Arm/Hand _____
_____ Leg/Foot _____
_____ Headache_____

Other Information:

_____
_____
_____
_____
_____
_____

_____ None _____ Occasional _____ Frequent _____ Constant

Objective Findings:

	L	R	
S TP P T N	_____	/ _____	Occipital/Splenius
S TP P T N	_____	/ _____	SCM/Scalenes
S TP P T N	_____	/ _____	Levator/U. Trapezius
S TP P T N	_____	/ _____	Rhomboid/M. Trapezius
S TP P T N	_____	/ _____	Latissimus/L. Trapezius
S TP P T N	_____	/ _____	Thoracic Paravertebrals
S TP P T N	_____	/ _____	SITS Group
S TP P T N	_____	/ _____	Pectoralis Group
S TP P T N	_____	/ _____	Serratus Anterior
S TP P T N	_____	/ _____	Lumbar Paravertebrals
S TP P T N	_____	/ _____	Quadratus Lumborum
S TP P T N	_____	/ _____	Iliopsoas Group
S TP P T N	_____	/ _____	Hip Rotators
S TP P T N	_____	/ _____	Hamstrings/TFL
S TP P T N	_____	/ _____	Quad Group
S TP P T N	_____	/ _____	Gastroc/Soleus
S TP P T N	_____	/ _____	Tibialis Anterior

			Response to Treatment:
S TP P T N ___ O ___	S-Spasm	1-Mild	
S TP P T N ___ T ___	TP-Trigger Point	2	_____ Excellent
S TP P T N ___ H ___	P-Pain	3 ↕	_____ Good
S TP P T N ___ E ___	T-Tenderness	4	_____ Fair
S TP P T N ___ R ___	N-Numbness/Tingling	5-Severe	_____ Poor

Treatment:

_____Therapeutic Massage 97124   _____Neuromuscular Reeducation 97112

_____Hot/Cold Pack 97010   _____Manual Therapy Techniques 97140

Other_____   Other_____

_____
Therapist's Signature

Rehab & Therapy, Inc.
437 West Main Street
West Palm Beach, FL 33415
PH. (000)000-0000 Fax (000)000-0000

Client History Form with SOAP Notes

CLIENT HISTORY FORM WITH SOAP NOTES

Client Name:_____ Date: _____

Address:_____

_____

Date of Birth:_____

Referred by:_____

Physician Name:_____

S: CHIEF COMPLAINT:

    ONSET

    DURATION

    PAIN LEVEL (Scale 1–10)

    WHAT INCR/DECR PAIN

    PAST MEDICAL HX (that may have an impact on chief complaint)

    FAMILY MEDICAL HX (that may have an impact on chief complaint)

    ACTIVITIES OF DAILY LIVING (ADLs)

O: ROM

    STRENGTH

    GAIT

A: ASSESSMENT/ACTION

P: PLAN/TREATMENT

    MODALITIES

    EDUCATION

    FREQUENCY

Client Information/Intake Form

EVERYDAY GOODFEELING MASSAGE CLINIC
CLIENT INFORMATION/INTAKE FORM

Name: _____ Birth date: _____

Address: _____ Home phone: _____

_____ Cell phone: _____

Occupation: _____ Work phone: _____

General health condition: _____ Usual blood pressure: _____

Have you had any serious or chronic illnesses, operations, infections, or trauma?

_____

_____

_____

Are you in recovery for addictions, emotional issues, or abuse? _____

Are you under a doctor's, chiropractor's, or other health practitioner's care? _____

If so, for what conditions? _____

Please list any medications, vitamins/minerals, or herbal supplements you may be taking, and what each is for.

_____

_____

_____

_____

Do you have any allergies? _____

Do I have permission to contact your doctor/practitioner/therapist? _____

Names of doctors/practitioners/therapists:

_____ Phone # _____

_____ Phone # _____

Why did you come in for our service? _____

What results would you like to achieve? _____

Is this your first massage/treatment? _____

How did you find out about our services? _____

In case of emergency, notify _____ Phone # _____

I have completed this information form to the best of my knowledge. I understand the massage services are designed to be a health aid and are in no way to take the place of a doctor's care when it is indicated. Information exchanged during any massage session is educational in nature and is intended to help me become more familiar and conscious of my own health status and is to be used at my own discretion. I agree to notify this clinic 24 hours in advance of any cancellation.

Date: _____ Signature: _____

Contributor Biographies

Janet Smith

Utilizing two decades of business and marketing experience, Janet founded a dynamic new company, www.ReferredHomeServices.com. She believes you should know who is in your home. Referred Home Services *screens contractors* by checking 10 references, licenses, insurance, BBB, corporate registration, the attorney general's office, and much more. Free and online, RHS presents only reputable, experienced home improvement and repair businesses so that homeowners, real estate professionals, and community managers get the job done right the first time.

Janet's "If there's no wind, row" approach to her new company has been the driving force in her career, carrying her to senior executive positions at A-list companies such as Siebel Systems, Informix Software, Tandem Computers, and what was then Arthur Andersen.

Janet also owns a consulting and advisory firm, 5th Dimension Marketing. She has written and implemented business plans for a wide range of companies, from start-ups to major corporations, and she has held board positions.

Janet is the recipient of corporate communication awards in Silicon Valley. She's a graduate of the University of Florida and resides in Jupiter, Florida, with her daughter, Veronica. She can be reached at janetrhs@comcast.net or 561.401.4004.

Valerie Wohl

Valerie Wohl, a writer and researcher, is President of Wohl Research and Consulting, Inc. Educated at the University of Michigan, in Ann Arbor (undergraduate), and the School of Education and Social Policy at Northwestern University, in Evanston, Illinois (graduate), she focuses on educational writing; sociocultural, behavioral, and economic research; and issues of social and public policy.

Renee Benrubi

Renee Benrubi has been teaching and training in the personal development field for the last 25 years. She trained with Bob Hoffman, founder of the Hoffman Process, and was responsible for bringing that program to Australia. As a Supervising Teacher, she established an Institute in Melbourne, Australia, where she trained teachers, taught, and had a private practice. Renee also delivered the Avatar Program internationally over the last 15 years. She has also served as a consultant to companies, with the purpose of facilitating alignment within organizations. Her passion is to support and empower others to enjoy their lives, facilitating the change any individual may seek. Her techniques are a synthesis of a variety of methods, her personal life experience, and spirituality.

She currently resides in Boca Raton, Florida, with her husband and two teenage sons. She continues her private practice with clients throughout the United States. For further information, you can contact Renee at rbenrubi@earthlink.net.

Glossary

A

advertising Making people aware of your business and what you offer.

alignment An arrangement in a straight line.

ambience The "feel" of the establishment.

artist A person who can present a more aesthetically pleasing way to do things.

assets The property of the business.

autonomy A principle based on respect for persons.

awareness The state of being conscious of something.

B

balance sheet A financial statement showing the value of your company at a given point in time.

beliefs The thoughts and ideas that a person holds as true.

beneficence The performance of acts of kindness or charity that go beyond strict obligation.

boundaries The extent and limitations of the relationship with your client.

brevity The quality of expressing much in few words.

budget A guideline that tells you how much money you have to spend on the items in your facility.

business financial needs The expenses of running your business, including paying yourself. (See Chapter 6.)

C

C corporation A separate entity from its owners or stockholders, formed in accordance with state regulation.

carrier The insurance company that carries the plan for the insurance program.

carrier identification number An insurance ID number.

choice The right, power, or opportunity to choose; an option.

clarity The quality of being free from obscurity and easy to understand.

client intake/history form A form that should consist of personal information, such as name, address, phone numbers, and the medical information required for specific types of treatment.

client's bill of rights A document explaining your clients' rights and the terms of your business.

coding An alphanumeric system applied to diagnoses and services and used on all insurance claims.

coinsurance An arrangement in which the customer pays a percentage, usually 20 percent, of the charges and the insurance company pays the remainder, usually 80 percent, but this amount is based on only the charges that the insurance company approves.

communication An exchange of thoughts, opinions, or information by speech, writing, or signs.

compensation The amount of money that a person is paid, either by the hour or by the job.

conflict of interest A situation in which an individual has a private or personal interest that is substantial enough to influence or appear to influence the individual's professional practice.

consciousness The potential or reservoir of all possible states you could experience.

co-pay A small fee that should be collected at the beginning of each visit.

cost-benefit analysis A means of determining whether something is worthwhile.

countertransference (1) A situation in which all the feelings experienced by the practitioner, related to his or her previous relationships and experiences, are stirred up during the session, including the practitioner's conscious and unconscious response to the client's transference of emotions; (2) a situation in which the professional tries to personalize the therapeutic relationship based on conscious or unconscious responses to the client's transfer of emotions.

customer A person you are going to provide service to.

customer interaction (1) Professional interaction during treatments, office visits, and home visits; (2) all other interaction that takes place under all other circumstances.

customer referral The process in which loyal customers who value your service refer others to you.

customer service Process that encompasses all aspects of taking care of the customer's needs.

D

deductible A fixed dollar amount that must be paid or met once a year before the insurance company will cover the charges.

defined-benefit plan A retirement plan in which the employer promises a specific benefit payment at retirement age. The benefit can be based on several criteria, including years of service and average pay, or it can be a flat dollar amount, such as $3,000 per month for life. The employer bears the investment risk.

desexualizing Making something with potential sexuality no longer sexual, or de-emphasizing that dimension.

doing business as (DBA) Operating a business under a fictitious name. (Contact the county clerk for specifics.) The DBA is usually required on business accounts.

dreamer A person who is able to see the big picture yet usually does not have the gift of seeing the details needed to achieve the goals set forth in the big picture.

dual-role (multiple) relationship A relationship in which you and/or your customer engages in more than one role, either at the same time or at different points in time, in your interaction with each other.

E

earnings per hour The amount figured by taking your gross income per week and dividing it by the total hours worked per week.

earnings per treatment The amount figured by dividing your gross income per week by the number of treatments per week.

employee An individual who works for an establishment and files a W-2 tax form.

employee handbook A document that outlines rules, policies, and job descriptions and is used as a guideline in the work environment.

Employer Identification Number Also known as a *Federal Employer Identification Number (FEIN)* or *Taxpayer Identification Number (TIN)*.

entrepreneur One who is ideologically a capitalist or industrialist, has a high tolerance for risk, and enjoys being his or her own boss.

essential (necessity) approach A fee-setting approach that is based on the amount of money you need to make during a given period of time.

establishment A place in which you are doing business and have some control over the environment.

ethics Principles of right or good conduct.

evidence Any information that supports what you are focused on.

expense The money that you spend in the normal course of your business.

F

federal 1040 form The form that you will file to report your personal income.

fiduciary relationship Relationship in which the client puts his or her trust in a professional practitioner with the expectation that both client and practitioner are working in the client's best interests.

401(k) with or without Roth A retirement plan that allows the most flexibility of all the defined-contribution plan structures.

functional Term pertaining to a location that is of big enough size for everyone to be comfortable.

G

general partnership A type of business in which partners share ownership and liability.

goal Something you strive to achieve.

goal setting Specifically planning how to get to a certain endpoint.

gratuity Extra money given to you by a satisfied customer for a job well done. It is optional and is not something that you should depend on. Also called *tip*.

gross income The amount of money that you earned during a week, month, or year.

gross sales The amount of money that you collect for the products and/or services that you provide to your customers over a period of time.

H

harassment A specific kind of misconduct or boundary violation in which an individual of equal or greater

authority is inappropriately familiar with a co-worker or junior employee.

health insurance claim The documentation submitted to an insurance plan requesting that money be paid for the service you, the therapist, provided.

Health Insurance Portability and Accountability Act (HIPAA) Designed to protect the privacy of customers and confidentiality of health records created by insurance companies, doctors, hospitals, and other health care providers.

Hippocratic Oath A 2,400-year-old ethical code that directs physicians, above all else, to "do no harm."

honesty The quality or fact of being truthful.

I

imagination In essence, the spiritual.

income The money that you earn from all aspects of your business.

income statement Financial statement showing the amount of money that you made during a specific period of time.

independent contractor A worker who pays his or her own self-employment and withholding taxes instead of filing a W-2 tax form.

individual 401(k) A retirement plan that covers only the business owner and his or her spouse.

individual retirement account (IRA) An individually funded retirement plan that is not company-sponsored.

informed consent A framework for termination of services because it specifies the need for an ongoing discussion between client and practitioner regarding the expected goals and anticipated timeline for therapeutic benefits.

insurance reimbursement Payment of a client's health care cost by an insurance company. It is not guaranteed. (If your services are not paid for by the insurance company, your customer is responsible for the balance due, unless his or her contract specifies that the individual is responsible for only a specific fixed co-payment.)

internal dialogue A mental conversation with yourself about your world and the people in it.

J

jack-of-all-trades Someone who does a lot of things well. He or she can perform different services that customers may need at different times.

L

liabilities Amounts owed by the business.

limited liability corporation (LLC) A type of corporation in which the owners are taxed as a partnership but their liability is limited, as in a corporation.

limited partner Someone who is not necessarily involved in the day-to-day operations of the business.

limited partnership A type of partnership in which the partners are financially invested in the business but do not play an active role in the operation of the business.

location The place at which you are going to provide your services.

long-term goal A goal that usually takes longer than one year to achieve.

loyal customers Customers who continue to come back and who refer others to your business.

M

macro view A view of the establishment as a whole.

macro view of hours The busiest times of the month and year; specifically, the busiest times during seasonal periods and holidays, beyond just the normal variations of a business week.

market approach A fee-setting approach that is based on the amount of money people are willing to pay for your services.

massage equipment Equipment that is specific to the performance of massage and has a useful life of more than one year.

micro view A view of one small aspect of the establishment.

micro view of hours The busiest hours of the day and the busiest days of the week.

misconduct Any inappropriate behavior that is the unintended result of thoughtlessness, errors in judgment, or improper planning. It risks potentially serious repercussions for the client and heavy penalties for the practitioner.

mission statement A statement that explains the purpose of your business—what you want to accomplish in your business today, tomorrow, and far off in the future.

mobile business A business in which you travel to your customers and treat them in their homes, places of business, or clubhouses.

N

net profit The amount remaining after subtracting total expenses from gross income for the period in question.

networking A means of expanding your client base through existing contacts so that people you don't know get to know you and your business.

nonmaleficence The avoidance of harm to the client or of anything that would be against the client's interests.

number of customers Your customer base.

number of treatments An indicator of how busy you really are making money.

number of units sold The number of products sold and/or services provided.

O

objective goal A goal that is quantifiable, that is, one that can be specifically measured.

office equipment Items that last more than one year and do not directly involve any therapy.

one-time expense Something that is bought only once.

opportunity cost A measure of the total cost of a purchase that takes into account the value of forgone alternatives.

other financial needs Debt reduction or future growth or savings that you may want to distinguish from your personal or business financial needs.

outcome A conclusion reached through a process of logical thinking.

owner's equity The value of a company after subtracting the liabilities from the assets.

P

partner A person who has an equal share in the running of the business and in the risks and rewards of the business.

paternalistic Term pertaining to a parental manner.

payment for services The means by which the customer pays you for your services.

personal financial needs The monthly expenses that you pay to run your household and support your family.

policy An established rule that serves as a guide to standard procedure for your employees, customers, and all who are involved in your business.

power differential The imbalance in authority, or power, between you and your client that results from your greater expertise in a health care discipline.

preauthorization The process of getting permission from the insurance company prior to the start of treatment for the services for which it will pay.

professional accountability The state of being accountable or responsible for professional obligations, including legal liability for failure to perform as expected.

professionalism A combination of individual responsibility—personal responsibility on the part of each member of the professional community—and the collective responsibility of a formal group or association of practitioners.

professor A person who should be the most critical adviser you have.

profit The total amount of money earned less the amount of money spent to run your business over a period of time.

profit-sharing plan A retirement plan that allows flexibility in eligibility criteria, formulas for allocating contributions, and vesting of contributions.

promotions Events that draw attention to your business and also help the community that you are serving.

public relations The process of keeping the public informed about what is new with your business.

Q

quality-of-life items Items that you buy to make your life easier and that allow you to do your job better.

R

recuperate To pay back debts.

recurring expense An expense that you have to pay over and over, such as the cost of Internet service.

referral The process in which existing customers who value your service refer others to you.

right of refusal (1) A client's right to refuse, modify, or terminate treatment regardless of any prior agreements or statements of consent; (2) a practitioner's right to refuse to treat any person or condition for just and reasonable cause.

Roth IRA A retirement plan that is funded with nondeductible contributions. Qualified distributions are not subject to income tax at the time of distribution. This means both the contributions and all subsequent earnings are tax free.

S

S corporation A corporation that has to meet IRS size and stock ownership requirements. Also called *subchapter S corporation*.

sale amount per customer (gross) The amount of money on average that a customer spends during each visit.

sale amount per customer (individual) The amount of money that a specific individual spends each time he or she walks into your business.

satisfied customer A customer who is happy with the treatment that he or she received and will likely return again.

Schedule C A federal government form you must file to report business losses or profits.

Schedule SE A federal government form used to report self-employment tax if there are net earnings on your form 1040.

scope of practice An area of competence, usually obtained through formal study, training, and/or professional experience, and one for which you've received certification or other proof of qualification.

services Everything that you provide to the customer.

short-term goal A goal that usually takes less than one year to achieve.

SIMPLE IRA A retirement plan that can be established by an employer with no more than 100 employees who earned $5,000 or more during the preceding calendar year.

simplicity The state of being easy to understand.

simplified employee plan (SEP) A simplified profit-sharing plan.

Small Business Administration An organization that acts as a quasi partner for your business by giving you input on how to run your business and providing loans for you to run your business.

SOAP notes Documentation that allows other practitioners to assume treatment of the client if you are not available, keeps physicians informed of a client's progress, and is a legal record that may be used in a court of law.

sole proprietorship A type of business in which one person has ownership of and liability for the business. It is the simplest form of business organization.

specialist Someone who does one type of service and does it well. He or she can be considered an expert or a leader in the performance of that type of service.

subjective goal A goal that cannot be measured in absolute terms.

suit The person to whom you will bring all the numbers to examine and see if they make sense or not.

T

1040-ES form The form used to make quarterly federal estimated tax payments.

1099 form A form, completed by an employer at the end of the year, showing the amount that was paid to an independent contractor during the year. The form is sent to the contractor, who must pay taxes on the amount reported on the 1099.

therapeutic relationship A relationship that cures or restores health.

time amount per customer (gross) The amount of time that you spend on average with a customer during each customer visit.

time amount per customer (individual) The amount of time that you spend with a specific individual each time that he or she walks into your business.

tip See *gratuity*.

total expenses The amount of money that you paid out during the period in question. This includes all the expenses that you incur and pay for.

total financial needs Needs that are calculated by adding your personal, business, and other financial needs together.

total hours worked The number of hours that you worked.

traditional IRA A retirement plan available to any individual under age 70½ who has earned income. The annual limit in 2008 was 100 percent of earned income up to $5,000.

transference (1) A situation in which all the feelings experienced by the client, related to his or her past experiences and relationships, are stirred up by or in the session; (2) a situation in which the client tries to personalize the therapeutic relationship on the basis of his or her projection of emotions from the past.

treatment The therapy services you provide to your customer.

V

value Term pertaining to something that the customer feels is worth his or her time and money.

Photo Credits

Index